WAR, PRESIDENTS
AND PUBLIC OPINION

WAR, PRESIDENTS AND PUBLIC OPINION

JOHN E. MUELLER
University of Rochester

JOHN WILEY & SONS, INC.
New York • London • Sydney • Toronto

Paper cover design and construction by
Roy Jones

Library of Congress Cataloging in Publication Data:

Mueller, John E.
    War, presidents and public opinion.

    Bibliography: p.
1. Korean War, 1950-1953—Public opinion.
2. Vietnamese Conflict, 1961-   —Public opinion.
3. Presidents—United States—Public opinion.
4. Public opinion—United States. I. Title.
E839.5.M8   301.15′43′1724   72-8072
ISBN 0-471-62299-0
ISBN 0-471-62300-8 (pbk.)

Printed in the United States of America

10 9 8 7 6 5 4 3 2 1

To J.A.M. and E.S.M.

PREFACE

In the years following World War II the United States became involved in two lengthy wars on the fringes of Asia. Because of the militarily limited and politically complex nature of these wars in Korea and Vietnam, they are often considered as having put a peculiar strain on the American public. Compared to World War II, the enemy is less obviously "evil," progress in battle is more difficult to measure and comprehend, the American entrance into the war is less easily rationalized, and the end of the war is more likely to prove puzzling and unsatisfying. Moreover, popular support influences the conduct of the conflict, since attitudes toward the war at home may be reflected in changes on the battlefield. Indeed, it is often argued that the chief target of enemy strategy in these wars has been American public opinion.

This book deals with American public opinion as it relates to these wars and to the presidents who have led the United States into and out of the conflicts.

To accomplish its purpose, this study relies almost entirely on data generated by the public-opinion polling agencies. Data from the polls must be handled carefully, partly because the instrument is crude, and partly because what it seeks to measure is frequently shapeless and elusive. Indeed, the polls often have been applied to questions for which they are incapable of supplying tangible answers. Chapter 1 examines these problems and suggests a number of approaches, stressing comparative ones, in which poll data can be used profitably to study human attitudes.

With this as background, Part 1 is devoted to a comparative examination of trends and patterns in popular support for the wars in Korea and Vietnam. It also considers the public's attitudes toward World Wars I and II.

Chapter 2 outlines the history of the Korean and Vietnam wars and compares them on a number of dimensions. Popular support for the wars is assessed and compared in Chapters 3 and 4. Chapter 3 deals mainly with the public's response to questions of this kind: "Do you think it was a mistake for the United States to have entered this war?" This query, known as the "mistake" question, was asked repeatedly during the course of both wars by the polling agencies and thus affords an opportunity for a fairly precise comparison and trend analysis. Popular support for the wars is further compared in Chapter 4, this time by using other poll questions, particularly those dealing with the public's preferences for various possible war policies such as escalation or withdrawal. In the process, the existence of an important group of people known as "followers" is suggested. Followers are citizens who take as cues for their own attitudes the accepted policy position of the nation's leadership, especially the president. Using the standard demographic categories included in the polls (age, education, and race, for example), Chapter 5 investigates the kinds of people who are most likely to support or to oppose the wars. Followers are contrasted with "partisans"—people who cue on the position of the party leadership—and with "believers"—those who cue on the issue itself because of ideology, predisposition toward force as a method of foreign policy ("hawks" and "doves"), or self-interest.

One conclusion of Chapters 3 to 5 is that the wars in Korea and Vietnam generated almost the same amount of support and, generally, received it from the same segments of the population— a rather odd finding, since *vocal* opposition to the war in Vietnam was far higher than that for the Korean War. Chapter 6 discusses possible explanations for this curious situation. Chapter 7 examines the degree to which wars have been supported after their conclusion. Limited data for the Korean War and for World Wars I and II are available for this purpose.

In Part 2 the focus shifts to public opinion about the presidency and particularly about the men who have held the office since 1945.

Chapter 8 places the presidency in context by examining the position that present and past presidents have achieved in various admiration sweepstakes conducted by the polling agencies. The meanderings of the presidential-popularity trend line for the period since World War II—the longest continuous substantive trend line in polling history—are assessed in Chapter 9. The effects on a president's popularity of time in office, international crises, and changes in the economy are explored, and special consideration is given to the impact of the wars in Korea and Vietnam on the popularity of wartime presidents. This analysis is extended a step further in Chapter 10 where patterns of presidential popularity are examined separately for three party groups: supporters of the president's party, supporters of the opposition, and independents. Finally, Chapter 11 deals briefly with the post-presidential popularity of several presidents.

Essentially, this book concentrates on popular reactions to certain events and personalities during a specific historical period. It also formulates and develops a number of notions and observations of a more general character. They concern trends and patterns of public opinion behavior, common psychological predispositions, and regularities of response to happenings and political figures. Chapter 12 summarizes some of them.

The research for this book was supported by grants from the National Science Foundation. Some of the material has appeared earlier in article form (Mueller 1970, 1971), but it has been updated, recalculated, and considerably revised. At various stages, helpful comments, criticisms, and complaints were contributed by Richard Fenno, Gerald Kramer, Richard Niemi, Peter Ordeshook, Alvin Rabushka, William Riker, and Andrew Scott. Secretarial work was ably handled by Peg Gross, and research assistance was given by Michael Coveyou, Karl Mueller, Masakatsu Kato, and Abraham Wagner.

April 1972

John E. Mueller

CONTENTS

LIST OF TABLES

LIST OF FIGURES

ABBREVIATIONS

AIPO	American Institute of Public Opinion, the Gallup organization, Princeton, N. J.
AIPOc	AIPO codebooks as a data source; housed in AIPO offices, Princeton, N. J.
AIPOr	AIPO press release
D & C	Rochester *Democrat and Chronicle*
DK	Don't know, usually synonymous with "No opinion"
GOI	*Gallup Opinion Index* (originally titled *Gallup Political Index*), published 1965-. In references only the issue number is usually given. To get some idea of the issue dates, the following may be helpful:

Issue Date	Issue Number
January 1966	8
January 1967	19
January 1968	31
January 1969	43
January 1970	55
January 1971	67
January 1972	79

Harris	The Harris Poll, New York
IISR	Institute for International Social Research, Princeton, N. J.
LAT	*Los Angeles Times*
Minn.	The Minnesota Poll
NORC	National Opinion Research Center, Chicago, Ill.
NORCc	NORC codebooks as a data source
NYT	*New York Times.* All references are to the City Edition
ON	*Opinion News,* published 1943 to 1948 by NORC
RC	Roper Public Opinion Research Center, Williams College, Williamstown, Mass.

SRC Survey Research Center, University of Michigan, Ann Arbor, Mich.

SRCc SRC codebooks as a data source. All SRC materials used in this study have been made available by the Inter-University Consortium for Political Research at the University of Michigan

WP *Washington Post*

WAR, PRESIDENTS
AND PUBLIC OPINION

CHAPTER 1

Public Opinion

Since the arguments, speculations, and conclusions of this book are based almost entirely on attitude data as generated by the public opinion polls, it is appropriate at the outset briefly to discuss the ways these polls are conducted, to comment on their "accuracy," and to suggest ways in which these data can be used meaningfully to understand popular attitudes.

1.1 INTERVIEWS, RESPONDENTS, IGNORANCE, THE WILL OF THE PEOPLE

The interview situation is an odd social experience. The respondent, on his doorstep or in his living room, is barraged with a set of questions on a wide variety of subjects by a stranger, usually a rather well-educated woman over 30, who carefully notes each response on a sheet of paper. Few people are accustomed to having their every utterance faithfully recorded and many find the experience flattering. And, aware that their views are being preserved for the ages, they do not wish to appear unprepared at that moment. Under these circumstances it is not surprising to find respondents pontificating in a seemingly authoritative, if basically "truthful," manner on subjects about which they know nothing or to which they have never given any thought whatsoever.

When they make efforts to assess the depth of this authoritative veneer, the polls disclose, in many areas, a rather monumental lack of knowledge and interest on the part of the American public. In fact, it is clear that many people simply do not *have* opinions on a number of questions, particularly on those that begin to get too complicated, remote, or vague. When the respondent is pressed by the interviewer for an opinion, therefore, many responses are likely to be capricious.

The most striking statistic in this area has been generated by Philip Converse's fine analysis of public reactions to the statement: "The government should leave things like electric power and housing for private businessmen to handle." According to his calculations, fully 81 percent of the American public either admits it has no opinion on this matter or else responds to the question in a manner that can only be adequately described as random (1964a: 26).

This matter is especially relevant to the analysis of public opinion about foreign affairs, since it is perhaps in this area that the analyst may most easily assume his own intense interest in the subject to be shared by the general public. Here, a couple of sobering statistics should be mentioned. In 1964 a cross section of the American public was asked: "Do you happen to know what kind of government most of China has right now—whether its democratic, or Communist, or what?" If the answer was unclear, the respondent was further asked, "Do you happen to know if there is any Communist government in China now?" Fully 28 percent admitted that they did not know (Patchen 1966:257). The question was again posed in a survey in 1968, at the height of the Vietnam War. At that time, the amount of self-confessed ignorance had dropped—to 24 percent (SRCc).

Thus the interview encounter can be viewed as a rather primitive stimulus-response situation in which quick and often poorly considered answers are fitted to an eclectic batch of questions in a social environment that is extraordinarily artificial. It is this image that should be carefully kept in mind when assessing the meaning of those little numbers generated by the polling process and published so grandly and authoritatively in the nation's press.

1.2 SAMPLING "ACCURACY"

But these are not the sorts of considerations usually brought up when the "accuracy" of polls is questioned. Rather, many people

are perplexed by the idea that the views of a tiny sample of people
—usually around 1500—can be taken to represent the attitudes
of the entire American population. On this score, the polling agencies have a reasonably sound defense.

They can point, first of all, to the considerable development of
sampling theory in this century which demonstrates that such
samples are quite adequate for the accuracy sought. That is, about
95 percent of the time one can expect the "real" value (the value
that would be found if the entire population were polled) to be
within a few percentage points of the sample value: if 42 percent
of the sample is of the view that the President is doing a fine job,
it is unlikely that his popularity among the population from which
the sample was drawn varies from that figure by much.

Furthermore, for those who want facts, not theory, the polling
agencies can relate their own practical experience in this area
which generally shows that even rather tiny samples of the population have given results very similar to those generated by much
larger samples (Cantril 1947: Chap. 12). And, of course, they
are quick to point to their considerable, if not unrelieved, success
at predicting elections from poll samples.

A sort of intuitive support to this defense can be derived from
the plot in Figure 1.1. Drawing from Gallup polls between 1945
and 1970 on which the presidential popularity question was asked
(as well as a few other polls for which data were readily available),
the plot displays the percentage of the population found in each
poll to be self-identified as Democrats, Republicans, or Independents. If the sampling methods used by the polls were unrepresentative and capricious, one might expect considerable fluctuation in
these figures from month to month. But, as can be seen, the
variation is generally a matter of only a few percentage points
around a set of gentle trends (discussed in Chapter 10).

The patterns of the lines suggest that Gallup poll data gathered
in the 1940s should be used more cautiously than that obtained
later. Of course here and there, even in the later periods, are skips
and turns of rather significant magnitude. These can be artfully
explained with the sampler's shrug: if you sample, you have to
expect to be pretty far off every once in a while—certainly 5
percent of the time.

One shift in the trend lines, however, is in no sense fleeting,

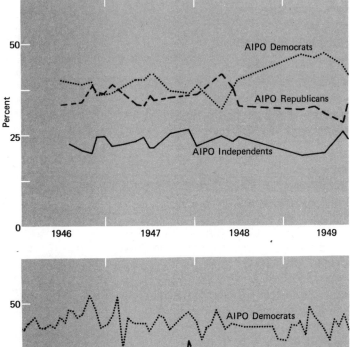

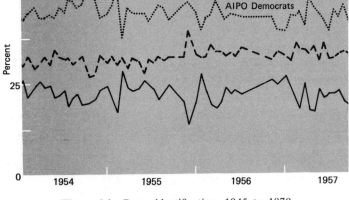

Figure 1.1 Party identification, 1945 to 1970.

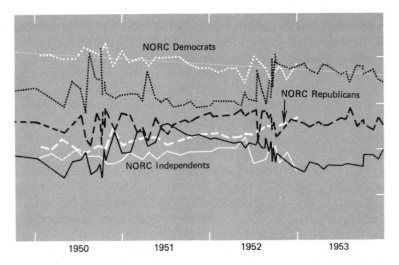

NORC Democrats

NORC Republicans

NORC Independents

1950 1951 1952 1953

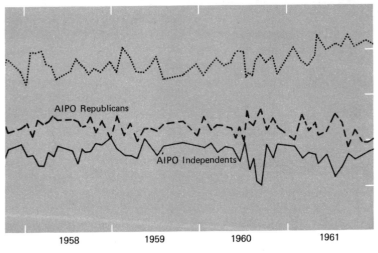

AIPO Republicans

AIPO Independents

1958 1959 1960 1961

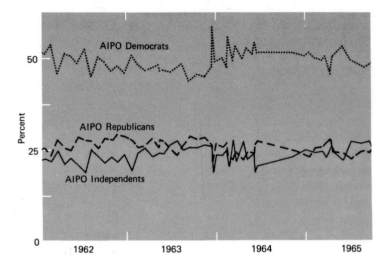

and it bears special examination. That is the noticeable, if less than spectacular, increase in the percentage of Democratic identifiers in the Gallup data and a corresponding drop in Republicans and Independents toward the end of 1952. A rather startling finding, it would seem, since it occurred at the very time when Dwight Eisenhower supposedly was successfully enticing Democrats into the Republican ranks.

One could generate a number of explanations for this strange finding. Perhaps Adlai Stevenson was effectively able to woo back to the Democrats those who had been alienated by President Truman over the course of his administration. A glance at identification figures for earlier years, however, should inspire a healthy skepticism for this hypothesis. For throughout the preceding two or three years (ignoring for the moment the sporatic wiggles) there was only the slightest tapering of Democratic identifiers—this despite the most spectacular decline in a president's popularity ever recorded, a decline to be examined more thoroughly in Chapter 9.

The probable explanation is more humdrum, but more relevant to present purposes. It appears that the Gallup poll anticipated the 1952 election with a degree of anxiety because of its disaster in attempting to predict the 1948 election. Accordingly, it appar-

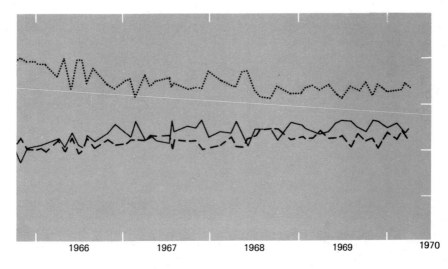

| 1966 | 1967 | 1968 | 1969 | 1970 |

ently took steps in late 1952 to improve the representativeness of its sample in line with professional criticisms of its sampling methods lodged after the 1948 experience (Mosteller et al. 1949). Specifically efforts were made to bring more lower class persons into the sample, since they had been found to be underrepresented by the 1948 methods. Therefore, since lower class people tend to be disproportionately Democratic, the increase in Democratic identifiers is probably largely a function of this change in sampling procedures. The new sampling methods were then apparently made standard. Related experiments probably explain the fluctuation at the time of the 1950 election (Gallup 1953; Perry 1960).

Superimposed on the Gallup party identification figures for the early 1950s are those obtained at the time by the National Opinion Research Center. Using more advanced methods, NORC achieved a better consistency of response and found, consonant with expectations, a small increase in Republican identifiers during the Eisenhower campaign. Estimates of identifier proportions obtained by the two agencies at the end of 1952, after the Gallup reappraisal, are quite similar.[1]

[1] The estimates cannot be compared in later years because NORC stopped asking its party identification question after 1952.

The Gallup shift represents a problem, of course, if one wishes to compare public opinion data gathered by the agency before the end of 1952 with data gathered later (Glenn 1970). For the purpose of this book, the problem is not very intense. The analysis of presidential popularity in Part 2 ends up treating each presidential term very much as a separate entity while, as will be seen in Section 5.2.1, the sampling differences make the arguments in Part 1 about the similarity of support for the wars in Korea and Vietnam, if anything, *stronger.*

As a final note on the sampling issue, it should be observed that the population sampled is not exactly the same as the entire adult American population. The polls sample *households,* not people, and persons institutionalized in prisons, asylums, army camps, and college campuses are not usually included. Furthermore, because people sometimes move, go on vacations, or refuse to be interviewed, the polls characteristically include only about three-quarters of the respondents designated in the original sample design. But it should be clear from the data examined that, as long as sampling procedures remain unchanged, polls are quite reasonably comparable: the biases remain constant.

1.3   QUESTION WORDING

Thus far it has been seen that, when sampling procedures are unchanged, the polls give reasonably consistent results from month to month and are not subject to wild and erratic fluctuations that might be expected if the sampling process were basically unsound. It has also been noted that the population sampled is not exactly the same as the total adult population and that, historically, when sampling procedures have been changed, somewhat different estimates of population parameters have been obtained.

After considerations like these are taken into account, however, there remains an additional aspect of the polls that is of special and rather continual concern in this book. This is the problem of question wording. The problem is familiar to all students of public opinion and has been frequently discussed in the literature, although more generally in past years than in recent times (Rugg 1941, Cantril 1947, Rogers 1949, Payne 1951, Selltiz 1962). However familiar, it has been often neglected in both scholarly and popular writings on public opinion.

The problem arises in large measure from the peculiarities of the interview situation and from the lack of knowledge found in many respondents as discussed in Section 1.1. Pronouncing on issues on which they have little knowledge and less interest, many respondents are found to react as much to cue words in the question and the tone of the language used as to the substance of the issue itself. The portion of the population in favor of "forbidding" speeches against democracy, for example, was found in one study to be 16 percentage points lower than the portion in favor of "not allowing" such utterances (Rugg 1941:92). Responses about the wars in Korea and Vietnam are shown in Chapters 3 and 4 of this book to be quite susceptible to the presence of the word, "communist," in the question. As Payne has observed (1951: Chap. 1), the differences caused by changing the wording of the question often can be far greater than any likely to result from sampling biases.

A consideration of the phenomenon, in fact, inspires the conclusion that *the polls are simply incapable of answering a very large number of the questions to which they have been applied.* When the poll reports boldly tell us to a tenth of a percentage point what portion of the population trusts the Russians, favors child-beating laws, advocates universal military training, or yearns for withdrawal from Vietnam, the numbers so displayed have almost no meaning by themselves. This is the case because the response percentages in many instances could be altered significantly by changes in the wording of the question stimulus—changes that would in no sense "load" the question or confuse the respondent.

1.4 USES OF POLL DATA; COMPARISON

As indicated, this concern about the precise nature of the stimulus delivered to the respondent in the polling situation is one that is considered carefully at many points in this study, particularly in Chapter 4. Since the rest of this book exists, it is obvious that it has not been concluded that the question-wording problem renders the analysis of poll data useless. There are several ways in which the data can be used to furnish evidence about human attitudes.

To begin with, as the polls' general success in predicting elections indicate, there are some very simple behavioral acts for which survey results can be taken to be tangible real-world estimates. Besides the voting act, questions about whether the respondent attended church last Sunday or what brand of coffee he happens to have in the house at the moment are among the ones that fit in this category.

Even here one has to be careful about how the question is worded: there are many ways of asking a man how he plans to vote next Tuesday, and some are distinctly better than others. Furthermore the response generated cannot be trusted perfectly: some respondents may misrecall their church activities and others may lie about them. Even the incredibly simple questions about the brand of coffee one has in the house are subject to biases of this kind. Commercial survey analysts, for example, often require the interviewer to ask the respondent to bring the can of coffee to the door so that the respondent's recollection does not have to be trusted (Selltiz 1962:252).

Nevertheless the percentages generated by these questions are far more likely to have tangible meaning by themselves than those inspired by queries that attempt to tap the respondent's opinion about NATO policy, the Bill of Rights, or the president's welfare program—subjects that most people spend almost no time thinking about. To deal with questions like these latter ones, it seems that one must adopt a *comparative* approach to be able to say anything really meaningful about public opinion. There are at least four ways in which a comparative approach can be employed.

1.4.1 Comparisons with Expectations

First, one can compare the results obtained with those one might "expect." Thus, during the Chicago Democratic Convention of 1968, many intellectuals based their expectations of public attitudes toward the riots there on the reactions of their liberal friends. Therefore when, as discussed in Chapter 6, the polls demonstrated that public reactions were rather intensely favorable to the Chicago police, many people were surprised. Or, to reapply an example from Section 1.1, one may find the degree to which Americans have expressed ignorance of China's form of government at variance with expectations.

This sort of "comparison" is, of course, a highly subjective thing and prey to all the vagaries of the polling process. Thus, as demonstrated in Chapter 4, if one expects or does not expect most Americans to favor withdrawal from Vietnam, it is quite easy to find a poll result that confirms or refutes either expectation. Nevertheless, the polling agencies continue to issue reports in which this sort of comparison is the only one possible. A question on some topical issue—birth control, taxes, J. Edgar Hoover—is formulated and posed to the poll sample. The results of this exercise are then soberly reported to be the public's "opinion" on the issue in question.

1.4.2 Comparisons of Subgroups

With an agreeable frequency, however, the poll reports often do contain a second form of comparison, one which is quite sound. This is a comparison of the reactions of various subgroups in the population to the same question. Whatever the problems of the wording of the stimulus, the biases, in this approach, are held more or less constant and a reasonably fair comparison can be made. Typically old people are compared with the young, Democrats with Republicans, rich with poor, or men with women. Sometimes, if rarely, the reports even include an analysis of how groups that respond differently to one issue question (approvers or disapprovers of the President, say) react to another issue question (attitudes toward a policy issue, for example).

In analyses like these, one does not seek to know how many people in the aggregate feel a certain way about an issue—as suggested above, often a rather unfruitful enterprise. Instead, given a question constructed in a reasonably sensible manner on the issue, one is content to declare, for example, that men are or are not more inclined to favor the issue than women.

The concern about the wording of the question does not evaporate, however, even in this case. For example, as noted in Section 5.1, a question about a political policy is more likely to get polarized reactions from Democrats and Republicans if a reference to a particular political personality or party is included in its wording. Similarly, generation gaps are more likely to yawn on the issue of political protest if protesters are identified as "young people" rather than as "demonstrators." And sometimes, in order to communicate to the poorly informed, a question may be worded so simplistically that it becomes meaningless to the sophisticated—in effect, a different question is being asked of the two groups.

1.4.3 Comparisons over Time

A third form of comparison, one applied frequently in this book, is trend analysis. In this approach one compares the response to a question on a poll with that obtained by the same question on a poll conducted at a different point in time. Assuming no changes in sampling procedure, the biases associated with the question are again held more or less constant and, again without saying what the "real" opinion on the issue is, one can fairly suggest how attitudes on the issue have shifted over time—whether in a favorable or unfavorable direction—if, indeed, they have shifted at all. (See also Hyman 1972.)

Although the wording of the question may remain unaltered, one still has to be careful that events have not substantially changed its meaning. In the 1950s, for example, questions about school desegregation were taken to apply to Southern schools (Little Rock, and the like); in the late 1960s, they would be seen to apply equally to Northern schools.

Data problems. But the greatest problem for the would-be analyst of trends is a lack of useful data. Except for a few items, such as the presidential popularity question, the polling agencies have not been particularly interested in asking a question repeatedly over extensive time periods. There appear to be several reasons for this. First, much of the interview time is spent discovering the respondents' attitudes toward rather specific current events. Data of this sort tend to be reasonably newsworthy and thus of interest to the newspapers and magazines that make up the polling agencies' clientele. But questions like this quickly lose their currency and, therefore, their news interest. Charles van Doren and the television quiz show scandals of the late 1950s were hot stuff at the time, but after the furor died down, they were no longer of interest to editors or readers.

This problem holds also for broader issues, for example, the question of racial relations in the United States—hardly a trivial or ephemeral matter. Extensive polling on the problem was only carried out in the 1960s when the issue burst forth so obviously that no one could possibly ignore it. Therefore, it is possible to trace changes in attitudes on the racial question during the 1960s, but very difficult to obtain data from earlier periods to compare it with (Sheatsley 1966). This, despite the fact that many people in the 1950s saw the racial situation as one of the country's greatest unsolved problems and one that would have to be dealt with frontally in the 1960s (Neustadt 1960: Chap. 8).

Perhaps another reason why the polling agencies have devoted so little effort to gathering trend data has to do with the rather remarkable stability of opinion on a number of matters. For issues of a rather general nature on which there have been no dramatic developments and on which there has been no pronounced change of position by major opinion leaders (especially the president), the public is often likely to react with about the same response today as it did 6 months ago or 3 years ago (see also Sheatsley and Feldman 1964:213–15).

Tables 1.1, 1.2, 1.3 and Figure 1.2 display data for 20-year

TABLE 1.1 Trends in Trust

"Do you think most people can be trusted?" Or, "Do you agree or disagree: Most people can be trusted?"

Year	Can	Cannot	No Opinion, Undecided
	(In Percent)		
1942	66	25	9[a]
1948	66	30	4
1952	68	30	2
1953	57	39	4
1954	62	34	4
1955	66	32	2
1957	75	22	3
1963	77	21	2
1966[b]	71	27	2

Sources. Cantril 1947:169; NORCc; RC.
[a] Includes 5 percent who were allowed "qualified" responses.
[b] Whites only.

TABLE 1.2   Trends in Support for Free Speech for Communists

"(In peacetime,) do you think members of the Communist party in this country should be allowed to speak on the radio?" (NORC)

	Yes	Yes, qualified	No	Undecided
	(In Percent)			
November 1943	48		39	13
November 1945	48		39	13
March 1946	45		44	11
April 1948	36		57	7
November 1953	19	9	68	4
January 1954	14	8	73	5
January 1956	16	6	76	3
December 1956	20	4	72	4
April 1957	17	5	75	3
November 1963	18	10	67	5

Sources. RC; NORCc; *ON,* September 15, 1948, p. 11.

periods for questions about trusting people, allowing Communists air time, and admitting Communist China to the United Nations —all of them items of interest in later chapters. In all three cases, there were attitude changes of importance when the trend is seen as a whole, but each also contained periods of 4, 6, or even 10 years during which there was virtually no change at all.

The trend on trust (Table 1.1) seems to have been modestly upward over the 20-year period with something of a dip during the McCarthy era in 1953 and 1954. Attitudes on civil liberties

TABLE 1.3 **Trends in Support for Admission of Communist China to the UN**

"Do you think Communist China should or should not be admitted as a member of the United Nations?" (AIPO)

	Approve	Disapprove	No Opinion
		(In Percent)	
June 1950[a]	11	58	31
December 1953[b]	12	74	14
March 1954[b]	11	79	10
June 1954	7	78	15
July 1954	8	79	13
May 1955	10	67	23
September 1955	17	71	12
September 1956[b]	17	73	10
December 1956	11	74	15
February 1957	13	70	17
January 1958	17	66	17
August 1958	20	63	17
March 1961	19	64	17
September 1961	16	64	20
February 1964	14	69	17
June 1964[c]	10	73	17
November 1964	20	57	23
November 1964[c]	25	56	19
February 1965	22	64	14
January 1966	22	67	11
March 1966	25	55	20
September 1966	25	56	19
February 1969	33	54	13
October 1970	35	49	16
May 1971	45	38	17

Sources. Hero (1966:441); Erskine (1971:125–26); GOI 72. Minor discrepancies between sources were settled arbitrarily.

[a] Before Korea. For full wording, see Erskine (1971:125).

[b] "Would you approve or disapprove of letting Communist China become a member of the United Nations?" (NORC) "No opinion" percentage includes "depends" responses.

[c] "As far as you are concerned, do you favor or oppose giving Red China a seat at the United Nations as a member?" (Harris)

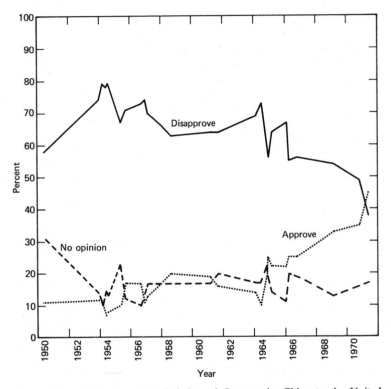

Figure 1.2   Opinion on the admission of Communist China to the United Nations, 1950 to 1971.

for Communists (Table 1.2) hardened firmly between the end of World War II and the mid-1950s, but showed no movement for the next 10 years. Opinions on the admission of Communist China to the United Nations (Table 1.3 and Figure 1.2) seemed to have become somewhat more favorable in the late 1960s, partly in response to policy modifications by the president, no doubt, but held firm, before then, at the same level for considerable stretches of time.

To a degree, this stability probably derives from a certain randomness in the public response to the question posed. One must assume, for example, that the quarter of the public that admits it does not know what form of government most of China has would be inclined to respond to the question about Communist

China in a rather capricious manner. So, when these people are repolled, it is to be expected that their composite response will average out about the same as in earlier polls. For those who do know what is going on, as long as the opinion cues remain about the same, they are likely to respond consistently.

But whatever the reason, the phenomenon does not seem to have encouraged the polling agencies to deal extensively with time comparisons. Trend lines that do not fluctuate usually make poor newspaper copy. There are important exceptions, fortunately, and it does seem to be the case that survey organizations are becoming more interested in analyses of this kind.

The data in Tables 1.1, 1.2 and 1.3 illustrate another problem for the would-be trend analyst even when extensive time series data are available: the often sparse and rather capricious timing of the question posings, a process often dictated, again, by newsworthiness. Apparently, the Communist radio question has not been asked in a national sample since 1963. And, while Gallup decided to pose the China-UN issue three times in 1966, the organization then proceeded to ignore it for $2\frac{1}{2}$ years.

1.4.4 Comparisons of Questions

A fourth form of comparison deals with the question-wording phenomenon itself. One can compare the reactions to differently worded questions about the same subject presented to the same or similar poll samples to see what variations in the stimulus result in variations in the response. When this is done, one is often in a good position to assess the opinion cues that go into making up an attitude response. The responses to the questions documented in Table 1.4, for example, say a good deal about the relative attraction in French politics in 1948 of "communism" as an ideology and "Communists" as representatives of a political party. They may also suggest to opposing parties vulnerability in the Communist image.

This comparative approach is applied from time to time in this book where the survey organizations happen to have asked at about the same time differently worded questions on a single topic. More desirable, however, would be the application of the "split ballot" technique frequently used in pretests of questionnaire items and in studies of questionnaire design (Payne 1951:73–74, 237

TABLE 1.4   Communist Support in France, 1948

A: "Are you more for the Communists, more for de Gaulle, or more for the 'Third Force?' "
B: "Are you more for Communism, more for de Gaulle, or more for the 'Third Force?' " (French Institute of Public Opinion, March 16, 1948).

	A	*B*
Communists	24%	
Communism		16%
de Gaulle	27	28
Third Force	27	31
No Opinion	22	25

Source. ON, May 1, 1948, p. 15.

and passim; Cantril 1947: Chap. 2 and passim). In this procedure, the poll sample is randomly divided in half, one part being asked the question as worded one way, the other part receiving an alternative wording. This makes direct, controlled comparison quite easy. Only in a few cases, however, are such data available on questions of relevance to this study. It may be an area that the polling agencies are reluctant to explore publicly, since the issue of wording sensitivity is often used by detractors to question the polls' "validity." But the technique could be of considerable benefit in many areas of political research (Mueller 1965, 1968).

There is one variety of comparison of this sort that is applied fairly frequently by the polling agencies. This is to ask the same question about a series of items (are you satisfied with your job, your housing situation, the schools your children attend, and the like) and to compare the responses. This can be a valuable exercise, although there is a danger that the order in which the items are posed can affect the responses generated.

The emphasis on question wording in this discussion should not lead one to conclude that *all* question responses are susceptible to extensive manipulation by minor wording changes (Gallup 1941). Where opinion is intense and commitment is strong on an issue, wording variations are unlikely to make much difference. In a 1941 study, for example, it was found that even the most loaded questions about Hitler could not alter American opinion about him one way or the other; on other subjects, however, attitude was found to be highly sensitive to changes in wording (Cantril 1947:45–46 and passim). The sensitivity of opinion to changes in the wording of the stimulus, in fact, can be taken as a sort of index of uncertainty, indecision, and lack of knowledge on the issue (see also Hochstim and Renne 1971 and Schuman 1972).

For the most part, the wording variations of interest in this study will be more of a substantive than semantic sort. Sometimes the tone of the words used in the stimulus can be seen to be vital determinants of an attitude response, as in the example above where people were found more willing to "forbid" something than they were to "not allow" it. But more commonly, issue cues of a more substantial sort—the evocation of a President's recommendation or of the anti-Communist cause—have direct bearing on the results generated by the poll stimulus.

1.5 PUBLIC OPINION DATA SOURCES

The sources for the public opinion data used in this book are varied. Most important has been the Roper Public Opinion Research Center at Williams College in Williamstown, Massachusetts. Stored there are hundreds of surveys and survey materials, including Gallup polls going back to the 1930s (Hastings 1964). Some additional Gallup data have been obtained from materials in the New York Public Library and in the library of the American Institute of Public Opinion in Princeton, New Jersey.

The other major archive of survey data is the Inter-University Consortium for Political Research at the University of Michigan, which has been the principal source for data from the Survey Research Center there (Miller and Converse 1964).

Data from the National Opinion Research Center at the University of Chicago have been obtained through the Roper Center and through the NORC library, ably run by Patrick Bova.

Data banks and libraries like these have greatly facilitated social research in recent years (Bisco 1966; Converse 1966). Other survey information derives from various published materials as indicated in references and footnotes throughout the book.

PART 1 War

CHAPTER 2

The Wars in Korea and Vietnam

To give a historical context for the survey data gathered during the Korean and Vietnam wars, this chapter is devoted to a brief discussion of these wars, giving special consideration to their similarities and differences. Events and developments that seem most relevant to popular reactions to the war are stressed. First, the chronologies of the two wars are sketched; for the most part, these are displayed in tabular form to more conveniently serve as a reference for later time trend analyses. Then some of the more important points of similarity and difference between the wars are assessed individually.

2.1 THE KOREAN WAR

An outline of the major events in the Korean War is given in Table 2.1.[1] The war began in June 1950 with a surprise attack by the Communist-controlled North Koreans across the 38th parallel which divided them from South Korea. President Harry Truman sent American forces to aid the South Koreans under

[1] The materials in Tables 2.1 and 2.3 were gathered from a number of sources, most importantly the *Congressional Quarterly* analysis of the postwar history of United States policy in the Far East (1967) and the *New York Times Index*.

23

TABLE 2.1 Chronology for the Korean War

1950	January	Statements by Secretary of State Acheson indicating first line of defense for United States included Japan, Okinawa, and the Philippines, but not Formosa or Korea
	June 25	North Korean attack; United Nations Security Council calls for cease-fire and withdrawal of invaders
	June 27	President Truman orders United States air and naval forces to aid South Korea; United Nations Security Council urges members to give assistance to South Korea
	June 30	Truman authorizes General MacArthur to send United States ground forces to Korea
	July 7	United Nations Security Council appoints MacArthur as United Nations commander in Korea
	August 15	United Nations and South Korean forces pushed to small perimeter around southern seaport city of Pusan
	September 15	Landing at Inchon, 150 miles north of the battlefront, beginning of major North Korean retreat
	October 7	United Nations General Assembly approves invasion of North Korea
	November 6	MacArthur reports United Nations forces are meeting a "new foe" in Korea: Chinese Communist forces
	November 24	United Nations forces launch a "final" offensive in the north
	November 26	Chinese forces open an enormous counteroffensive sending United Nations troops into major retreat
	December 14	United Nations General Assembly asks China for a cease-fire; rejected
1951	January 13	United Nations General Assembly asks again for cease-fire; rejected
	January 30	Communist China branded an aggressor by United Nations General Assembly

TABLE 2.1 (Continued)

February 18	Chinese unable to break United Nations front in central Korea; United Nations launches counteroffensive, driving most Communist forces back across the 38th parallel
March 27	Defense Secretary Marshall vetoes idea of full-scale invasion of North Korea by United Nations forces
April 11	MacArthur dismissed for violating orders not to make public statements demanding expansion of the war against Communist China; replaced by General Ridgeway
April 19	MacArthur addresses joint session of Congress after hero's welcome; asserts China should be bombed
April 22	Communists begin expected spring offensive
May 1	Communists abandon first phase of offensive, retreat to regroup
May 3	Senate hearings on MacArthur dismissal begun, continue into summer
May 16	Second Communist spring offensive; soon abandoned after heavy losses
June 23	Soviet Union calls for cease-fire negotiations on Korea
July 10	Truce talks begin in Kaesong
August 23	Communists break off truce talks because jeep carrying their chief negotiator had been strafed by a United Nations plane; United Nations later admitted the incident, said it was accidental
October 25	Truce talks resume in Panmunjom
November 27	Agreement to make cease-fire line at existing battleline
November 28	Fighting on front largely stops
1952 April	Truce talks deadlocked, principally over the issue of the exchange of prisoners: Communists insist all their prisoners must be returned, even the ones who do not wish repatriation

TABLE 2.1 (Continued)

March 29	After losing a primary, Truman announces he will not be a candidate for reelection
June 23–26	Hundreds of United States planes bomb North Korean hydroelectric power plants in largest bombing raid of the war to that time
July 11	Republicans nominate Eisenhower for president; North Korean capital heavily bombed, warnings issued of more to come
July 26	Democrats nominate Stevenson for president
October 8	Truce talks recessed indefinitely
October 24	Eisenhower pledges to "go to Korea" to end the war if elected
November 4	Eisenhower elected president
November 17	India proposed neutral commission to handle prisoner repatriation; United States accepts idea, Soviets and Chinese reject
December 2–5	President-elect Eisenhower visits Korea
1953 January 20	Eisenhower assumes office
March 5	Stalin dies
April 11	Agreement reached on repatriation of sick and wounded prisoners; prisoners who did not wish to return sent to a neutral nation
April 26	Truce talks resume
June 8	Prisoner agreement reached: neutral commission established, home country given 90-day period to attempt to change the minds of those unwilling to return
June 18	President Rhee of South Korea releases 25,000 anti-Communist prisoners in defiance of United Nations command; Communists, outraged, break off truce talks
July 11	Rhee agrees to armistice terms
July 13	Chinese launch largest offensive since May 1951; halted by United Nations
July 26	Armistice signed
August 5	Exchange begins of prisoners wishing repatriation

TABLE 2.1 (Continued)

September 6	First stage of prisoner exchange completed; begin processing prisoners who do not wish repatriation
1954 January 21	Prisoner exchanges completed
1972 July	North and South Korea agree to discuss reunification and to refrain from armed provocations

United Nations auspices. The North Koreans, highly successful at first, were forced into retreat after a few months of fighting and finally were chased back across the 38th parallel with United Nations forces in hot pursuit. At the end of the year, the United Nations offensive was itself turned around by a massive attack of Chinese Communist troops, who entered the battle by the hundreds of thousands.

By mid-1951, battle lines more or less stabilized at the 38th parallel and truce talks began. A cease-fire line was agreed to by the end of 1951, and the level of fighting was reduced considerably, although far from eliminated. An armistice, delayed mainly because of disagreement over the exchange of prisoners of war, was finally signed in mid-1953.

Two events of domestic political impact are worth special mention. One was the firing in the spring of 1951 of General Douglas MacArthur by President Truman. The President maintained that the General had been insubordinate by repeatedly making public statements in conflict with official policy despite orders not to do so. The Truman-MacArthur controversy is discussed more fully in Chapter 9 where its possible application to some peculiarities of Truman's presidential popularity is discussed. The other political phenomenon was the election of Dwight Eisenhower to the presidency in 1952 partly because of a popular discontent over the war in Korea.

2.2 THE VIETNAM WAR

The history of the war in Vietnam to 1972 is outlined in Tables 2.2 and 2.3. The war grew out of gradually increased aid commitments to the South Vietnamese government which went back to the mid-1950s. These commitments had been made in part to

TABLE 2.2   United States Troop Strength in South Vietnam

1954 to 1960	650 (annual average)
End of 1960	800
1961	3,200
1962	11,300
1963	16,300
1964	23,300
1965	184,300
1966	389,400
1967	485,600
1968	549,500
1969	474,400
1970	339,200
1971	161,000

Sources. Congressional Quarterly (1967:170); *New York Times Index.*

avoid the mistake of 1950 when aggression was supposedly encouraged by statements by government spokesmen that had suggested the United States would not aid South Korea in a war there. By the end of the 1950s the South Vietnamese were engaged in an increasingly intense war with Communist-led guerrillas who received verbal, and then more tangible, support from North Vietnam.

In 1965, fearing a collapse of the South Vietnamese government, the United States altered its policy to one of more direct participation in the war. American troops entered the combat, and United States air power was used against Communist targets in North as well as South Vietnam.

The buildup on both sides continued over the next few years, and the fighting quickly reached Korean War magnitudes. At the same time an increasingly vocal opposition to the war grew within the United States.

A sort of turning point was effectively reached in the spring of 1968 in the wake of a major Communist offensive. President Johnson essentially placed a ceiling on the United States buildup and halted the American bombing of most of North Vietnam. At the same time Johnson announced that he would not be a candi-

TABLE 2.3   Chronology for the War in Vietnam

1954	July 21	Geneva accords end Indochina war between French and Communist-led guerrillas
	September 8	South East Asia Treaty Organization created
	October 23	President Eisenhower offers aid to South Vietnamese government
1955	February 12	United States advisers take over training of South Vietnamese army from French
	October 23	Diem becomes president of South Vietnam
1958		Growth of Viet Cong guerrilla war against government of South Vietnam
1960	November 8	South Vietnamese government charges North Vietnam is infiltrating troops into South Vietnam
	November 10	Revolt of South Vietnamese paratroopers against Diem fails
1961	Fall	Decision by Kennedy Administration to increase military and economic aid to South Vietnam, raise numbers of military advisers from 685 to several thousands
1962	October 9	Diem says war against Viet Cong now going well
1963	October 2	Defense Secretary McNamara predicts most of the 14,000 United States military personnel in South Vietnam can be withdrawn by the end of 1965
	November 1	After months of internal political and religious turmoil, Diem ousted from office and killed in coup
	November 22	Kennedy assassinated; Johnson becomes president
	December 21	McNamara abandons plan to withdraw by end of 1965, notes gains of Viet Cong after Diem coup
1964	January 30	Another coup in South Vietnam
	March 17	United States pledge of continued assistance to South Vietnam as long as required to control "Communist aggression"; warnings to North Vietnam repeatedly issued

TABLE 2.3 (Continued)

August	In response to two firings on American ships in Gulf of Tonkin, North Vietnamese PT boat bases are bombed; Congress passes resolution supporting action and other such measures to protect United States forces and "prevent further aggression"
November 3	Johnson reelected president
1965 January 27	Coup in South Vietnam after months of political and religious turmoil
February 7	North Vietnam bombed by United States planes in retaliation for Viet Cong attack on United States bases in South Vietnam
February 16	Coup in South Vietnam
February 24	United States planes bomb Viet Cong targets in South Vietnam for first time
February 27	State Department White Paper on aggression from the North
March 8	Marines land in South Vietnam to defend United States base
March 21	Communist China says it will fight in Vietnam if United States invades the North or if aid is requested by the North Vietnamese
April 2	United States to increase troops in South Vietnam, increase air strikes
April 17	15,000 demonstrators in Washington protest bombings; teach-ins follow
May	Five-day suspension of air raids
June 21	Ky becomes premier of South Vietnam
July 28	Johnson announces increased draft calls to allow buildup in Vietnam from current 75,000 to 125,000
September 23	North Vietnam reaffirms earlier rejections of United States offers to negotiate
September 30	Attempted coup by Communists in Indonesia fails, leads to massive anti-Communist movement there
December 24	Month-long bombing halt begins

TABLE 2.3 (Continued)

1966	February	Senate hearings on war in Vietnam
	Spring	Many antiwar demonstrations
	April 12	First B-52 raids over North Vietnam
	May	Rise of Lin Piao in China; beginnings of purges, Red Guard movement, Great Proletarian Cultural Revolution
	June 29	Extension of bombing raids to oil dumps near Hanoi
	September 11	Elections in Vietnam for constituent assembly
	December	Reports from North Vietnam by *New York Times* correspondent on civilian damage caused by United States air strikes
1967	February	Wilson-Kosygin probes for negotiations on war; North Vietnam continues to demand unconditional bombing halt before talks can begin
	April 15	Mass antiwar rally of 100,000 in New York
	September 3	Elections of Thieu and Ky in South Vietnam
	October 21	Antiwar demonstrators storm Pentagon
	November	Bunker-Westmoreland visit to United States, voice optimism on war
1968	January 30	Beginning of major offensive by Communists during Tet cease-fire
	February 28	Military requests 206,000 more men
	March 1	McCarthy gets sizeable vote in challenge to president in New Hampshire primary
	March 22	General Westmoreland removed as commander in Vietnam and promoted
	March 31	Johnson declares partial bombing halt, calls for talks, announces he will not run for reelection
	April 3	North Vietnam agrees to preliminary peace talks
	April 9	Defense Secretary Clifford announces policy of 549,500 troop ceiling and gradual transfer of war responsibility to South Vietnamese
	Spring	Many antiwar demonstrations
	May	Further Communist offensives
	August 8	Nixon nominated by Republicans

TABLE 2.3 (Continued)

August 29	Humphrey nominated by Democrats at tempestuous convention
October 31	Full bombing halt agreed to, "productive discussions" to be begun
November 6	Nixon elected president
1969 Spring	Communist offensives
June 8	Nixon announces beginning of troop withdrawals: 25,000 by August
September 3	President Ho Chi Minh of North Vietnam dies
September 16	Nixon announces withdrawals of 35,000 more men as pace of war slackens
October	Nationwide protests against the war (moratorium)
November 15	Mass antiwar march in Washington of 250,000 to 300,000
November 16	Reports of civilian massacre by United States troops in March 1968 at Mylai
December 15	Nixon announces further withdrawal of 50,000
1970 April 20	Nixon pledges to withdraw 150,000 troops over the next year
May	Joint United States-South Vietnamese invasion of Cambodia; massive protest in the United States
1971 February	South Vietnamese troops, with United States support, invade Laos
Spring	Trial and conviction of Lt. Calley for mass murder at Mylai
June 13	*New York Times* begins its controversial publication of the "Pentagon Papers"
October	Reelection of Thieu
December	Series of bombing raids on North Vietnam
1972 March 23	United States declares indefinite suspension of Paris peace talks
April	Major Communist offensive; United States resumes massive bombing of North Vietnam
July	Peace talks resume; one battalion remains as the only American combat unit in South Vietnam

date for reelection. In the ensuing election, the Republicans won the presidency. Truce talks, begun at the time of the bombing halt, proved unproductive through mid-1972.

By 1969, with the pace of the war slackening, the Nixon Administration found it possible to begin withdrawing American troops, relying increasingly on the South Vietnamese for the fighting manpower. By the end of 1971, troop levels were back down to 1965 strengths, and American troops were involved in very little actual ground combat, although they were still considerably involved in logistical and air support. A major Communist offensive in the spring of 1972 was confronted on the ground almost entirely by South Vietnamese forces.

2.3 A COMPARISON OF THE WARS

The wars in Korea and Vietnam were probably as similar to each other as any pair of wars in United States history. Nevertheless, on several points there were striking differences. A number of these similarities and differences deserve emphasis.

2.3.1 The battlefield: Locale, Scope, Tactics, Limitation

The wars in Korea and Vietnam both found the United States aiding the government of a small Asian country against a Communist enemy who used comparatively primitive methods of warfare and who was seeking to unite his divided country under Communist leadership.

Both wars were limited: they took place within a fairly specific area, and in both cases the United States refrained from using the most powerful weapons in its arsenal. There was domestic political pressure to expand the wars, particularly with respect to bombing policy, and this pressure was resisted at least to the extent that certain areas in North Vietnam in the Vietnam War and all of China in both wars were exempted from bombing. Unlike North Korea, North Vietnam was never invaded, but certain areas —Cambodia and Laos—once held to be sanctuaries in the Vietnam War, were invaded.

Within these general similarities there were, of course, a number of important specific differences. Ones that are most relevant to the purposes of this book include the following: the Truman-MacArthur controversy on tactics, which has no parallel in Vietnam;

the participation of the United Nations as a combat organization in the earlier war but not the later one; the existence of battle lines in Korea but not in Vietnam; and the sheer length of the Vietnam War, which eventually made the 3-year Korean venture seem short indeed.

2.3.2 Popular Justification

Compared to World War II, in particular, the enemy engaged in the Korean and Vietnam conflicts was less obviously "evil," and it was far more difficult to find convincing ideological or humanitarian reasons to justify the wars to the public. Neither war produced in any number romantic heroes, stirring songs, patriotic slogans, or novels of dashing adventure. Both were "dirty little wars." Furthermore, because of their limited, faraway nature, it was more difficult to view the wars as necessary from the standpoint of direct American security, although the idea of "stopping the Communists" was related to this concern. In addition, neither war was ever formally "declared" although, in this, they were hardly unique in American history. The Korean War was most often justified as a "police action" under United Nations auspices, the war in Vietnam as the carrying out of alliance and treaty commitments.

2.3.3 Domestic Presidential Politics

Both wars became important in domestic partisan politics. Both were begun under Democratic presidents who decided not to seek reelection at a time when the unpopular war was still continuing. In both elections, the Democratic party was removed from the White House by a Republican candidate who promised new, inspecific initiatives to bring the war to a speedy end.

2.3.4 The Start of the Wars

Although the wars looked alike in many important respects once they were underway, their beginnings were quite different. The Korean War was begun under highly dramatic circumstances with a rather clear-cut Communist attack and an American decision over a few days to come to the aid of the attacked under United Nations auspices (Paige 1968).

The war in Vietnam grew out of a gradually increasing commitment to the South Vietnamese government, and the greatly increased American involvement in 1965 was accomplished over several months and in piecemeal fashion with the administration consciously trying to downplay its significance. It is difficult even to date the beginning of the war. For the purpose of public opinion analysis, however, it seems sensible to take mid-1965 as the starting point. Before that, Americans were strikingly ignorant of the war. In spring, 1964, Gallup determined that 63 percent of the public was giving little or no attention to developments in South Vietnam (AIPOr, May 27, 1964); in June, the Survey Research Center found fully 25 percent of its respondents willing to admit they had heard nothing about the fighting in Vietnam (Patchen 1966:294); and SRC in its 1964 election study, after months of campaign debate over the war, escalation, and the incidents in the Bay of Tonkin, found that 20 percent still were paying no attention to what was going on in Vietnam (SRCc).

2.3.5 The Wars' End

The wars also ended in different ways. The Korean War concluded with a negotiated truce and an exchange of prisoners. However, this hardly guaranteed tranquility in the area. There was considerable concern that the war would erupt again at any moment. Although that never happened, the United States in the late 1960s still found it necessary to retain 50,000 troops in South Korea and could suffer about 50 battle deaths per year in various border incidents.

The end of the war in Vietnam is as difficult to fix as its beginning. Since it is the American aspect of the war and its relation to public opinion that are of principal concern here, the end of the war could be taken to be the time that the United States ceased to participate actively in the fighting—particularly in the ground combat. By 1971 this point apparently was being reached.

2.3.6 Casualties

Although American casualties in the two wars were roughly of the same order of magnitude (compared, for example, to World War II or the Spanish-American War), the rate at which these casualties were suffered differed markedly. The cumulative battle casualty figures (killed, hospitalized, wounded, and missing) for the two wars are plotted in Figure 2.1.[2]

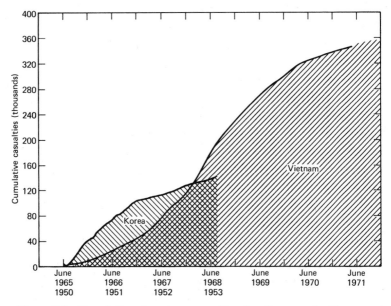

Figure 2.1 Cumulative American casualties for the wars in Korea and Vietnam.

Casualties in Korea came heavily at the beginning of the war as Americans were thrown into combat to help stop the Communist gains. The intensity increased throughout 1950, especially in September as Americans took up a major part of the counterattack that drove the enemy back across the 38th parallel. And then, of course, with the Chinese intervention at the end of the year and the disastrous United Nations retreat, casualty figures soared.

With the beginning of peace talks in mid-1951, the casualty rate dropped. However, while casualties were suffered in the last 2

---

[2] Casualty figures used in this book are taken from tables helpfully supplied by Thomas C. Thayer of the Defense Department with supplementary information gathered from the *New York Times*.

years of the war at an average rate quite a bit lower than during the first year, the accumulative costs were still considerable: some 45 percent of the American casualties in the war occurred after peace talks began.

In Vietnam, by contrast, the costs were accumulated at a more gradual rate. In mid-1965, when, as noted above, the war could be considered to have started as far as the American public was concerned, total American casualties from previous years of combat in Vietnam stood at about 2500, about 400 of these deaths. It was two or three years later before American ground troops really were heavily involved in the action and, therefore, before casualties were suffered at peak rates. The most costly period of the war was the first half of 1968, at the time of several major offensives by the Communists, when American deaths were being registered at several hundred per week. As the fighting declined in following years and as the South Vietnamese took on a larger share of the combat burden, American casualty rates were reduced.

The contrasts between the two wars, therefore, are considerable. Korean War casualties were suffered disproportionately in the first year of the war and at much lower rates thereafter, while it took several years before the United States reached comparable casualty totals in Vietnam. Of course, Vietnam did finally become a more costly war. American combat casualty totals passed Korean War levels in March 1968, as did combat death totals in April 1969.[3]

As will be shown in Chapter 3, the differing rates at which casualties were suffered is an important consideration when comparing patterns of popular support for the two wars.

2.3.7 The Economy

For the most part, the economy behaved in similar ways during the two wars. As shown in Figure 2.2, both wars were accom-

---

[3] The difference in these two dates is partly attributable to another difference between the wars: improvements in medical treatment for the wounded in the decade separating the wars. Although about some 30 percent of American casualties in the Korean War represented combat deaths, only 13 percent did so in the war in Vietnam. Another factor was the great punishment taken by American troops in Korea in the retreat in the winter of 1950 to 1951, when thousands of troops were missing in action and later officially declared dead.

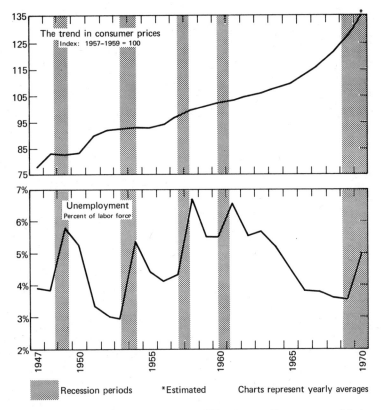

Figure 2.2 Economic trends 1947 to 1970. (*Source*. Department of Labor as reported in the *New York Times,* January 10, 1970.)

panied by rising prices and declining unemployment, except that unemployment rose markedly in the last years of the war in Vietnam as (but not necessarily because) United States troops were being withdrawn. There was also an unemployment effect connected with the Korean War, but this did not occur until after the truce was signed.

2.3.8 The Amount and Source of Local Domestic Opposition

An extraordinarily important difference between the two wars, if one is interested in popular opinion, concerns the extreme contrasts in the amount of opposition to the wars as openly expressed by demonstrations, petitions, speeches in Congress, newspaper commentaries, and organized political campaigns. Judging from these alone, the Vietnam War would seem to have been far the more unpopular. Indicative are some data furnished in a study by James Rosenau (1968:17):

> A good measure of the difference in the domestic controversies generated by the limited wars in Korea and Vietnam is provided by a comparison of the number of persons and organizations associated with policy-oriented advertisements placed in the "News of the Week in Review" section of the Sunday edition of the *New York Times* during the two periods. For the first year after the inception of American bombing raids on North Vietnam in February 1965, a total of 27 advertisements were placed in this medium by 25 different groups or organizations. Some of the advertisements indicated support of U.S. policy, but most opposed it. All together, the 27 advertisements contained the names of 9,476 individuals as sponsors of the positions advanced in their texts. On the other hand, similar expressions of opinion for the entire Korean War, from July 1, 1950, through August 1, 1953, totaled two advertisements, one without signatures placed by the American Friends Service Committee asking for contributions to send clothing to Korean children and one placed by Eugene Greenhut of 10 East 44th Street, New York, proposing a plan for ending the Korean conflict and "insuring democracy's survival in the Free World."

At least as important as the amount of opposition to the wars was the source of this opposition. In the Korean case, what opposition there was seems to have come from the Right. It was the conservative Senator from Ohio, Robert Taft, after all, who called the Korean action "an utterly useless war." By contrast, vocal opposition to the war in Vietnam seems to have come predominantly from the intellectual, nonunion Left, a group that has been called the journalistic-academic complex. The role of this group will be assessed more fully later, especially in Chapter 6.

2.3.9 The Cold War Atmosphere

The reasons for the intellectual Left's acceptance of the Korean War and its opposition to the war in Vietnam are partly linked, it would seem, to differences in the cold war atmosphere under which the wars were conducted. To many on the Left, Korea may have seemed an unpleasant, but necessary, episode in the cold war against Stalinist Russia.

The intellectual Left was hardly alone in viewing the Korean War in cold war terms. Table 2.4 gives the trend for a poll ques-

TABLE 2.4 Attitudes toward Russia, 1946 to 1950

"As you hear and read about Russia these days, do you believe Russia is trying to build herself up to be *the* ruling power of the world, or do you think Russia is just building up protection against being attacked in another war?"

	June 1946	March 1948 (After Czech coup)	May 1949	January 1950	November 1950 (After Korea)
Ruling power	58%	77%	66%	70%	81%
Protection	29	12	15	18	9
Don't know	13	11	19	12	10

Sources. AIPOr July 14, 1950, November 29, 1950.

tion about perceived Russian intentions in world affairs. It is clear that the war served to magnify and harden anti-Soviet attitudes in the country. Little differentiation between the Russians and the Chinese Communists was made: in late 1950, 81 percent of the public was of the view that China had entered the war on direct orders from the Soviet Union.[4]

By the mid-1960s, however, particularly after the Cuban missile crisis of 1962, the Russian cold war threat had abated considerably. It is to be expected that, among individuals attentive to world affairs, those on the Left would be the first to conclude that the

[4] AIPOr December 30, 1950. A sort of parallel can be found in the public's reaction to Japanese participation in World War II. Asked for the "underlying reasons" explaining why Japan was fighting the United States, 48 percent—far the most popular answer—suggested she had been urged into the war by Germany (Cantril and Strunk 1951:1078).

evidence about changed Russian behavior should lead to a modification in American foreign policy. For them, the wisdom of another anti-Communist war in Asia under the changed cold war circumstances was found to be difficult to grasp. Hans J. Morgenthau, the political scientist and antiwar activist, is probably reasonably representative of this view. At the time of Korea, he says, "Communism was monolithic. Since we were committed to the containment of the Soviet Union, we were also committed to the containment of Communism throughout the world—Communism being a mere extension of Russian power. I have been frequently criticized by supporters of our Vietnam policy because of this alleged inconsistency. I supported the Korean intervention, but I was from the very beginning opposed to the Vietnam intervention. The Vietnam intervention is of an entirely different character in its foreign policy from what it was twenty years ago."[5]

In 1965, the Johnson Administration's position (more or less) was that, while Russia may have become less of a threat than previously, China still posed a significant challenge, at least in the Southeast Asian area. Thus, the standard cold war policy of containment was applicable there. Of particular concern was the potential development of a China-Indonesia anti-American axis capable of gaining control of all of Southeast Asia through a sort of political pincers move.[6]

Some of the cold war types within the intellectual Left may have been willing, in 1965, to grant this position. Within a year, however, this point was considerably weakened by two events. The first was the abortive Communist coup attempt in Indonesia that led to Sukarno's downfall and to a sharp reversal of the country's pro-Chinese political trends. The second was the beginning of the highly diverting Red Guard movement within China. Therefore, for the cold warriors of the Left, the rationale for the Vietnam venture was no longer valid, and they could turn to opposition.

How members of the general public reacted to the changed cold war atmosphere as reflected in their attitudes toward the Vietnam War is a subject of the next chapter.

---

[5] Comment in a round table discussion, *The University of Chicago Magazine,* Sept.–Dec. 1969, pp. 17–18.

[6] For a discussion of this concern, see Sulzberger (1966).

CHAPTER 3

Trends in Popular Support for the Wars in Korea and Vietnam

Using poll data, this chapter assesses trends in support by the American public for the wars in Korea and Vietnam and compares the wars with each other and with earlier wars on this basis.

It is possible to generate a number of plausible hypotheses about what shape trends in support for a war should take. The most popular proposition, at least for the wars in Korea and Vietnam, suggests a continually declining level of support. As the war drags on, it is suggested, more and more Americans become disillusioned with the war and their support changes to opposition.

An alternative hypothesis would suggest increasing support for the war. The public, horrified at the start by the thought of war, soon becomes propagandized by the government into supporting the war policy. Furthermore as costs and casualties mount, opposition to the war becomes more difficult, since such a position seems callously to write off the sacrifices of the combat dead. Thus the war might gain a certain "popularity" to justify these sacrifices.[1]

---

[1] This is a possible interpretation of William Gladstone's observation that all English wars gained popular approval within eighteen months of their commencement. See Waltz (1967:272)

A third hypotheses, among many possible, might suggest that no general trends in war support are likely. Rather the excitable American public is found to swing capriciously from support to opposition and back again depending on the events of the hour. A military setback, it is expected, will send much of the public into opposition while good news from the battlefield or negotiating table causes support to blossom.[2]

As will be seen, none of these three hypotheses is entirely adequate.

3.1 MEASURING WAR SUPPORT: THE "MISTAKE" QUESTION

For the purposes of this analysis, it was necessary to find a poll question that tapped a sort of generalized support for the war and that was asked repeatedly in both wars. Only one question fits these requirements really well: Gallup's query during Korea, "Do you think the United States made a mistake in going into the war in Korea, or not?" and his Vietnam version: "In view of the developments since we entered the fighting in Vietnam, do you think the United States made a mistake sending troops to fight in Vietnam?"

This basic question was asked in a variety of ways, especially during the Korean War. Sometimes the question was put in positive form: "Did we do the right thing?" rather than "Did we make a mistake?" and sometimes there were phrases added that helped to boost the percentage expressing support while at other times a variant seemed to lower support. Rather than obfuscating the patterns of support, these question variants, used with care in the manner suggested in Section 1.4.4, can help to broaden the trend analysis.

Whatever the variation, however, the question always asks for the respondent's general opinion on the wisdom of the war venture itself, and thus it seems to be a sound measure of a sort of general support for the war. But it says little about policy preferences at any given moment: Should the war be escalated or deescalated? Nor does it give much indication of how the respondent feels the incumbent president is handling the war at the moment. For various reasons, questions like these are less satisfactory than the

[2] Such fluctuations have been stressed by Almond (1950).

"mistake" question for present purposes. They receive separate and extended examination in Chapter 4.

3.2 ELEMENTS OF SUPPORT FOR THE KOREAN WAR

The responses for the "mistake" question and its variants for the Korean War period are given in rather elaborate form in Table 3.1.[3] The basic question asked by Gallup (American Institute of Public Opinion—AIPO) is given in Column A. Included with it is the Survey Research Center (SRC) question asked in 1950 and 1952, "Do you think we did the right thing in getting into the fighting in Korea last summer (two years ago) or should we have stayed out?" The positive-negative "right thing"—"mistake" comparison seems to make little difference, as can be seen in a comparison of responses to polls conducted at approximately the same time. The Minnesota poll asked a support question quite similar to the AIPO-SRC version and, despite the limited sampling area, generated similar responses as displayed in Column D.

In the first years of the war, the National Opinion Research Center (NORC) included an additional element in its formulation of the question. The respondent was asked if he felt the United States was right to send troops "to stop the Communist invasion of South Korea" (see Column B). Clearly the added reference to the "Communist invasion" was an important cue to the respondents, for the NORC question generally found a 15 to 20 percentage point increase in "support" over that indicated by the AIPO-SRC version and a noticeable drop in the percentage without opinion.

The words "Communist invasion" seem to have served more ably as a clarion call than the words "defend South Korea." When the AIPO question was first asked (the items with the *b* superscript in Column A) it included these latter words but with no apparent impact on war support. This can also be seen in the responses to a question asked in Minnesota early in the war and documented in Table 3.2. Despite the leading tone of the question, a desire to defend the Koreans was found to be rather less than a major motivating force in opinion on the war.

These data suggest somewhat conflicting observations. On the

[3] For other analyses of some of these data, see Scott and Withey (1958); Campbell and Cain (1965); Waltz (1967); and Erskine (1970).

TABLE 3.1 Support and Opposition in the Korean War

A: "Do you think the United States made a mistake in going into the war in Korea, or not?" (AIPO)

B: "Do you think the United States was right or wrong in sending American troops to stop the Communist invasion of South Korea?" (NORC)

C: "As things stand now, do you feel that the war in Korea has been (was) worth fighting, or not?" (NORC)

D: "Looking back over the Korean War since it started last June (in June last year, last year, two years ago, in June of 1950) would you say now that you feel the United States (we) did the right thing in sending American forces to Korea?" (Minn.)

For each question the numbers represent, in order, the percentages in support of the war (Pro), in opposition (Con), and with no opinion (DK).

	A			B			C			D		
	Pro	Con	DK	Pro	Con	DK	Pro	Con	DK	Pro	Con	DK
July 1950												
August 1950	66[b]	19	15	75[a]	21	4						
Inchon landing												
September 1950				81	13	6						
China enters war												
December 1950	39[b]	49	12	55	36	9				47[d]	42	11
February 1951	41	49	10	57	32	11				46[d]	38	16
March 1951	43	44	13	60	30	10						
MacArthur recalled												
April 1951	45	37	18	63	27	10						
May 1951				59	30	11						
Early June 1951	42[c]	41	17							39[d]	46	15

TABLE 3.1 (Continued)

	A			B			C			D		
	Pro	Con	DK	Pro	Con	DK	Pro	Con	DK	Pro	Con	DK
Mid June 1951	39	43	18									
Peace talks begin												
July 1951	47	42	11							46[a]	43	11
Early August 1951												
Late August 1951				60	30	10						
September 1951										52	35	13
Early December 1951				54	36	9				45	39	16
Early January 1952				56	34	9						
March 1952	37	50	13	50	40	10						
June 1952				55	38	7				41	43	16
September 1952	39[c]	41	20									
Early October 1952	36	46	18									
Late October 1952	37	42	20				31	56	12			
Eisenhower elected												
November 1952							34	58	8	48	38	14
Ike visit to Korea												
January 1953	50	36	14				39	53	9			
April 1953							36	55	9			
Late April 1953												
Late June 1953							32	58	9	52	36	12
Talks resume, truce signed												

46

TABLE 3.1 (Continued)

	A			B			C			D		
	Pro	Con	DK	Pro	Con	DK	Pro	Con	DK	Pro	Con	DK
August 1953							27	62	11			
Prisoner repatriation												
September 1953				64e	28	8						
November 1953							38	50	11			
November 1954							39	51	10			
September 1956							46	41	13			
March 1965										67f	16	17

Sources. RC; *Polls*, Spring 1966, p. 76; SRC. The data come from the following surveys. In Column A: AIPO 460, 469, 471, 473, 474; SRC S-101; AIPO 476, 478, 487; SRC 1952 election study; AIPO 506, 507, 510; in Column B: NORC 287, 288, 295, 298, 300, 302, 307, 312, 314, 315, 320, 327, 348; in Column C: NORC 332, 333, 334, 339, 341, 347, 349, 365, 393; in Column D: Minn. 89, 92, 94, 95, 97, 99, 104, 111, 116, poll in *Polls*, Spring 1966, p. 76.

[a] "Do you approve or disapprove of the decision to send American troops to stop the Communist invasion of South Korea?" (NORC)

[b] "In view of the developments since we entered the fighting in Korea, do you think the United States made a mistake in deciding to defend Korea (South Korea), or not?" (AIPO)

[c] "Do you think we did the right thing in getting into the fighting in Korea last summer (two years ago) or should we have stayed out?" (SRC)

[d] ". . . that you feel it was the right thing or the wrong thing to send American . . ." (Minn.)

[e] "As you look back on the Korean war, do you think the United States did the right thing in sending troops to stop the Communist invasion, or should we have stayed out of it entirely?" (NORC)

[f] "Do you think the United States did or did not do the right thing by entering the Korean War in 1950?" (Minn.)

TABLE 3.2 Popular Rationales for the Wars in Korea and Vietnam

August 1950. On the whole do you approve or disapprove of President Truman's action in sending American military forces to help the people of South Korea? Why? (Minn.)

Approve 75% Disapprove 19% No Opinion 7%

Reasons given for approval

53%	Must stop Russia, the Reds, only thing to do, have to sooner or later
17	Serving our own interests, keep them from coming over here
10	Help oppressed people, they needed help
7	Bound to help because of United Nations ties, United Nations action, etc.
2	Approve, but other nations should help too
1	We should have fought the Reds even sooner
8	Other reasons
3	Don't know why, no reason given

Reasons given for disapproval

31%	Not our business, let them fight their own battles
13	Other nations should help too
12	We weren't prepared, not ready, not equipped
5	Don't like war, don't want war
34	Other reasons
6	Don't know why not, no reason given

one hand, support for the war was clearly tied to the anti-Communist spirit in America at the time. To generate a kind of war fever, one merely had to toss the words, "Communist invasion," into the discussion. On the other hand, the Communist element was not entirely built into the response to the war because Americans had to be reminded of it before their anti-Communism was fully activated. To an extent these notions conform at the international level to the survey findings of Samuel Stouffer from the domestic level: while Americans were devotedly and illiberally anti-Communist in the early 1950s, in no sense did a national anxiety syndrome prevail on the issue (1955: Chap. 3). There was concern, but not hysteria.

Another formulation of the question was asked by NORC in the last years of the war (and into the postwar period, a concern of

TABLE 3.2 (Continued)

February 1968. Here is a list of arguments that have been given for our military effort in Vietnam. I'm going to ask you to read over this card carefully. Then I'm going to ask you to tell me . . . which *two or three* of these, yourself, feel are the *very strongest arguments?* (ISSR)

49% If we do not continue, the Communists will take over Vietnam and then move on to other parts of the world

48 We must support our fighting men

33 If we quit now, it would weaken the will of other countries to defend their freedom

33 If we give up, the whole expenditure of American lives and money will have been in vain

24 The United States should never accept defeat

23 If we do not continue, we will lose prestige and the confidence of our friends and allies abroad

19 We are committed to South Vietnam

14 If we pull out and the Communists take over, they will kill many of the Vietnamese who have opposed them

8 If we persevere, we are sure to gain our objectives

Sources. RC; A. Cantril 1970:A-15, A-16.

Chapter 7). In this, the mention of the Communists was eliminated as well as the reference in the AIPO-SRC version to the idea that the United States or "we" somehow "made a mistake" or "did wrong." The respondent was simply asked if he thought the war "worth fighting." This elegantly bland formulation (Column C) seems to have dropped "support" for the war substantially below that tapped by the other queries.

These findings suggest another manipulable element in measured war support: loyalty to governmental policy, reluctance to admit that "we" might have erred. Again, however, this element has more response impact when it is explicitly included in the stimulus. It is clear that *support for the war does not come simply from those who find war a congenial way of solving problems, but also from those who support it because, right or wrong, it is "ours."* This theme, an important one, is developed at greater length in Chapters 4 and 5.

These considerations suggest, therefore, that it is clearly nonsense to designate the amount of "support" for the war by a single number. The question, "How many people support the war?" has no simple answer. For popular "support" for the Korean War was noticeably raised whenever the respondent to oppose the war was required (a) to admit that the United States had made a mistake, or (b) to oppose the halting of the Communists. Both a desire to support the country and its leadership and a penchant for anti-Communism seem to have been important factors in determining support for the war. At any given point in time, support should be considered a chord, rather than a note.

3.3 TRENDS IN SUPPORT FOR THE KOREAN WAR

The support percentages for the questions in Columns A, B, and C of Table 3.1 are plotted in Figure 3.1. As can be seen, the chords progress in parallel fifths, making for consistently patterned, if inelegant, harmony.

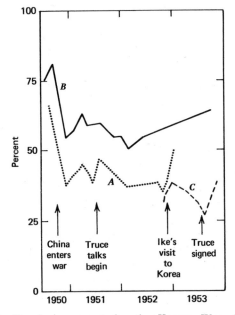

Figure 3.1 Trends in support for the Korean War. (Letters refer to questions in Columns A, B, and C in Table 3.1.)

Support for President Truman's reaction to the North Korean invasion was extremely high at the beginning of the war. When asked in early July, approximately 77 percent responded that they approved his "decision to send United States military aid to South Korea" despite the fact that 43 percent in the same Gallup poll felt this action would "lead to another world war."[4] Support remained high through the summer and into the fall of 1950 as the North Korean thrust was stopped at Pusan and reversed at Inchon.

This high level of support was maintained probably because the public was convinced that the war would be a short one. In July, only 14 percent expected the war to last more than a year (AIPOr July 29, 1950).

It was the entry of China into the war that apparently altered such perceptions and, with them, the basic support for the war. As the Chinese swarmed across the Yalu River, blunting and then turning the Allied "home by Christmas" offensive, the war took on a new and far more painful appearance.[5] By the time the "mistake" questions were again posed in the last days of 1950, support for the war had dropped some 25 percentage points.

More striking than the drop in support caused by the Chinese entry is the near-absence of further decline for the remaining 2½ years of war. From early 1951 until the end of the war in the summer of 1953, basic support for the war, shown not only in the A and B figures, but also in those from Minnesota in Column D of Table 3.1, remained largely constant—this, despite the continually mounting casualties and despite a number of important events: the recall of General MacArthur; the beginning, breaking off, and then intermittent restarting of peace talks; the launching of offensives and counteroffensives; the 1952 campaign and election.

Thus, although there seems to have been an important shift of

---

[4] RC. See also Roper (1957: 144-45) and the Minnesota data in Table 3.2 on p. 49.

[5] Most Americans, however, were probably not surprised by the Chinese entry into the war. In September 1950, Gallup asked, "The 38th parallel is the border between North and South Korea. Do you think Russia and Communist China will enter the fighting in Korea if the U.S. and her allies continue the fight north of this line?" Fully 64 percent replied affirmatively; 22 percent negatively. (RC)

opinion on the war after one major event, events thereafter had comparatively little impact on the aggregate support for the Korean War. The Chinese intervention seemed to shake from the support ranks those who were tenuous and those who felt that they could support a short war, but not a long one. The war was then left with a relatively hard core of support that remained generally at a constant level for the duration; changes of fortune and climbing casualty figures apparently became less important. Notions about the shifting moods of the American public do not seem to fit these findings at all well.[6]

Of course, a constant result like this in aggregate figures can mask substantial changes among subgroups. Thus the result suggests either no change or else subgroup changes that happen to be countervailing. The trends in responses to this question for various poll subgroups are assessed in Chapter 5 and, in general, they are found to display much the same imperturbability.

A number of small changes in the aggregate support figures are worth noting. Support for the war rose somewhat and opposition declined in the A, B, and D figures in the first half of 1951 after the initial depression over the Chinese entry began to wear off, and as the Chinese drive was blunted. By June this marginal increase of enthusiasm showed signs of waning when the opening of peace talks, viewed by some with cautious optimism, seems to have caused a rise of support (but a much smaller decline in opposition), evident in the A and D figures. And the election of General Eisenhower in 1952 together with his postelection trip to Korea seems to have generated some temporary enthusiasm, judging from the behavior of the data in the A, C, and D columns.

3.4 TRENDS IN SUPPORT FOR THE VIETNAM WAR

Survey trend data on war support are less rich in the Vietnam than in the Korean period, despite the increased popularity of polling in the decade separating the wars. Gallup was still there and asking the right questions for present purposes, but NORC had gone into more specialized polling and the new Harris polling organization never really asked over any length of time a war support question that was in the right spirit.[7]

---

[6] See also Caspary (1970). But see also the discussion in Chapter 4.

[7] From time to time between 1966 and 1968 the Harris Poll reported a

Table 3.3 displays the results of the relevant questions from the Vietnam period. The three questions listed are all quite similar in basic format to the AIPO-SRC questions from Korea listed in Column A of Table 3.1: all ask whether "we" or "the United States" did the right thing; none add anything about stopping Communism.[8] The AIPO question in Column B of Table 3.3 is separated out only because there is room. The SRC question in Column C, however, must be kept separate because it sometimes was asked only of those respondents who said they had been paying attention to what was going on in Vietnam. The support scores from Columns A and B are combined and plotted in Figure 3.2.

Judging from these materials, support for the war in Vietnam rose very considerably as American troops joined the fighting during the last half of 1965. There seems, therefore, to have been at the time a fairly considerable "rally-round-the-flag" effect, a phenomenon of interest also in other chapters. At the same time the percentage with no opinion dropped, suggesting that, as the war began to gather more popular attention, people seem to have been led to form an opinion on it, not led to confusion and doubt from cross-pressures or value conflicts. It is also notable that, as the Vietnam war debate broadened over the next years, the no opinion percentage tended somewhat to decline further.

General approval for the war remained at its high level into 1966. Comparable support in Korea is found only in the early months of the conflict. By mid-1966, however, support had dropped to levels more familiar from the Korean case, although still on the high side. The Buddhist crisis and the frustrating South Vietnamese political instability of the time—Americans advocated summary withdrawal by a 54 to 28 margin if the internal fighting increased (GOI 12)—undoubtedly affected this change. In addition, the increasing disaffection of prominent American politicians and intellectuals, voiced in the Fulbright hearings of February and March 1966, probably helped to make dissent respectable.

"war support index." However, although it was not always clear from the news releases, the questions on which this index was based varied somewhat from time to time and usually tapped policy preferences (discussed in Chapter 4) rather than the sort of general war support in the Gallup question.

[8] There is evidence from other questions asked during the Vietnam War, however, to suggest that the word, "Communist," still was capable of increasing measured support for the war (see Section 4.2.2).

TABLE 3.3 Support and Opposition in the Vietnamese War

A: "In view of the developments since we entered the fighting in Vietnam, do you think the U.S. made a mistake sending troops to fight in Vietnam?" (AIPO)

B: "Some people think we should not have become involved with our military forces in Southeast Asia, while others think we should have. What is your opinion?" (AIPO)

C: "Do you think we did the right thing in getting into the fighting in Vietnam or should we have stayed out?" In 1964 and 1966 asked only of those who said they had been paying attention to what was going on in Vietnam (80 percent of the sample in 1964, 93 percent in 1966). (SRC)

For each question the numbers represent, in order, the percentages in support of the war (Pro), in opposition (Con), and with no opinion (DK).

	A			B			C		
	Pro	Con	DK	Pro	Con	DK	Pro	Con	DK
November 1964							47	30	23
January 1965				50	28	22			
May 1965				52	26	22			
August 1965	61	24	15						
November 1965				64	21	15			
March 1966	59	25	16						
May 1966	49	36	15						
Bomb oil dumps									
September 1966	48	35	17						
November 1966	51	31	18				47	31	22
Early February 1967	52	32	16						

May 1967	50	37	13			
July 1967	48	41	11			
October 1967	44	46	10			
Bunker, Westmoreland visit						
December 1967	46	45	9			
Tet offensive						
Early February 1968	42	46	12			
March 1968	41	49	10			
April 1968	40	48	12			
GOP Convention						
August 1968	35	53	12			
Dem. Convention						
Early October 1968	37	54	9	30	52	18
Nixon elected						
February 1969	39	52	9			
September 1969	32	58	10			
January 1970	33	57	10			
March 1970	32	58	10			
April 1970	34	51	15			
Cambodia invaded						
May 1970	36	56	8			
November 1970				30	49	20
January 1971	31	59	10			
May 1971	28	61	11			

Sources. SRC; GOI 6, 52, 56, 59, 61, 69, 73.

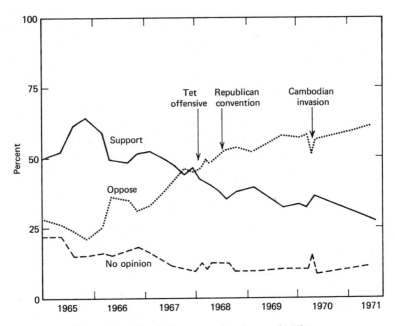

Figure 3.2 Trends in support for the war in Vietnam.

Also important was the fact that, like Korea at the end of 1950, the war was increasingly seen to be a long, bloody affair, not one that American troops could bring to a hasty end. The percentage expecting a long war rose from 54 to 72 between the end of 1965 and mid-1966.[9] At the same time, United States casualties soon attained an order of magnitude comparable to Korea: 5000 Americans had been killed in Vietnam by September 1966 and another 1000 had died by the end of the year.

In the years following mid-1966, support for the war suffered a slow and somewhat ambiguous decline while opposition grew at a slightly faster rate. Support dropped by 1969 to levels as low as any attained in Korea. And then at the end of the year support for the first time finally reached levels clearly lower than those found

[9] Harris Poll, *Newsweek,* July 10, 1967, p. 22.

in the earlier war. By that time, however, the war had been going on over a year longer than the Korean conflict, and American losses in Vietnam had well surpassed those suffered in Korea—as noted in Section 2.3.6, casualties reached Korean War levels in early 1968 and combat deaths did so a year later (see Figure 2.1).

As in the Korean case, events do not seem to have set up major perturbations in these trends. It is particularly notable in this regard that support for the war changed so little between the fall of 1967 and the spring of 1968, despite a series of presumably momentous events: the Tet offensive, the replacement of General Westmoreland, President Johnson's decision not to run again and his partial bombing halt, the opening of preliminary peace talks, miscellaneous offensives in the South, and the emergence of explicit challenges to the Johnson policy by prominent Democratic presidential candidates. Of course, the support question was not asked frequently enough to sort out the various effects of each of these incidents, but the combined, net impact of all of them seems limited at most.[10]

It appears then that public support for and opposition to the war in Vietnam hardened, somewhat as in Korea, to the point where events were less likely to make much of an impression. This is not to say that Americans became unaware of events in the war: Gallup found that the number who believed that the allies were "losing ground" in Vietnam rose 15 percentage points after the Tet offensive in 1968 and those of the opinion that the war

---

[10] It is tantalizing to suggest that perhaps an event which did noticeably decrease support for the war was the 1968 *Republican* convention, for a new low support score for the war was registered in August 1968 after the Republican but before the Democratic convention. Perhaps the televised display of that respectable, conservative body denouncing the war, albeit in highly unspecific terms, served to convert to war opposition some conservatives who had been utterly unaffected by the antiwar agitation from the Left. However, it should be acknowledged that the trend was downward throughout the spring and possibly this depth of support would have been reached by August anyway. In a report on some unpublished research based on a series of daily polls conducted during the last half of 1968, Richard Maisel notes: "public response to the Republican convention was greater than to the Democratic convention particularly for noncollege graduates" (1969: 456).

would be over in less than two years dropped 13 percentage points (NYT, March 10, 1968). But support or opposition as a matter of general policy seems to have changed only gradually.

As in the case of Korea, public support had little to do with the defense of the local ally there. This is suggested by the data in the second half of Table 3.2 (p. 49). Further evidence for this notion is proffered in Section 4.2.2.[11]

3.5 A COMPARISON OF THE WARS

3.5.1 The Beginning

It is somewhat surprising that the wars in Korea and Vietnam generated about the same amount of support at the beginning—where the "beginning" of the Vietnam War is taken to be mid-1965. As noted in Section 2.3.4, the Korean War was begun under far more dramatic circumstances with a rather clear-cut Communist attack and an American decision over a few days to come to the aid of the attacked under United Nations auspices. In Vietnam the greatly increased American involvement in 1965 was accomplished over several months and in piecemeal fashion with the administration consciously trying to downplay its significance.

The comparability of war support at this point suggests that the principal motivating element in the public response to the Korean decision was similar to that in Vietnam—a desire to support the country's leadership in time of trouble, the rally-round-the-flag phenomenon.

It also suggests that as long as the president has the power to commit troops, proposals that suggest wars would be avoided if the public (or Congress) were required to vote on their desirability are naive. After the commitment, there is a strong tendency to support the leadership. Even votes taken before the commitment is made are likely to be heavily influenced by the position of the leadership.[12]

[11] In this, the public was in accord with some official thinking. In a memo of March 1965, reprinted in the *Pentagon Papers,* Assistant Secretary of Defense John T. McNaughton specifically excluded as a "U.S. aim" in Vietnam "to 'help a friend' " (Sheehan 1971:432).

[12] See also the discussion in Chapters 5 and 6. One might also extrapolate

3.5.2 Trends in Support

As seen in Sections 3.3 and 3.4, support in both wars declined from initial high levels to lower levels. The transitions were similar in that events, particularly in later stages of the wars, seem to have had relatively little impact on the overall trend. However, the pace of the transitions differed considerably: the drop of support in Korea was precipitous after the Chinese entered the war, but support for Vietnam declined considerably more gradually. Therefore, in comparing the wars, it does not seem to be the case that the decline of war support has been related to the duration of the war in any simple manner. Such a relation works fairly well in the Vietnam case, but in Korea there was a large drop in support over a relatively short period of time during the winter of 1950 to 1951; thus, unlike Vietnam, support did not decline continually as time went by.

Part of this difference can be taken into account if one seeks to relate support for the war to the number of casualties suffered at the time of the poll (see Figure 2.1). The relevant measure then becomes the amount of pain caused by the war—as reflected in the total casualty figures—rather than simply the amount of time the war has been going on. The assumption is that people react more to the cumulative human costs of the war than to its duration.

In the Vietnam case this does not change the picture too much because casualties mounted gradually as time went by. In the Korean case, however, things are improved considerably. The large drop in war support that occurred with the Chinese entry into the war is associated, of course, with a corresponding jump in the cumulative casualties suffered.

But problems remain. While casualties continued to mount in the last two years of the Korean War, there was no corresponding drop in support. And, after a few years in the Vietnam War, casualties were being suffered at increasing rates; yet support continued

tentatively to suggest the possibility that the impact of the Pearl Harbor attack was not as vital to public attitudes toward World War II as might be supposed. President Roosevelt might have been able to carry much of the public with him had he simply led the country directly into war without benefit of this dramatic stimulus. Popular attitudes toward World War II are discussed briefly in Section 3.6.

to decline at a relatively gentle pace not really reflecting this mounting casualty rate.

These concerns can be incorporated into the analysis by seeking to relate popular support for the wars to the *logarithm* of the total number of American casualties that had been suffered at the time of the poll. That is, one assumes that the public is sensitive to relatively small losses at the start of the war but only to rather large ones toward its end. Specifically, one does not expect casualties to affect attitudes in a linear manner with a rise from 100 to 1000 being the same as one from 10,000 to 10,900. Rather, a rise from 100 to 1000 is taken as the same as one from 10,000 to 100,000. Thus the distance between the numbers, 10, 100, 1000, 10,000, 100,000 and 1,000,000 is made equal.

This sort of a transformation is applied for Table 3.4 and the result is a set of equations suggesting strikingly similar drops in popular support for the two wars: *in each war, support is projected to have started at much the same level (the intercept figure), and then every time American casualties increased by a factor of 10, support for the war dropped by about 15 percentage points.*[13] Results are not so neat when the dependent variable is the percentage opposing the war, but the patterns remain largely similar: opposition to Vietnam is taken to have begun at a somewhat lower level than in Korea and then to have increased at a somewhat faster rate. Part of this difference is due to the generally lower frequencies of no opinion responses during the Vietnam period.[14]

To summarize, then. When one takes support or opposition for

---

[13] For example, the amount of support for the war in Vietnam at any point in time would be equal to 124.98 minus 16.51 times the logarithm of the United States casualties at that point. The intercept figure is a backward extrapolation to an imaginary starting point percentage of 114 for Korea and 125 for Vietnam at the point when casualties would have been zero. To avoid this absurdity a transformation of the dependent variable could have been undertaken, but this would have complicated the analysis without adding any important new information.

[14] The similarities between the equations for the wars increase when the NORC cases and the NORC dummy variable are removed from the Korean consideration, thus comparing only questions almost identical for the two wars. The Korean equations then generate intercepts of 117.44 and −22.74 and regression coefficients of −15.51 and 13.40 for the approval and disapproval scores, respectively.

TABLE 3.4 Regression Results: War Support as a Function of the Logarithm of American Casualties

| | Dependent variable | | | |
| | Percent Support | | Percent Opposed | |
	Korea	Vietnam	Korea	Vietnam
Mean	51.4	43.0	36.2	44.8
Standard Deviation	12.1	10.0	9.4	12.1
Intercept	114.46	124.98	−16.12	−55.07
Independent variables				
$\quad$ Log_{10} casualties	−14.89	−16.51	12.02	20.12
	(2.39)	(1.16)	(2.60)	(1.34)
$\quad$ NORC dummy	15.49		− 9.45	
	(2.10)		(2.30)	
Standard error of estimate	5.21	3.20	5.68	3.70
R^2	.83	.90	.67	.91

The regression equations are displayed vertically. The number of items in the Korean case is 25: all items in Columns A and B of Table 3.1 except for that of September 1953 (which was taken after the war had ended). The number of items in the Vietnam case is 24: all items in Columns A and B of Table 3.3 after mid-1965 (which is when the war is taken to have begun for the American public). The NORC dummy variable in the Korean case takes on a value of 1 if the item in question comes from Column B of Table 1 and is zero otherwise. It reflects, therefore, the general added boost given to measured war support by the wording of that question. The figures in parentheses are the standard errors for the respective regression coefficients. To be regarded statistically significant a regression coefficient should be, conventionally, at least twice its standard error. All equations are significant (F test) at well beyond the .01 level. The standard error of estimate and the R^2 figure measure how well the equation fits the data points. An R^2 of 1.00 would indicate a perfect fit.

the wars in Korea or Vietnam and correlates either of them (1) with the casualties suffered at the time the poll was conducted or (2) with the duration of the war at the time of the poll, one gets, at least, a reasonably good fit—as would be the case if one correlated support or opposition with *any* variable that increased (or decreased) continually during the wars. But in all cases, correlating the *logarithm* of the number of casualties suffered at the time of the poll gives the best fit. Furthermore, and most important, because of the differing patterns under which casualties were suffered in the two wars, the equations relating support or opposition to the logarithm of the casualties are much more similar for the two wars than are the equations generated when the logarithm of the casualties is related to the simple casualty figure or the duration figures. The plots in Figures 3.1 and 3.2, relating support to duration, do not look greatly similar; if the percentage support were plotted against the logarithm of casualties, however, the lines would be highly similar for the two wars.

What this suggests, then, is that *Americans, in the aggregate, reacted in similar ways to the two wars.* While they did weary of the wars, they generally seem to have become hardened to the wars' costs: they are sensitive to relatively small losses in the early stages, but only to large losses in later stages. Another way of looking at the trends is to see subgroups of the population dropping off sequentially from the war's support as casualties mount. In the early stages the support of those with considerable misgivings is easily alienated; in later stages the only advocates left are the relatively hardened supporters whose conversion to opposition proves to be more difficult.

Numbers. Although the casualty figures can be taken to be a good composite indicator of the intensity and costs of the wars as well as their length, and although public opinion seems to relate to these figures, it should not be assumed that Americans are reacting in a direct sense to the numbers themselves. On occasion, the public has been asked to estimate the American casualty or death figures for a war, and it is possible to compare these estimates with the respondents' policy preferences on the war. Four surveys of this kind were investigated: two taken at the beginning of the Vietnam War, one from the midst of the Korean War, and one from shortly after World War II. No consistent patterns could be found. There was no clear tendency for high (or low) estimators to support or oppose the wars, and few demographic relations of interest emerged.

3.6 KOREA, VIETNAM, AND WORLD WAR II

To put the poll statistics from Korea and Vietnam in somewhat broader perspective it may be useful to look at poll data from World War II, presumably the most "popular" in American history. A question comparable to the one under consideration here was posed by Gallup in early 1944, "Do you think you, yourself, will feel [in years to come] it was a mistake for us to have entered this war?" Only 14 percent answered affirmatively with 77 percent in the negative, a support rating solidly more favorable than those attained by the two later wars (Cantril and Strunk 1951:978).

Still, the picture is not quite so clear-cut. In 1967 Gallup posed an updated version of a question that had been asked frequently during World War II: "Do you feel you have a clear idea of what the Vietnam War is all about—that is, what we are fighting for?" Not surprisingly, great confusion was found—only 48 percent felt they knew (GOI 25). The comparable question during World War II elicited a more confident judgment—but not as much greater as might be expected. In fact in June 1942, 6 months after Pearl Harbor, only 53 percent of the public felt it had a clear idea of what the war was about. This proportion increased after that but approached 80 percent only in 1945 and at one point, the spring of 1944, dipped below 60 percent (Cantril and Strunk 1951:1077–78; Cantril 1967:48).

Sentiment for withdrawal from the Korean and Vietnam wars may very crudely be compared to an affirmative reply to the following query posed frequently during World War II: "If Hitler offered peace now to all countries on the basis of not going further but of leaving matters as they now are, would you favor or oppose such a peace?" Few supported the proposition in the early years of the war, but in early 1944—while Hitler still held France—it was endorsed by more than 20 percent of the population and by about 15 percent thereafter (Cantril and Strunk 1951:1077–78).

Thus World War II, although unquestionably much more highly supported by the public than the Korean and Vietnam wars, seems

TABLE 3.5   Opinion on Concentration Camps, World War II

January 1943. It is said that two million Jews have been killed in Europe since the war began. Do you think this is true or just a rumor?

True	47%
Rumor	29
No opinion	24

November 1944. Do you believe the stories that the Germans have murdered many people in concentration camps are true or not true?

True	76%
Not true	12
No opinion	12

Nobody knows how many may have been murdered, but what would be your best guess? Asked of the 76 percent of the sample who believed stories of German murders of concentration camp inmates.

100 thousand or less	27%
(including answers of "thousands")	
Over 100 thousand to 500 thousand	5
500 thousand to 1 million	1
(including answers of "hundreds of thousands")	
1 million	6
2 million to 6 million	8
6 million or more	4
No opinion	25

May 1945. What do you think of the reports that the Germans have killed many people in concentration camps [prisoner of war camps] or let them starve to death—are they true or not true?

	Concentration Camps	Prisoner of War Camps
True	84%	87%
Probably true	–	1
Partly true, exaggerated	9	6
Believe some, doubt others	–	*
Doubtful, hard to believe	1	1
Untrue	2	3
Didn't say	3	3

Nobody knows how many have been killed or starved to death [in German concentration camps], but what would be your best guess?

Median = 1,000,000 people

Source. Cantril and Strunk (1951:383, 1070, 1071)

to have been rather less consensual than might be supposed. This may be so in part because the truth about Hitler's death camps only reached the American public in 1945 (see Table 3.5). In mid-1943 only half the population thought that the death camp "rumors" were true. At the end of 1944 this portion had risen to 76 percent, but few anticipated that the death toll would be greater than "thousands." Therefore a major reason for supporting the war was largely unappreciated while it was going on.

3.7 CONCLUSION

The situation with regard to the data from Korea and Vietnam is rather extraordinary. As observed in Section 2.3.8, the amount of *vocal* opposition to the war in Vietnam was vastly greater than that for the war in Korea. Yet it has now been found that support for the wars among the general public followed a pattern of decline that was remarkably similar. Although support for the war in Vietnam did finally drop below those levels found during Korea, it did so only after the war had gone on considerably longer and only after American casualties had far surpassed those of the earlier war.

An effort to explain this state of affairs is deferred until Chapter 6. The intervening chapters, however, attempt to broaden the comparison of the wars by assessing other possible measures of war support and by looking at subgroups of the population as they have responded to the wars and to war issues.

CHAPTER 4

Support for the Wars as Reflected in Questions About Withdrawal, Escalation, Leadership, Isolationism

The analysis in Chapter 3 is based almost entirely on an examination of the responses to one kind of poll query about the wars, the "mistake" question. On this measure, levels of support seem quite similar for the two wars.

But it might be argued that these measures are insufficiently sensitive to important nuances of opinion. For example, of those who classify the war a "mistake," it is possible that more are intense about their opposition in Vietnam than in Korea. This could help to explain the difference in vocal opposition to the wars. These and other subtleties might become obvious if one were to look at other poll queries. The purpose of this chapter then is to examine other questions posed during the wars in an effort to gain some depth about attitudes toward the conflicts and to compare them from other angles.

Of particular interest will be questions about war policy and strategy as they reflect attitudes toward escalation and deescalation and as they bear on the consideration of groups commonly known as "hawks" and "doves." Although there is a correlation, such questions about policy options by no means probe the same attitudes as the "mistake" questions. As Converse and Schuman

(1970) have shown for the Vietnam War, it is entirely possible for a respondent to find the war a mistake but still to prefer escalation as a strategy, or to favor withdrawal as a present strategy while finding the war not to have been a mistake. Table 4.1 displays some comparable evidence from the Korean period.

TABLE 4.1   The Mistake Question and Policy Options, November 1952

Suppose the truce talks in Korea break down completely. Which one of these three things do you think we should do then?	As things stand now, do you feel that the war in Korea has been worth fighting or not?	
	Support, worth fighting	Oppose, not worth fighting
Pull our troops out of Korea and bring them home	7%	32%
Keep our troops in Korea and hold the present line there	43	21
Go ahead and attack the Chinese Communists	43	38
No opinion	7	9

Source. NORCc.

Although many questions were posed by the polling agencies during the Korean and Vietnam wars, none were asked with anything approaching the constancy and persistency of the "mistake" questions. Therefore, when one tries to use these questions to compare wars, or even to analyze trends within a single war, conclusions can be reached only with more tedium and uncertainty. Both the conclusions and the difficulties are discussed (belabored perhaps) in this chapter.

4.1   TWO PRELIMINARY CONSIDERATIONS

Two considerations deserve special examination before the poll results are directly assessed. One of these is a continuation of a concern of Chapter 1: the elusive, but absolutely vital, matter of question wording. The other is the importance of the position of the leadership, particularly the presidential leadership, in influencing public responses to questions about foreign policy. These two concerns must be carefully kept in mind when assessing public opinion data on the wars. They are particularly stressed here because, in the extraordinary debates in recent years over Vietnam policy, they have been so often ignored by partisans—and sometimes professional analysts—seeking to use public opinion data to buttress a substantive position.

4.1.1 Question Wording, Again

An advantage of the "mistake" question was, as noted, the persistent way it was asked without wording change, or with wording changes whose effects could be rather directly assessed. In the case of most other questions this constancy is absent, and thus one is usually confronted with a set of responses to questions which, though similar in basic content and purpose, contain variations in wording that often render comparison extremely difficult.

Consider, by way of example, two questions posed by Gallup about a month apart shortly after the Chinese had entered the Korean War. One was an open-ended query: "If the Chinese Communists continue to send hundreds of thousands of troops into Korea, far outnumbering our forces there, what do you think we should do?" The other gave the respondent two specific options: "Now that Communist China has entered the fighting in Korea with forces far outnumbering the United Nations troops there, which one of these courses would you, yourself, prefer that we follow—A. Pull our troops out of Korea as fast as possible, or B. Keep our troops there to fight these larger forces?"

To begin with, the questions are framed in such a remarkably tendentious manner that the only really safe inference is that the Gallup organization, itself, favored United States withdrawal from Korea at the end of 1950.[1] Beyond this, the change from an open-ended format to a strict two-way choice between withdrawal and American slaughter alters radically the proportion who are presumed to favor withdrawal apparently because it forces would-be escalators to choose between, for them, second-best alternatives.

---

[1] Nevertheless, the questions are taken to have meaning for some analysts. See GOI 3, p. 26; Lipset (1966:24).

About 28 percent were found to "favor" withdrawal in the first question, while fully 66 percent took the withdrawal option on the second. (The full results are given in Table 4.4, questions *C* and *D,* on p. 75.)

Of course, the problems of question wording need not be this gross. It will be seen that the American public will respond in quite different ways to these three comparatively similar options: "withdraw immediately," "withdraw as fast as possible," and "begin to withdraw." Therefore *if one wants to demonstrate the popularity or unpopularity of various war issues, considerable power is in the hands of the author of the question.*[2]

Following the discussion in Chapter 1, then, the very sensitivity of opinion to changes in the wording of the stimulus question can be taken to suggest that public opinion on many war issues has been marked by a good deal of uncertainty and indecision.

4.1.2　The Position of the President; "Followers"

To deal with this uncertainty and indecision, many in the population grope for cues on which to base their opinion. The perceived issue position of various opinion leaders is very often taken as an important guide. While many public figures and institutions influence public opinion in this way, the most important by far is the president.

Thus there exists, particularly in the area of foreign affairs, an important group of citizens—they can be called "followers"—who are inclined to rally to the support of the president no matter what he does.[3]

The president's strength in this area seems to derive from the majesty of the office and from his singular position as head of state. Followers seem to identify with the country and with its leadership and tend to be susceptible to social and political influences in this direction. They swim in the mainstream, to apply the jargon of yesteryear. For them, the president *is* the country for many purposes and, therefore, there is a certain popular loy-

---

[2] The problems of varying question wording are also discussed for the Vietnam case in Converse and Schuman (1970) and Rosenberg et al. (1970: Chap. 2).

[3] See also the discussion of the "mainstream model" in Gamson and Modigliani (1966).

alty to the man that comes with the office which tends to place him above politics. As will be seen in Chapter 8, whatever his party, the president invariably comes out at or near the top on Gallup's yearly most admired man sweepstakes. In 1968, eight of the ten most admired men were present or past Presidents or were prime contenders for the office.

A feature of the "mistake" question, thus far unappreciated in this discourse, is the consistency of the presumed presidential position on the issue posed by the question: for both wars, the official policy would assert that the war was not a mistake. Therefore the decline of the wars' popularity on this dimension could be fairly safely attributed to factors other than shifts of official policy, principally, of course, to a growing weariness with the costs of the war itself.

On other issues, however, especially those dealing with questions of war policy and strategy in the Vietnam War, changes of official policy did occur. And, because of the follower phenomenon, one finds major shifts in public opinion on questions of policy after policy changes. Table 4.2 illustrates this with an

TABLE 4.2   Responses to Questions about the Bombing of Hanoi and Haiphong, 1965 to 1966

	Percentage of Those with Opinion	
	Favor Bombing	Oppose Bombing
Do you think the administration is more right or more wrong in not bombing Hanoi or Haiphong?		
September 1965	30	70
February 1966	42	58
May 1966	50	50
BOMBING BEGUN		
Do you think the administration is more right or more wrong in bombing Hanoi and Haiphong?		
July 1966	85	15

Source. Harris poll, LAT, June 13, 1966, July 11, 1966.

example from the Vietnam period. The Harris poll reports that support for bombing the Hanoi-Haiphong area increased in a major way after the bombing of military targets there was begun in 1966. Lest one conclude these data suggest that administration-supporters are simply latent hawks, Table 4.3 illustrates a dovish shift after the partial bombing halt of 1968. Question *F* was asked after the bombing halt but before the North Vietnamese had responded by agreeing to preliminary talks. As can be seen, the shift in opinion is striking if the response is compared to the prehalt response generated by question *E,* which is worded in a manner rather favorable to a bombing halt, and the shift is spectacular if some of the other early questions are used as the base of comparison.[4]

Substantively, what this phenomenon means, of course, is that, if one wishes to assess the American public's "opinion" on an issue of this sort, it is essential that consideration be taken of what the administration's policy was at the time the poll question was posed. It is clear from Tables 4.2 and 4.3 that data exist to argue that Americans were basically either "hawkish" *or* "dovish" about bombing policy in the Vietnam War.

What the tables actually suggest, however, is that the "hawk"-"dove" categorization is quite inadequate to explain popular opinion on the wars, a topic to be developed more fully in Chapter 5. Followers tend to reject proposals for forceful or accommodating policies in the abstract if they imply an alteration of "our" present course, but once the president has adopted the new policy many in the group will follow his lead. Thus followers cannot be classified in hawk-dove terms: if the administration is using force, followers will respond like hawks; if it is seeking peace, they will respond like doves.

Sometimes the propensities of the follower group can be activated in an extraordinarily simple manner on polls. One can simply frame a hypothetical question: "Suppose policy x *were* the president's policy, then would you go along with it?" When asked about supposedly unpopular policies, such questions often

---

[4] See also Rosenberg (1970:25–29) where a related example, concerning popular reaction to President Nixon's 1970 decision to invade Cambodia, is discussed.

TABLE 4.3   Responses to Questions about the Halting of Bombing, 1967 to 1968

	Favor Bombing	Oppose Bombing	No Opinion
A1 Should the bombing of North Vietnam be halted "to see if the Communists will come to the negotiating table?"			
September 1967	48	37	15
A2 Same as A1. October 1967	53	29	18
B "Continue to bomb selected targets in North Vietnam as at present and keep military pressures on until we get word from North Vietnam that they will reduce their military efforts and agree to talk about a solution to the war. Do you favor or oppose this plan?"			
October 1967	55	35	10
C1 "Some people say that a halt in bombing will improve our chances in Vietnam for meaningful peace talks. Others say that our chances are better if the bombing is continued. With which group are you more inclined to agree?"			
October 1967	63	26	11
A3 Same as A1. December 1967	63	24	13
TET OFFENSIVE			
C2 Same as C1. February 1968	70	16	11

TABLE 4.3 (Continued)

	Favor Bombing	Oppose Bombing	No Opinion
D "The North Vietnamese have said that if we agree to stop the bombing of North Vietnam, they will agree to peace negotiations. How do you feel—should we stop the bombing or not?"			
March 1968	51	40	9
PARTIAL BOMBING HALT			
E "Do you approve or disapprove of President Johnson's decision to stop the bombing of North Vietnam?"			
April 1968	26	64	10
NORTH VIETNAMESE AGREE TO PRELIMINARY PEACE TALKS			
F "Do you approve or disapprove of the President's decision to halt bombings of North Vietnam to get the Communists to start peace negotiations?"			
April 1968	24	57	19

Sources. A: WP December 23, 1967, full text of question not given; *B:* GOI 29; *C:* GOI 33; *D:* GOI 34; *E:* GOI 35; *F:* WP, April 8, 1968.

stimulate considerable changes in public response. An example can be seen in question Z in Table 4.5 (p. 90) where the public is asked if it would support a government approved policy of withdrawal from Vietnam. The policy garners unusually high support, compared for example to question $Y1$ where there is no suggestion of government sponsorship of the idea. A second example concerns United States policy toward Communist China. A study conducted by SRC in 1964 (Patchen 1966) clearly showed a public willingness to support hypothetical presidential initiatives for the relaxation of tensions with Communist China although, as shown in Figure 1.2 (p. 16), opposition at the time on the issue of admitting her to the United Nations was about as strong as it had ever been. As later data in Figure 1.2 show, successful initiatives in this area, particularly under President Nixon in 1970, did lead to a considerable shift of opinion (see also Free and Cantril 1968:86–89).

The existence of the followers means the president, particularly in the short run, has more flexibility in foreign policy than might at first appear, a proposition rarely noted by journalists or politicians, but often by public opinion analysts (Rosenberg et al. 1970: Chap. 2; Waltz 1967; Verba et al. 1967; Converse and Schuman 1970; Lipset 1966). Of course, it is important for him to consider not only the short-range popularity of such initiatives but also the potential long-range damage if the opposition should be able to exploit the initiative to its advantage in an election contest.

4.2 QUESTIONS ABOUT WITHDRAWAL

American withdrawal from the war was a policy option that was available throughout both wars, and it was frequently asked about by the polling agencies. Because of the diffuse array of questions used to assess popular support for this strategic alternative, there is no approach to it that is at once thorough and concise. The effort in Tables 4.4 and 4.5 is for thoroughness and the results may strike some as an exercise in tabular overkill. Listed in chronological order are questions and responses on the withdrawal issue for each of the wars. Questions of identical wording are given the same identifying letter. Table 4.4 covers pp. 75–80; Table 4.5 covers pp. 81–98.

TABLE 4.4 Support for Withdrawal from Korea

Identical questions are given the same identifying letter. The identification for the last question in a series is underlined.

A   Some people say that the United States should pull our troops out of Korea and stop fighting there. Other people say that we should go on fighting in Korea. With which point of view do you agree? (Late July 1950)

    12% Pull out, stop fighting
    77   Go on fighting
    11   No opinion

B   Some people say the United States should stop fighting and take her troops out of Korea to avoid a third world war. Other people say we should keep our troops there even if it does mean a world war. What do you, yourself, think—should we take our troops out of Korea, or not? (November 1950)

    25% Stop fighting, take troops out
    65   Keep troops, risk world war
    10   No opinion

C   If the Chinese Communists continue to send hundreds of thousands of troops into Korea, far outnumbering our forces there, what do you think we should do? (Early December 1951)

    28% Withdraw
    4   Strategic retreat
    2   Negotiate
    25   Intensify against Red China
    27   Use atomic bomb
    1   Miscellaneous
    12   No opinion

D   Now that Communist China has entered the fighting in Korea with forces far outnumbering the United Nations troops there, which one of these courses would you, yourself, prefer that we follow? (Early January 1951)

    66% Pull our troops out of Korea as fast as possible
    25   Keep our troops there to fight these larger forces
    9   No opinion

TABLE 4.4 Support for Withdrawal from Korea (Continued)

E Do you think we should pull our troops out of Korea now, or should we try to stay on as long as possible? (January 1951)

    20% Pull troops out
    67   Try to stay on
    13   No opinion

F What do you think we should do to bring the war in Korea to an end? (March 1951)

    12% Withdraw
    11   Arbitration
     1   Negative, oppose war, "it's a mess"
    22   Stay there, finish
    11   Bomb them, use A-bomb
    29   Don't know

G1 Do you think we should continue to keep our troops in Korea, or should be pull them out? (March 1951)

    18% Pull them out now
    71   Continue
    11   No opinion

G2 Do you think we should continue to keep our troops in Korea, or should we pull them out now? (April 1951)

    21% Pull them out now
    68   Continue
    11   No opinion

G3 Do you think we should continue to keep our troops in Korea, or should we pull them out now? (May 1951)

    18% Pull them out now
    73   Continue
     9   No opinion

H Here is a list of things that might be done in handling the Korean situation. Which of these things do you feel the United States should do and which ones shouldn't we do? Get out of Korea and stay out. (June 1951)

    19% Should get out and stay out
    63   Should not
    18   No opinion

TABLE 4.4   Support for Withdrawal from Korea (Continued)

*I*1   What do you, yourself, think we should do now about the war in Korea? (October 1951)

    9% Withdraw
    5   Negative, have no business there
    10   Make peace
    2   Continue
    25   "End it"—don't say how
    24   Intensify
    10   Use A-bomb
    4   All out or get out
    11   Don't know

*I*2   What do you, yourself, think we should do now about the war in Korea? (November 1951)

    7% Withdraw
    4   Negative, have no business there
    9   Make peace
    6   Continue
    21   "End it"—don't say how
    27   Intensify
    9   Use A-bomb
    4   All out or get out
    11   Don't know

*J*1   Which one of these three things comes closest to your idea of what we should do in Korea? (November 1951)

    17% Pull our troops out of Korea and bring them home
    35   Continue the war on the present basis while the peace talks are going on
    43   Attack the Communist forces now with everything we have
    5   No opinion

*J*2   Which one of these three things comes closest to your idea of what we should do in Korea? (December 1951)

    16% Pull our troops out of Korea and bring them home
    36   Continue the war on the present basis while the peace talks are going on
    43   Attack the Communist forces now with everything we have
    5   No opinion

TABLE 4.4 Support for Withdrawal from Korea (Continued)

J3 Which one of these three things comes closest to your idea of what we should do in Korea? (February 1952)

 28% Pull our troops out of Korea and bring them home
 27 Continue the war on the present basis while the peace talks are going on
 39 Attack the Communist forces now with everything we have
 6 No opinion

K1 Suppose the truce talks in Korea break down completely. Which one of these three things do you think we should do then? (March 1952)

 24% Pull our troops out of Korea and bring them home
 37 Keep our troops in Korea and hold the present line there
 30 Go on the attack against the Chinese Communists
 9 No opinion

K2 Suppose the truce talks in Korea break down completely. Which one of these three things do you think we should do then? (April 1952)

 28% Pull our troops out of Korea and bring them home
 31 Keep our troops in Korea and hold the present line there
 34 Go on the attack against the Chinese Communists
 7 No opinion

L What do you think we should do now in Korea? (May 1952)

 13% Pull out of Korea as quickly as we can and let them settle their own problems
 22 Keep on trying to work out a way to stop the fighting in Korea
 53 Stop fooling around and do whatever is necessary to knock the Communists out of Korea once and for all
 12 No opinion

M Suppose the truce talks in Korea break down completely. What do you think we should do then? (May 1952)

 11% Pull out
 14 Stay
 32 Take offensive

TABLE 4.4 Support for Withdrawal from Korea (Continued)

10	Attack China
6	Attack China and Russia
4	Use A-bomb (additional 6% suggests A-bomb in connection with other answers)
2	All out or nothing
3	Miscellaneous
18	Don't know

N Do you think United States troops should be withdrawn (pulled out) from Korea, or should they continue to fight there? (May 1952)

36% Withdraw
48 Continue to fight
16 No opinion

*K*3 Suppose the truce talks in Korea break down completely. Which one of these three things do you think we should do then? (June 1952)

21% Pull our troops out of Korea and bring them home
28 Keep our troops in Korea and hold the present line there
44 Go ahead and attack the Chinese Communists
7 No opinion

*K*4 Suppose the truce talks in Korea break down completely. Which one of these three things do you think we should do then? (August 1952)

28% Pull our troops out of Korea and bring them home
30 Keep our troops in Korea and hold the present line there
35 Go ahead and attack the Chinese Communists
7 No opinion

O Which of the following things do you think it would be best for us to do now in Korea? (October 1952)

10% Pull out of Korea entirely
46 Keep on trying to get a peaceful settlement
38 Take a stronger stand and bomb Manchuria and China
1 Either the first or third
5 No opinion

TABLE 4.4 Support for Withdrawal from Korea (Continued)

K5 Suppose the truce talks in Korea break down completely. Which one of these three things do you think we should do then? (October 1952)

     30%   Pull our troops out of Korea and bring them home
     30   Keep our troops in Korea and hold the present line there
     29   Go ahead and attack the Chinese Communists
     11   No opinion

K6 Suppose the truce talks in Korea break down completely. Which one of these three things do you think we should do then? (November 1952)

     23%   Pull our troops out of Korea and bring them home
     29   Keep our troops in Korea and hold the present line there
     38   Go ahead and attack the Chinese Communists
     10   No opinion

I3 What do you, yourself, think we should do next in the Korean War? (November 1952)

     2%   Withdraw
     2   Negative, have no business there
     10   Make peace
     10   Use South Koreans
     4   Rely on Ike
     2   Continue
     13   "End it"—don't say how
     20   Intensify
     7   Use A-bomb
     4   All out or get out
     25   Don't know

P Which one of these three things comes closest to your idea of what we should do in Korea? (December 1952)

     23%   Pull our troops out of Korea and bring them home
     27   Keep our troops in Korea and hold the present line
     39   Go ahead and attack the Chinese Communists
     11   No opinion

Sources. *A,B,C,F,I:* AIPOc; *D:* GOI 3; *E,G,J,K,M,N,P:* NORCc; *H:* SRC; *L:* RC; *O:* Robinson et al. 1968:582.

TABLE 4.5 Support for Withdrawal from Vietnam

Identical questions are given the same identifying letter. The identification for the last question in a series is underlined.

A   Have you given any attention to developments in South Vietnam? What do you think should be done next in Vietnam? (May 1964) (See also *B*)

        4% Get out
        1   Raise South Vietnamese standard of living
        6   Send U.N. force
        3   Maintain present policy
        5   Get tougher, put on more pressure (nonmilitary)
        4   Take definite military action
        4   Either fight or get out
        3   Other
      63   Have given little or no attention to Vietnam

*B*1   What do you think should be done next in Vietnam? (August 1964)

        4% Get out
      10   Avoid all out war, talk
      27   Keep troops there, don't be pushed around
      12   Get tougher, put on more pressure (nonmilitary)
        9   Take definite military action
        3   Either fight or get out
        9   Other
      30   Don't know

*B*2   What do you think should be done next in Vietnam? (November 1964)

        9% Get out
        3   Avoid all out war, talk
        5   Keep troops there, don't be pushed around
      10   Get tougher, put on more pressure (nonmilitary)
        9   Take definite military action
      15   Either fight or get out
      19   Other
      30   Don't know

TABLE 4.5 Support for Withdrawal from Vietnam (Continued)

C   There would seem to be three basic courses the United States could follow in Vietnam. On balance, which one of these courses [listed on card] would you favor? (Fall 1964)

> 16% Pull out entirely
> 37   Keep on about the way we have been
> 29   Step up the war by carrying the fight to North Vietnam, through more air strikes against Communist territory
> 18   No opinion

D1   Have you been paying any attention to what is going on in Vietnam? Which of the following do you think we should do now in Vietnam? (Fall 1964) (See also CC)

> 8%   Pull out of Vietnam entirely
> 22   Keep our soldiers in Vietnam but try to end the fighting
> 29   Take a stronger stand even if it means invading North Vietnam
> 15   No opinion
> 18   No interest

E   Should the United States continue its present efforts in South Vietnam or should it pull our forces out? (Early February 1965) (Percentage of those who have followed the war.) (See also G)

> 18% Pull out
> 64   Continue present efforts
> 18   No opinion

F1   Which of these three courses do you favor for the United States in Vietnam: carry the war into North Vietnam at the risk of bringing Red China into the war; negotiate a settlement with the Communists and get out now; continue to hold the line there to prevent the Communists from taking over South Vietnam? (February 1965)

> 23% Negotiate and get out
> 40   Hold the line, prevent Communist takeover
> 13   Carry war to North Vietnam at risk of war with China
> 24   No opinion

TABLE 4.5   Support for Withdrawal from Vietnam (Continued)

*F*2   Same as previous question. (March 1965)

    35%   Negotiate and get out
    46   Hold the line, prevent Communist takeover
    12   Carry war to North Vietnam at risk of war with China
    7   No opinion

*G*1   Should the United States continue its present efforts in South Vietnam or should it pull our forces out? (March–April 1965)

    19%   Pull out
    66   Continue present efforts
    15   No opinion

*F*3   Which of these three courses do you favor for the United States in Vietnam: carry the war into North Vietnam at the risk of bringing Red China into the war; negotiate a settlement with the Communists and get out now; continue to hold the line there to prevent the Communists from taking over South Vietnam? (Early April 1965)

    31%   Negotiate and get out
    48   Hold the line, prevent Communist takeover
    17   Carry war to North Vietnam at risk of war with China
    9   No opinion

*F*4   Same as previous question. (Late April 1965)

    28%   Negotiate and get out
    43   Hold the line, prevent Communist takeover
    20   Carry war to North Vietnam at risk of war with China
    9   No opinion

*B*3   In your opinion, what would you like to see the United States do next about Vietnam? (April 1965)

    17%   Withdraw completely
    12   Start negotiations, stop fighting
    14   Continue present policy
    12   Step up present efforts
    19   Go all out, declare war
    5   Other responses
    12   No opinion

TABLE 4.5 Support for Withdrawal from Vietnam (Continued)

*B*4   Same as previous question. (May 1965)

    13% Withdraw completely
    12   Start negotiations, stop fighting
    13   Continue present policy
    8   Step up present efforts
    15   Go all out, declare war
    6   Other responses
    35   No opinion

*B*5   Same as previous question. (Early June 1965)

    13% Withdraw completely
    11   Start negotiations, stop fighting
    16   Continue present policy
    6   Step up present efforts
    17   Go all out, declare war
    4   Other responses
    33   No opinion

*B*6   Same as previous question. (June 1965)

    12% Withdraw completely
    11   Start negotiations, stop fighting
    20   Continue present policy
    4   Step up present efforts
    17   Go all out, declare war
    5   Other responses
    28   No opinion

*G*2   Should the United States continue its present efforts in South Vietnam or should it pull our forces out? (June 1965) (See also *Q*)

    20% Pull out
    66   Continue present efforts
    14   No opinion

H   If the South Vietnam government decides to end the war and stop fighting, what should the United States do—continue the war by itself, or should we withdraw? (July 1965) (See also *O*)

    65% Withdraw if South Vietnam quits
    19   Continue war
    16   No opinion

TABLE 4.5 Support for Withdrawal from Vietnam (Continued)

*I*1   All in all, what do you think we should do about Vietnam? We can follow one of three courses: carry the ground war into North Vietnam at the risk of bringing Red China into the fighting, withdraw our support and troops from South Vietnam or continue to try to hold the line there to prevent the Communists from taking over South Vietnam. Which do you favor? (September 1965) (Percentage of those with opinion)

      25% Withdraw
      49   Hold the line, prevent Communist takeover
      26   Carry war to North at risk of war with Red China

*I*2   Same as previous question. (December 1965) (Percentage of those with opinion)

      7% Withdraw
      65   Hold the line, prevent Communist takeover
      28   Carry war to North at risk of war with Red China

J   Would you approve or disapprove of the following action to end the fighting: Gradually withdrawing our troops and letting the South Vietnamese work out their own problems? (February 1966)

      39% Approve gradual withdrawal
      56   Disapprove
      5   No opinion

K   If President Johnson were to announce tomorrow that we were going to withdraw from Vietnam and let the Communists take over, would you approve or disapprove? (February 1966)

      15% Approve Johnson-led withdrawal, Communist take-over
      81   Disapprove
      4   No opinion

L   Suppose you have to choose among continuing the present situation indefinitely, fighting a major war with hundreds of thousands of casualties, or a withdrawal of American troops leading to an eventual Communist takeover. Which would you choose? (February 1966) (See also *T*)

      19% Withdraw, allow Communist takeover
      49   Continue present situation indefinitely
      23   Fight major war
      9   No opinion

TABLE 4.5 Support for Withdrawal from Vietnam (Continued)

M   If Red China decides to send a great many troops, should we continue to fight in Vietnam, or should we withdraw our troops? (March 1966)

      8% Withdraw if China comes in
     73   Continue
     19   No opinion

N   What are your overall feelings about the Vietnam situation? (March 1966)

     15% United States should get out
     5   Too many lives being lost
     11   General fear of war
     10   Wish for quick ending
     43   It's a necessary evil
     12   We should be more aggressive
     6   Other
     6   No opinion

I3   All in all, what do you think we should do about Vietnam? We can follow one of three courses: carry the ground war into North Vietnam at the risk of bringing Red China into the fighting, withdraw our support and troops from South Vietnam or continue to try to hold the line there to prevent the Communists from taking over South Vietnam. Which do you favor? (May 1966) (Percentage of those with opinion)

     15% Withdraw
     47   Hold the line, prevent Communist takeover
     38   Carry war to North at risk of war with Red China

O   If the South Vietnam government decides to stop fighting, what should the United States do—continue the war by itself, or should we withdraw? (May 1966) (See also *H*)

     72% Withdraw if South Vietnam quits
     16   Continue war alone
     12   No opinion

P   Suppose the South Vietnamese start fighting on a big scale among themselves. Do you think we should continue to help them, or should we withdraw our troops? (May 1966)

     54% Withdraw if South Vietnamese fight among themselves
     28   Continue to help
     18   No opinion

TABLE 4.5 Support for Withdrawal from Vietnam (Continued)

Q Suppose you were asked to vote now on the question of continuing the war in Vietnam or withdrawing our troops during the next few months. How would you vote? (June 1966) (See also G)

    35% Withdraw
    48 Continue
    17 No opinion

R1 Just from what you have heard or read, which of these statements comes closest to the way you, yourself, feel about the war in Vietnam? (October 1966)

    18% The U.S. should begin to withdraw its troops
    18 The U.S. should carry on its present level of fighting
    55 The U.S. should increase the strength of its attacks on North Vietnam
    9 No opinion

D2 Have you been paying any attention to what is going on in Vietnam? Which of the following do you think we should do now in Vietnam? (Fall 1966) (See also CC)

    9% Pull out of Vietnam entirely
    36 Keep our soldiers in Vietnam but try to end the fighting
    36 Take a stronger stand even if it means invading North Vietnam
    12 No opinion
    7 No interest

S1 If you have to choose, which of these courses would you choose in Vietnam: have both sides withdraw under United Nations supervision, win a total military victory, get a neutralist government of South Vietnam, or have U.S. troops moved out? (November 1966) (Percentage of those with opinion)

    7% Move United States troops out
    57 Both sides withdraw under United Nations
    5 Get neutralist South Vietnam
    31 Win total military victory

S2 Same as previous question. (February 1967) (Percentage of those with opinion)

    6% Move United States troops out
    44 Both sides withdraw under United Nations
    7 Get neutralist South Vietnam
    43 Win total military victory

TABLE 4.5 Support for Withdrawal from Vietnam (Continued)

T	Suppose you had to choose continuing the present situation indefinitely, fighting a major war with thousands of American casualties, or a withdrawal of American troops leading to an eventual Communist takeover in Vietnam. Which would you choose? (Spring 1967) (See also *L*)

        19% Withdraw, allow Communist takeover
        39   Continue present situation indefinitely
        30   Fight major war
        13   No opinion

S3 If you have to choose, which of these courses would you choose in Vietnam: have both sides withdraw under United Nations supervision, win a total military victory, get a neutralist government of South Vietnam, or have United States troops moved out? (May 1967) (Percentage of those with opinion)

        6% Move United States troops out
      41   Both sides withdraw under United Nations
       8   Get neutralist South Vietnam
      47   Win total military victory

U1 If you had to make a choice about the Vietnam war right now, which one would you favor: fighting on to a total military victory, fighting until we achieved a negotiated peace, or trying to end the war and get out as quickly as possible? (July 1967)

        24% Try to end war, get out quickly
      51   Fight to negotiated peace
      21   Fight to total military victory
       4   No opinion

U2 Same as previous question. (August 1967)

        34% Try to end war, get out quickly
      37   Fight to negotiated peace
      24   Fight to total military victory
       5   No opinion

R2 Just from what you have heard or read, which of these statements comes closest to the way you, yourself, feel about the war in Vietnam? (August 1967)

        32% The U.S. should begin to withdraw its troops
      10   The U.S. should carry on its present level of fighting
      50   The U.S. should increase the strength of its attacks on North Vietnam
       8   No opinion

TABLE 4.5 Support for Withdrawal from Vietnam (Continued)

U3   If you have to make a choice about the Vietnam war right now, which one would you favor: fighting on to a total military victory, fighting until we achieved a negotiated peace, or trying to end the war and get out as quickly as possible? (September 1967)

       37%   Try to end war, get out quickly
       37   Fight to negotiated peace
       20   Fight to total military victory
       6   No opinion

R3   Just from what you have heard or read, which of these statements comes closest to the way you, yourself, feel about the war in Vietnam? (October 1967)

       31%   The U.S. should begin to withdraw its troops
       10   The U.S. should carry on its present level of fighting
       53   The U.S. should increase the strength of its attacks on North Vietnam
       6   No opinion

V   The war in Vietnam is not worth the cost in lives and money. We should withdraw our troops now. Even if we win, the South Vietnamese will start fighting among themselves as soon as the war is over. And if we don't get out now we may get involved in World War III. Do you favor or oppose this plan? (October 1967)

       35%   Favor withdrawal
       56   Oppose
       9   No opinion

W   Fighting the war is primarily the responsibility of the South Vietnamese and they should begin to take a more active part militarily. Let them draft many more men, who are available, and see to it that they are better trained and have greater fighting spirit. As each new group of one hundred thousand South Vietnamese is trained a similar number of United States troops would be released to come home. We would continue to supply all war materials and provide economic aid. Would you favor or oppose this plan? (October 1967)

       71%   Gradual withdrawal, Vietnamization
       20   Oppose
       6   No opinion

TABLE 4.5 Support for Withdrawal from Vietnam (Continued)

X   Turn the entire problem of Vietnam over to the United Nations. Ask the United Nations to try to find a peace solution. Both sides would agree in advance to accept the decision even if it calls for withdrawing United States troops. The United Nations would then police the border between North and South Vietnam. Do you favor or oppose this plan? (October 1967)

    60% Favor United Nations solution even if it includes United States withdrawal
    32   Oppose
    8   No opinion

B7   In your opinion, what would you like to see the United States do next about Vietnam? (November 1967) (only responses listed)

    10% Withdraw completely
    34   Start negotiations, decrease fighting
    4   Continue present policy
    48   Step up present efforts
    7   Go all out, declare war, use nuclear weapons

Y1   Options on Vietnam (no question given) (February 1968)

    24% Discontinue the struggle and begin to pull out of Vietnam gradually in the near future
    4   Continue the war but cut back the American military effort to a defense only of key areas in South Vietnam where most of the population is located
    10   Continue the war at the present level of military effort
    25   Gradually broaden and intensify our military operations
    28   Start an all-out crash effort in the hope of winning the war quickly even at the risk of China or Russia entering the war
    9   No opinion

Z   If our government were to decide at this time that the best things for us and the Vietnamese would be for United States forces to stop the bombing and the fighting and gradually withdraw from Vietnam, would you approve or disapprove of this decision? (March 1968)

    56% Approve government-led withdrawal
    34   Disapprove
    10   No opinion

TABLE 4.5   Support for Withdrawal from Vietnam (Continued)

Y2   Options on Vietnam (no question given) (June 1968)

42%   Discontinue the struggle and begin to pull out of Vietnam gradually in the near future

7   Continue the war but cut back the American military effort to a defense only of key areas in South Vietnam where most of the population is located

8   Continue the war at the present level of military effort

10   Gradually broaden and intensify our military operations

25   Start an all-out crash effort in the hope of winning the war quickly even at the risk of China or Russia entering the war

8   No opinion

AA   Suppose that in the coming presidential campaign one candidate said that we should turn over more of the fighting in Vietnam to the South Vietnamese and that as of next January 1, the United States should withdraw some of our troops. Other things being equal, would you vote for or against this candidate? (July 1968)

66%   Favor Vietnamization, begin United States withdrawal

18   Oppose

16   No opinion

BB   Suppose the Vietnam war is not over by the time the next president takes office. If you had to choose one, which one of the following courses would you favor his following in Vietnam? (Options apparently presented in reverse of order shown) (September 1968)

13%   Get out of Vietnam altogether

18   Withdraw United States troops gradually but keep supplying the South Vietnamese militarily

17   Pull United States troops back to the cities and let the South Vietnamese do more of the fighting until Communists make peace

17   Keep military pressure on until the Communists make peace

18   Pour in troops and bombs to win war with conventional weapons

8   Use nuclear weapons and win the war once and for all

9   No opinion

TABLE 4.5 Support for Withdrawal from Vietnam (Continued)

CC1 Which of the following do you think we should do now in Vietnam? (Fall 1968) (See also *D*)

    19% Pull out of Vietnam entirely

    37   Keep our soldiers in Vietnam but try to end the fighting

    34   Take a stronger stand even if it means invading North Vietnam

    10   No opinion

DD1 Some people think the time has come to begin to reduce month by month the number of United States soldiers in Vietnam. How do you feel—do you think the time has come to do this, or not? (January 1969)

    57% Approve monthly troop reduction

    28   Disapprove

    15   No opinion

B8 In your opinion, what would you like to see the United States do next about Vietnam? (March 1969)

    26% Withdraw completely

    19   Continue present policy

    32   Go all out, escalate

    19   End as soon as possible

    21   No opinion

EE1 Some United States Senators are saying that we should withdraw all our troops from Vietnam immediately. Would you favor or oppose this? (June 1969)

    29% Favor Senators' plea for immediate withdrawal

    62   Oppose

    9   No opinion

FF As you know, President Nixon has ordered a withdrawal of 25,000 American troops from Vietnam. Which of these statements comes closest to describing the way you feel about troop withdrawals? (June 1969)

    20% Disapprove, no withdrawal until war is over

    18   Approve, but go slow in withdrawing more troops until we are more sure the war is really ending

    48   Approve, but should withdraw more troops, even if no peace agreement

    10   Disapprove, get all our troops out as fast as possible

    4   No opinion

TABLE 4.5   Support for Withdrawal from Vietnam (Continued)

<u>DD</u>2   Some people think the time has come to begin to reduce month by month the number of U.S. soldiers in Vietnam. How do you feel—do you think the time has come to do this, or not? (Late June 1969)

    59%   Approve monthly troop reduction
    24   Disapprove
    17   No opinion

GG   Have you given any thought about what this country should do next in Vietnam? What, specifically, do you think the United States should do? (July 1969) (See also *B*)

    12%   Stop fighting, withdraw immediately
    2   Give economic but not military aid to South Vietnamese
    9   Let South Vietnamese take over
    32   Gradual United States withdrawal
    9   Stay in Vietnam as long as necessary; keep military pressure on; work for cease-fire at Paris
    4   Step up military efforts
    3   Bomb them, blow them up
    4   Either go all out or get out
    5   Other and no opinion
    29   Have given no thought to what should be done

HH   President Nixon has recently announced an additional withdrawal of 35,000 American troops from Vietnam. Do you approve or disapprove of this troop withdrawal? (October 1969)

    71%   Approve Nixon's withdrawal announcement
    15   Disapprove
    14   No opinion

II   A United States Senator has proposed legislation to require the withdrawal of ALL United States troops from Vietnam by the end of next year. The fighting would be turned over entirely to the South Vietnamese, with the United States providing military supplies and financial help. Would you like to have Congress pass or defeat such a proposal? (October 1969)

    56%   Favor Senator's plan to withdraw by end of 1970
    30   Oppose
    14   No opinion

TABLE 4.5   Support for Withdrawal from Vietnam (Continued)

*JJ*1   If the reductions of United States troops continued at the present rate in Vietnam and the South Vietnamese government collapsed, would you favor or oppose continuing the withdrawal of our troops? (October 1969)

> 47% Favor continued withdrawal even if South Vietnam government collapses
> 38   Oppose continued withdrawal
> 15   Not sure

KK   Do you think the United States should withdraw troops from Vietnam at a faster rate, a slower rate, or at about the present rate? (October 1969)

> 45% Withdraw at faster rate
> 31   At present rate
> 11   At slower rate
> 13   No opinion

LL   Are you satisfied or dissatisfied with the rate at which the U.S. is withdrawing its troops from Vietnam? (November 1969)

> 56% Satisfied with withdrawal rate
> 31   Dissatisfied
> 13   No opinion

*EE*2 Some United States Senators are saying that we should withdraw all our troops from Vietnam immediately. Would you favor or oppose this? (November 1969)

> 21% Favor Senators' plea for immediate withdrawal
> 73   Oppose
> 6   No opinion

MM   Here are four different plans the United States could follow in dealing with the war in Vietnam. Which one do you prefer? (December 1969) (See also *NN* and *OO*)

> 19% Withdraw all U.S. troops from Vietnam immediately
> 22   Withdraw all troops by the end of 1970
> 39   Withdraw troops but take as many years to do this as are needed to turn the war over to the South Vietnamese
> 11   Send more troops to Vietnam and step up the fighting
> 9   No opinion

TABLE 4.5 Support for Withdrawal from Vietnam (Continued)

*EE*3 Some United States Senators are saying that we should withdraw all our troops from Vietnam immediately. Would you favor or oppose this? (February 1970)

    35% Favor Senators' plea for immediate withdrawal
    55   Oppose
    10   No opinion

NN Here are four different plans the United States could follow in dealing with the war in Vietnam. Which ONE do you prefer? (March 1970) (See also *MM* and *OO*)

    21% Withdraw all troops from Vietnam immediately
    25   Withdraw all troops by end of 18 months
    38   Withdraw all troops but take as many years to do this as are needed to turn the war over to the South Vietnamese
     7   Send more troops to Vietnam and step up the fighting
     9   No opinion

*JJ*2 If the reductions of United States troops continued at the present rate in Vietnam and the South Vietnamese government collapsed, would you favor or oppose continuing the withdrawal of our troops? (April 1970)

    56% Favor continued withdrawal even if South Vietnamese government collapses
    27   Oppose continued withdrawal
    17   Not sure

*JJ*3 Same as previous question. (May 1970)

    58% Favor continued withdrawal even if South Vietnamese government collapses
    29   Oppose continued withdrawal
    13   Not sure

*OO*1 Here are four different plans the United States could follow in dealing with the war in Vietnam. Which one do you prefer? (May 1970) (See also *MM* and *NN*)

    23% Withdraw all troops from Vietnam immediately
    25   Withdraw all troops by July, 1971—that is, a year from this coming July
    31   Withdraw troops but take as many years to do this as are needed to turn the war over to the South Vietnamese
    13   Send more troops to Vietnam and step up the fighting
     8   No opinion

TABLE 4.5 **Support for Withdrawal from Vietnam (Continued)**

*OO*2 Same as previous question. (July 1970) (See also *MM* and *NN*)

    22% Withdraw all troops from Vietnam immediately

    26 Withdraw all troops by July, 1971—that is, a year from this coming July

    34 Withdraw troops but take as many years to do this as are needed to turn the war over to the South Vietnamese

    10 Send more troops to Vietnam and step up the war

    8 No opinion

*JJ*4 If the reductions of United States troops continued at the present rate in Vietnam, and the South Vietnamese government collapsed, would you favor or oppose continuing the withdrawal of our troops? (July 1970)

    58% Favor continued withdrawal even if South Vietnam government collapses

    24 Oppose continued withdrawal

    18 Not sure

PP It has been proposed that Congress pass a resolution requiring that all United States troops be withdrawn from Vietnam by the end of 1971. Opponents say such a resolution would tie the hands of the President. Would you favor or oppose a resolution in Congress which would require all United States troops to be withdrawn from Vietnam by the end of 1971? (Late July 1970)

    44% Favor Congressional requirement of withdrawal by end of 1971

    35 Oppose

    21 No opinion

*QQ*1 A proposal has been made in Congress to require the U.S. government to bring home all U.S. troops from Vietnam before the end of next year. Would you like to have your congressman vote for or against this proposal? (September 1970)

    55% Favor congressional requirement of withdrawal by end of 1971

    36 Oppose

    9 No opinion

TABLE 4.5 Support for Withdrawal from Vietnam (Continued)

CC2 Which of the following do you think we should do now in Vietnam? (Fall 1970) (See also *D*)

    32% Pull out of Vietnam entirely
    32   Keep our soldiers in Vietnam but try to end the fighting
    24   Take a stronger stand even if it means invading North Vietnam
    11   No opinion

QQ2 A proposal has been made in Congress to require the U.S. government to bring home all U.S. troops from Vietnam before the end of the year. Would you like to have your congressman vote for or against this proposal? (January 1971)

    72% Favor congressional requirement of withdrawal by end of 1971
    20   Oppose
    8   No opinion

QQ3 Same as previous question. (February 1971)

    66% Favor congressional requirement of withdrawal by end of 1971
    26   Oppose
    8   No opinion

QQ4 Same as previous question. (May 1971)

    68% Favor congressional requirement of withdrawal by end of 1971
    20   Oppose
    12   No opinion

RR Would you favor withdrawal of all United States troops by the end of 1971 even if it meant a Communist takeover of South Vietnam? (May 1971)

    29% Favor withdrawal by end of 1971 even if it meant Communist takeover
    55   Oppose
    16   No opinion

TABLE 4.5   Support for Withdrawal from Vietnam (Continued)

SS   Would you favor withdrawal of all United States troops by the end of 1971 even if it threatened the lives or safety of United States POWs held by North Vietnam? (May 1971)

      11%   Favor withdrawal by end of 1971 even if it endangers United States POWs

      75   Oppose

      14   No opinion

Sources. *A:*AIPOr 5/27/64; *B*1, *B*2:AIPOr 11/29/64; *C:*Cantril and Free 1968:200; *D, CC:*SRCc; *E:*AIPOr 2/16/65; *F:*LAT 5/3/65; *G*1:AIPOr 3/12/65; *B*3:LAT 4/23/65; *B*4:LAT 5/16/65; *B*5, *B*6: GOI 2; *G*2:LAT 6/19/66; *H:*GOI 3; *I:*LAT 6/13/66; *J, K, L:*Stanford University release, 3/15/66; *M:*GOI 10; *N:*AIPOr 4/3/66; *O, P:*GOI 12; *Q:*GOI 13; *R*1:GOI 16; *S:*WP 5/16/67; *T:*Stanford materials; *U:* WP 8/28/67; *R*2, *R*3, *V, W, X:*GOI 29; *B*7: NYT 11/11/67; *Y*:A. Cantril 1970:6, *OO*2:p. 8; *Z:*GOI 34; *AA:*GOI 38; *BB:*WP 10/7/68; *DD*1: GOI 44; *B*8:NYT 3/28/69; *EE*1, *DD*2:GOI 49; *FF:*D & C 7/7/69; *GG:*GOI 50; *HH:*D & C 10/27/69; *II, KK:*GOI 53; *JJ*1–3:D & C 6/4/70; *JJ*4:Harris 1971:111; *LL, EE*2:GOI 54; *MM:*GOI 55; *EE*3: GOI 57; *NN:*GOI 58; *OO*1:GOI 61; *PP:*Harris 1971:115; *QQ*1:GOI 69; *QQ*2, *QQ*3:GOI 71; *QQ*4, *RR, SS:*Opinion Research Corporation Release, 5/8/71.

4.2.1   Withdrawal from the Korean War

The data in Table 4.4 suggest that about 15 to 35 percent of the American population generally favored withdrawal from the Korean War at various times. The precise response, of course, depended very much on circumstances and question wording. The questions were of three general types: those asking the respondent whether he preferred withdrawal to a continued prosecution of the war (*A, B, D, E, G, H, N*), those asking him to choose between withdrawal, the status quo, and escalation (*J, K, L, O, P*), and those asking in an open-ended fashion for his suggestions about what to do next in the war (*C, F, I, M*).

If one looks particularly at the first two types of questions, it does seem that the sentiment for withdrawal gained somewhat in popularity over the course of the war, although it certainly never reached overwhelming proportions. As would be expected from the discussion in Chapter 3, the popular support for the president's actions in the summer of 1950 was accompanied by few pleas for withdrawal (question A). After the trauma of the Chinese intervention, support for withdrawal settled in 1951 into the 15 to 20 percentage point range. The alternative became somewhat more popular in 1952 (compare especially $J2$ and $J3$) with the withdrawal response usually hanging around the 30 percent mark.

The open-ended questions are difficult to deal with. They garner a higher "no opinion" response and few specific pleas for withdrawal: compare $I1$ or $I2$ with $J1$, $I3$ with $K6$, M with $K3$ or, for a more spectacular consideration, the already discussed C and D. Some of the withdrawal supporters may be masked in the "End it" or other categories, of course. In general, however, it does seem that these questions tended to stimulate a considerable bounty of escalatory sentiment (especially in a comparison of $I2$ with $J1$ or M with $K2$), a topic to be considered in Section 4.3. Because so little data from open-ended questions are available and because of the changes in coding categories used by the survey organizations, little can be gleaned from these questions about trends over the course of the war.

Support for withdrawal is much lower in O than in $K5$ or $K6$, despite similarities in question structure. The status quo alternative, "Keep on trying to get a peaceful settlement," seems to be quite attractive to would-be supporters of withdrawal, and this perhaps suggests a certain lack of tenacity among many of those oriented toward that option.

4.2.2 Withdrawal from Vietnam and a Comparison

A letter from a political scientist printed in the *New York Times* of July 3, 1971 observed that, after years of debate, "opinion has fully matured and crystallized" on the Vietnam issue. "The polls show," he asserted, "that an overwhelming majority of Americans want the troops out of Vietnam by years' end."

A poll result that could be used to support his contention is numbered $QQ4$ on p. 97 in the rather mammoth Table 4.5, which contains the withdrawal queries for Vietnam. How "fully" opinion had "crystallized" on the issue is in some doubt, since the response to the question had fluctuated by more than 15 percentage points over the preceding nine months ($QQ1$ to $QQ4$).[5] In addition, two related questions on the same poll as $QQ4$ give some illumination about the makeup of the popular sentiment for withdrawal in 1971. Identified RR and SS, the results show that majority support fell apart if it was suggested that withdrawal would mean a Communist takeover in South Vietnam, and the support utterly disintegrated if withdrawal would threaten the lives or safety of United States prisoners of war. The latter result rather graphically demonstrates the potency of the "support our boys in Vietnam" slogan that antiwar politicians were continually being confronted with (as do the data in Table 3.2 on p. 49).

As noted in Section 3.2, support for the Korean war was dramatically raised when the "Communist" issue was included in the "mistake" question. The comparison of the QQ and RR responses in Table 4.5 demonstrates that the issue also could sharply alter responses to questions about the war in Vietnam. This can be seen in several other questions in the table. Although it is rather remarkable how rarely the Communist takeover issue was asked about during the war, it does appear, connected to the withdrawal option, in questions K, L, and T which were asked in 1966 and 1967. In each case, the sentiment for withdrawal is less than 20 percent depite the fact that, in one case (K) the proposed withdrawal is president-led (compare with Z where no takeover issue is broached) and in the other two the alternatives to withdrawal are a costly major war or an indefinite continuation of the conflict.

On the other hand Americans were quite willing to withdraw if the South Vietnamese should stop fighting (H, O, P) while, later in the war, continued withdrawal remains a popular policy even if it is suggested that the South Vietnamese government would collapse in the process (JJ—no mention of a Communist takeover). As with the Korean War, the idea of stopping Communism

---

[5] As suggested in Chapter 1, however, a constant result over time would not necessarily be proof that opinion had crystallized, since a constant result would be expected if people were responding purely randomly to the question. To establish crystallization it would be helpful to be able to demonstrate, in addition, that *individuals* (not just the collectivity) respond the same way over time, that opinion is not easily manipulable by minor wording changes, and that individuals can respond consistently to logically related questions.

triggers support; the idea of defending the local government does not.

It was argued earlier that sentiment for withdrawal from Korea may have grown somewhat in the course of the war. There is evidence in the tabular thicket for Vietnam that a similar progression may have occurred during the later war, but as in the Korean case the data are far from unambiguous. A deliberate reading of the entire table will leave this impression, and it can be grasped with a moderate degree of precision by comparing such questions as $B7$ and $B8$; $D2$ and CC; $R1$, $R2$, and $R3$; $U1$, $U2$, and $U3$; $Y1$ and $Y2$; $EE1$ and $EE3$; $JJ1$, $JJ2$, $JJ3$, and $JJ4$.

In examining the questions in this manner, however, two important differences with the Korean case are worth special mention. One is the existence in some of the Vietnam queries of the prospect of "gradual" withdrawal, an option not considered in the earlier war. Questions that suggest such a policy, or that imply it by setting a final date substantially in the future for completion of withdrawal, rather uniformly garner considerable support. This can be seen as early as February 1966 in response to question J. Thus the popularity of this approach and of the related policy of "Vietnamization" (see especially question W), as long as there was no suggestion of Communist victory, was predictable fairly early in the war.

The second difference concerns the ultimate acceptance in mid-1969 by the Nixon Administration of a policy of gradual withdrawal while it also continued and formalized the policy of Vietnamization that had been begun more or less with the Johnson policy changes of the spring of 1968. For, with that, withdrawal of a sort became official presidential policy and administration followers could move to its support. At the same time, of course, leaders of the Democratic opposition became increasingly withdrawal conscious, and people inclined to follow *their* lead had a model. Since no sort of withdrawal ever became official policy in the Korean case, there is no parallel in the earlier war with the post-1969 period for Vietnam.

With these considerations in mind, it appears that the sentiment for withdrawal for the two wars was roughly the same. Particularly for the pre-1969 period, support for withdrawal from Vietnam in the blunt Korean-style question ("pull our troops out") ranges upward, as in Korea, to a maximum of around 35 percent. The closest thing to a direct comparison between the wars occurs on two SRC questions, O in the Korean table (p. 79) and CC on the Vietnam table (p. 92), although the meaning of the escalation option probably is quite different: bombing Manchuria and China in the Korean War, a policy advocated by many opinion leaders at the time, is hardly equivalent to invading North Vietnam, a policy rarely supported publicly. At any rate, the differences in the results attained by the two questions are of much the same order of magnitude.

It seems as easy as in the Korean case to drop expressed support for withdrawal by an adroit selection of alternatives. As compared to most of its contemporaries, the S questions, posed by Harris in 1967, find many supporters of United States withdrawal grasping eagerly at a proposed United Nations supervised end to the fighting. Question X (p. 90) also suggests handing the whole thing over to the United Nations and garners great acceptance.

Through forest and quagmire, therefore, it does seem that the wars in Korea and Vietnam stimulated popular yearning for the policy option of withdrawal to much the same degree. The conclusion of Chapter 3 that the wars were about equally supported, at least for the period in which the wars were generally comparable in casualties, remains reasonably firm. Again, this is not a conclusion one would predict from a consideration of vocal opposition to the wars. The outcry against the Vietnam War was much the greater, and the demands for withdrawal were far more commonly and noisily voiced.

4.3 QUESTIONS ABOUT ESCALATION

As the discussion of the Vietnam bombing issue in connection with Tables 4.2 and 4.3 already suggests, the escalation issue is an extraordinarily slippery one. It becomes even more so when one seeks to compare the wars in Korea and Vietnam.

However if one scans through the questions in Tables 4.4 and 4.5 that contain escalation as well as withdrawal options, it seems that the wars generated escalatory yearnings to about the same degree. With rather considerable gyrations, between 20 and 50 percent are generally found to take the escalation options when several are presented. The major exception to this, as would be expected, occurs in the Vietnam War after 1969 when the administration had shifted solidly to a withdrawal policy and the bottom utterly dropped out of the escalation position—compare its attainments in the *MM, NN,* and *OO* questions in Table 4.5 with those in earlier years or compare *CC2* with *CC1* (pp. 92, 97).

With this in mind, the rest of this section investigates various specific escalation issues.

4.3.1 Bombing

The major escalation issue during the course of the Korean War concerned the advisability of bombing Communist supply bases inside China. The elite was considerably divided on this issue and, therefore, the followers presumably were a bit puzzled. President Truman strongly opposed such an escalatory measure while General MacArthur strongly favored it. Needless to say, poll data can be found to argue either that the majority of the public supported the president or that it went along with the General on the issue. Throughout most of 1951 and 1952, NORC asked: "Do you think United States airplanes should or should not cross the Korean border and bomb Communist supply bases inside China?" Rather consistently 55 or 60 percent supported this idea while about 25 or 30 percent opposed it. A reformulation of the question, asked in mid-1952, however, generated considerably different results: "Some people think we should *force* the Communists to sign a truce in Korea by staging a number of sea and air attacks against China itself. Do you agree, or should we avoid extending the war while the truce talks are going on?" Only 36 percent agreed with this proposal while 52 percent opposed it (NORCc). Bombing China was a good idea—unless, of course, it meant "extending the war" while the peace talks dragged on.

Instead of being viewed as saying much about opinion on the bombing issue, data like these can be used better to illustrate the public's considerable frustration over what to do next in the war. Appeals to belligerent escalation had a quick appeal—unless it was suggested that such a policy might have some undesirable side effects. This can be seen also in parts of Table 4.4 for Korea in questions that contain escalatory as well as withdrawal options. In a three-way strategy choice in question *L* (p. 78), posed at the same time as the bombing questions just discussed, Roper phrased his escalation option this way: "Stop fooling around and do whatever is necessary to knock the Communists out of Korea once and for all." Fully 53 percent grasped this intemperate option, significantly more than opted for the escalation option on any of the other tripartite questions in the entire war. Also support for withdrawal, when this escalatory option is proffered, drops greatly (compare L with any of its tripartite neighbors).

During the Vietnam conflict, Harris twice asked about extending the bombing that was then going on to include supply lines and airfields in China (WP March 25, 1968). Only 25 percent bought the idea while 52 or 53 percent opposed it, proportions about the reverse of those obtained in Korea. But the issues are not really comparable, of course, since China was a direct and immediate enemy in the earlier war but not in the later one.

The bombing of North Vietnam is more relevant because this *was* an enemy directly opposing American forces who was operating from a sort of sanctuary accessible to United States bombers. The issue was reversed, however: from the beginning of the war in 1965 until 1968, bombing was carried out in the North (with pauses) and the principal political issue was the limitation of this bombing, not, as in Korea, its extension. And, of course, the various shifts of policy by the Johnson Administration make the data difficult to sort out. The bombing questions displayed in Table 4.3 (p. 72) show a considerable approval of the bombing even when the question suggested that a bombing halt might lead to meaningful peace negotiations.

Probably the closest parallel to the Korean case was the situation in 1966 when the administration was being urged by latter-day MacArthurs to extend the bombing of the North to include industrial areas and cities. As shown in Table 4.2, public support for the administration's restraint crumbled markedly during the first half of 1966. A fairly direct question on this issue, asked by Gallup in March 1966, generated bombing supporters of Korean magnitude: to the question, "Would you favor or oppose bombing industrial plants and factories in North Vietnam?" 60 percent responded affirmatively, 26 percent negatively (GOI 9).[6]

---

[6] Despite the hypothetical tone of the question, however, it is possible that some respondents saw this question as a query about present bombing policy,

4.3.2 Use of Atomic Weapons

There does seem to be an area of escalation in which public opinion differs between the wars. The American public apparently was more willing to recommend the use of atomic weapons in the Korean War than in Vietnam. Direct questions about the use of nuclear weapons were asked at least three times during the Korean War. In the second month of the war Gallup asked whether the United States should "use the atom bomb in Korea." Approximately 19 percent approved the idea with another 8 percent giving qualified approval. Toward the end of 1951 Gallup again raised the question, this time more specifically focused on the use of the atom bomb "on enemy military targets in Korea" by United Nations forces. Fully 39 percent were willing to go along with this idea while another 10 percent gave qualified approval. Finally, at the very end of the war the public was asked, "If the truce talks in Korea break down, would you favor or oppose the United Nations using atomic artillery shells against Communist forces?" To this proposal 56 percent were in approval, only 23 percent in disapproval. (All statistics RC.)

In Vietnam, far less approval was in evidence. In 1965 and 1966 Harris found only 10 or 15 percent who thought "the administration" to be "more wrong" than right in its policy of "not using atomic ground weapons" (D & C September 13, 1965; LAT June 13, 1966). In December 1967 and March 1968, shortly before and shortly after the Tet offensive, Harris again asked about the use of "atomic ground weapons" apparently without reference to the administration. The results were virtually identical for the two polls: about 25 percent in favor, 55 percent opposed (WP March 25, 1968). A more intemperate question, originally posed by Gallup in May 1967, was also asked in the post-Tet atmosphere of March 1968: "Some people say we should go all-out to win a military victory in Vietnam, using atom bombs and weapons. Do you agree or disagree with this view?" Again, no change was found between the two polls as some 26 percent approved and, higher than on the Harris "ground weapon" questions, about 65 percent disapproved (GOI 34).

not about a possible escalatory one. It should also be added that Gallup asked at the same time about "bombing big cities in North Vietnam." Only 28 percent approved, while 60 percent opposed.

These data may be taken to indicate a greater frustration in the earlier war, but they probably reflect better a certain casualness toward the weapons in the early years of the atomic age, a casualness that diminished with the acquisition of the hydrogen bomb in enormous stockpiles and with the development of the missile.[7]

4.3.3 Hawks and Doves; the Impact of Events, Particularly Tet

It was a repeated observation of Chapter 3 that, particularly after the war had been going for a while, specific events had relatively little impact on support for the war as measured by the "mistake" trend line. It was especially notable that the Tet offensive and the events surrounding it seem to have had only a rather small impact on war support (although it was pointed out that expectations about the progress and the length of the war *were* altered). And now it has just been shown that Tet also did not change the public's willingness to use atomic weapons.

There is some evidence, however, to indicate a somewhat greater sensitivity to war events on issues of more general escalation and deescalation than was found either on the "mistake" question or on the atomic issue. The data in Table 4.6 from the Vietnam period suggest that the Tet offensive caused an initially hawkish reaction but that this effect was revised in a month or two to levels significantly more dovish than prevailed in the days before Tet. With President Johnson's speech and the bombing halt at the end of March 1968, the administration became, at least by implication, "dovish" in the terms of the poll question and followers, formerly hawks, could now begin to think like doves.[8] And later

---

[7] A reading of *The Pentagon Papers* suggests that this bearing was also reflected in some official military thinking. At the time of major decisions over American participation in Indochina in 1954, the Joint Chiefs rather casually proposed, in the event of direct United States intervention, the employment of atomic weapons if it appeared militarily advantageous (Sheehan et al. 1971:44). Bombing plans proposed by the same body for the later war seemed conspicuously to ignore the possible use of nuclear arms (Sheehan et al. 1971:330).

[8] The combined impact of these events can also be seen in the Y questions in Table 4.5. Between February and June 1968 notable improvement in the fortunes of the gradual withdrawal option and declines in those of the gradual escalation option are evident.

TABLE 4.6 Policy Preferences in Vietnam: Hawks and Doves

People are called "hawks" if they want to step up our military effort in Vietnam. They are called "doves" if they want to reduce our military effort in Vietnam. How would you describe yourself—as a "hawk" or a "dove?"

	December 1967	Late January 1968	Early February 1968	Late February 1968	March 1968	April 1968	Early October 1968	November 1969
Hawk	52%	56%	61%	58%	41%	41%	44%	31%
Dove	35	28	23	26	42	41	42	55
No opinion	13	16	16	16	17	18	14	14
		Tet			Bombing halt			

Source. GOI 54.

course, when the Nixon Administration as well as most of the Democratic party adopted a very distinctly dovish position (again, in terms of the question), hawks became a clear minority group—and Gallup became bored with the poll question.

4.4 QUESTIONS ABOUT WAR LEADERSHIP

Besides the "mistake" question, one poll query posed repeatedly during the two wars might be expected to reflect in some way support for the wars. This was the "presidential popularity" question: "Do you approve or disapprove the way (the incumbent) is handling his job as president."

If the responses to this question are taken to be stimulated in large measure by attitudes toward the war, one would conclude that, if anything, the war in Korea was somewhat more unpopular than the one in Vietnam. As will be seen in Chapter 9, popularity ratings of Presidents Truman and Johnson were in clear and rather steady decline during the terms in which the wars occurred, but President Truman managed to descend to a popularity rating a full 10 percentage points lower than that attained by President Johnson.

It is doubtful whether the wars can be connected in any simple manner to presidential popularity, however. Indeed, as argued in Chapter 9, the Korean War had a substantial negative independent impact on President Truman's popularity while Vietnam had no independent impact on President Johnson's popularity at all after other effects, including a general overall downward trend in popularity, had been taken into account.

A related potential indicator of war support might be the question posed repeatedly during Vietnam by the Gallup and Harris organizations: "Do you approve or disapprove of the way President Johnson is handling the situation in Vietnam?" The responses to this question closely parallel those generated by the presidential popularity question.[9] This may suggest that the question does not discriminate war support very well from presidential popularity: it may be that it is the "approve . . . President" part of the question

[9] For the first war years, Milstein and Mitchell find a correlation of .80 for the "approve" responses and .89 for the "disapprove" responses (1968: 168).

that activates most of the response, not the "handling . . . Vietnam" part. This impression is strengthened by some data from Korea. During that period NORC repeatedly asked their respondents whether they approved or disapproved "of the way the officials in Washington are handling our foreign affairs"—a large part of which, presumably, included the war in Korea. (In fact, in a NORC poll of October 1951, people who gave disapproving responses were asked why they were unhappy, and discontent with policy in Korea and the Far East was a large part of the answer.) In general, the responses over time to this question, which did not directly mention the president, fell into a pattern that closely imitated the trend on the "mistake" question—a substantial decline of approval after the Chinese entry into the war and then something of a leveling off—*not* the continual decline of the Truman popularity trend line (NORCc). Thus questions asking about the president and the wars in the same breath may stimulate reactions to the president more than to the war.[10]

4.5   ISOLATIONISM

Cold Warriors during the Vietnam venture often voiced their concern over what they perceived to be a rising isolationism in the American public. Poll data could be—and were—used to support this notion. Although comparison is difficult and the evidence somewhat mixed, it does seem that isolationism grew during the Korean conflict as well.

The data for consideration are given in Table 4.7. Four relevant questions, two for each war, were asked. The questions in Columns

[10] Another repeated NORC question also followed the pattern of the "mistake" trend line. This was a question asked 14 times between March 1951 and June 1953: "Do you think the people in this country have been asked to make too many sacrifices to support the defense program, not enough sacrifices, or about the right amount?" As with the "mistake" question during the same time period, there was rather little variation in response to this question. About half the population thought the sacrifices "about right," a bit more than 20 percent thought the sacrifices "too many," and a bit fewer than 20 percent found the sacrifices "not enough" (NORCc). A similar, but not identical, question asked during World War II found the percentage thinking the government had not gone far enough in asking for sacrifices for the war to be in rather pronounced and continual decline during the course of the war (Cantril 1967:48, 173).

TABLE 4.7 Questions on Isolationism

A. Do you think it will be best for the future of this country if we take an active part in world affairs, or if we stay out of world affairs? (NORC, AIPO)

B. Do you feel that since the war this country has gone too far in concerning itself with problems in other parts of the world, or not? (NORC, SRC)

C. Would it be better for the United States to keep independent in world affairs—or would it be better for the United States to work closely with other nations? (AIPO)

D. The United States should mind its own business internationally and let other countries get along as best they can on their own. Do you agree or disagree? (IISR)

For each question the numbers represent, in order, the percentages responding with an isolationist response, an interventionist response, and no opinion.

| | A | | | B | | | C | | | D | | |
	Stay Out	Active Part	No Opinion	Too Far	Not	No Opinion	Keep Independent	Work Closely	No Opinion	Mind Business	No	No Opinion
April 1949				41	50	9						
September 1949	25	67	8	48	41	11						
October 1949	24	67	9									
January 1950												
June 1950				36	54	10						
November 1950	25	64	11	36	48	13						
December 1950	25	66	9									
October 1952	23	68	9	55ᵃ	32	12						
February 1953	22	73	5									
August 1953							15	78	7			
September 1953	21	71	8									
April 1954	25	69	6									
October 1954				41ᵃ	46	12						
March 1955	21	72	7									
November 1956	25	71	4									
April 1963							10	82	8			
October 1964							16	79	5			
1967							22	72	6			
February 1968										18	70	12
February 1969										27	66	7

Sources. RC; NORCc; SRCc; A. Cantril 1970:40.

ᵃ Some people think that since the end of the last world war this country has gone too far in concerning itself with problems in other parts of the world. How do you feel about this? (SRC) Qualified isolationist and internationalist responses are included in the figures given. They total

A and B cover the Korean period and responses to the B question show an increased isolationist impulse as the war wore on with a return to more internationalist leanings in 1954. A more modest, but still quite perceptible, isolationist shift during the Vietnam War is chronicled in Columns C and D.

The puzzle involves the question in Column A with its rather remarkable imperturbability through war and peace—although it should be stressed that the shifts of opinion documented in the other columns are far from massive. It may be that the peculiar blandness of the internationalist response in the Column A question, "take an active part in world affairs," something the United States can hardly fail to do simply by existing, accounts for this phenomenon (see Payne 1951:150).

A related issue has to do with the question of the advisability of instituting more Koreas or Vietnams in other parts of the world. Results of an NORC question from the Korean period are given in Table 4.8. The popularity of the idea dropped during the course of the war, especially after the Chinese intervention, and rose again only after the war was over.[11]

TABLE 4.8 Popular Support for Other Koreas

If Communist armies attack any other countries in the world, do you think the United States should stay out of it, or should we help defend the countries, like we did in Korea? (NORC)

		Stay Out	Help Defend	It Depends	No Opinion
1950	September	14	66	15	5
	December	28	48	15	9
1951	August	28	53	13	6
	December	30	52	13	5
1952	June	33	45	15	6
	October	31	45	18	6
1953	August	36	45	13	6
	November	26	52	17	5
1955	October	28	52	14	6
1956	November	24	52	20	4

Source. NORCc.

[11] Given the understandable frustration over the war in 1952 and 1953,

Limited data from the Vietnam War generate similar results. In December 1967, after 2½ years of escalated warfare there, Harris asked (WP December 30, 1967): "In the future, do you feel the United States has an obligation to defend other Vietnams if they are threatened by Communism?" He also asked if the United States should go to the defense of Thailand if that country were threatened by Communism. The responses were, respectively, 39 and 36 percent in opposition to such ventures, and 44 and 42 percent in favor—statistics very close to those found in Table 4.8 for the Korean War during the 1952–1953 period.

At the risk of tedious repetition on the question wording issue, it should be observed that the set of questions considered from the two wars are comparable in two important respects: they all mention the Communist threat and, while they ask about "defending" threatened lands, they do not specifically mention sending American troops. Far less support for intervention is found when these conditions are altered. At about the time of the Harris queries, Gallup posed a question that dropped the Communist element while it included the troop issue: "If a situation like Vietnam were to develop in another part of the world, do you think the United States should or should not send troops?" Approximately 57 percent opposed such an idea while only 29 percent favored it, a difference of 15 to 20 percentage points from the Harris findings.[12]

4.6 CREDIBILITY GAPS

A concept of considerable popularity among journalists during the war in Vietnam has been the "credibility gap," the idea that the administration has been holding from the public (and its tribunes) essential information about the war. The public was polled several times on this issue and seemed to perceive a gap itself. Three times in 1967 Gallup asked: "Do you think the John-

---

the willingness of about half the population to get involved in other Koreas seems rather remarkable. The NORC survey of November 1953 also asked whether the war in Korea had been worth fighting (the question in Column C of Table 3.1). Fully 40 percent of the respondents who thought the Korean War *not* to have been worth fighting were willing, nonetheless, to help defend other countries so attacked (NORCc).

12 GOI 29. Gallup repeated his question in January 1969 and found hostility to the idea had gone up slightly (GOI 45).

son Administration is or is not telling the public all it should know about the Vietnam War?" Only 21 to 24 percent thought it was, while 65 to 70 percent thought it wasn't (GOI 23, 29). The question was resurrected and applied to the Nixon Administration in February and April 1971 after the Cambodian and Laotian invasions but before the publication of *The Pentagon Papers*. If President Nixon brought any special credibility to the office, it had been eroded by that time for the results to the questions were virtually identical to those tallied for Johnson in 1967.[13]

During the Korean War, a similar gap was perceived by the public, but it was not obvious to quite so many partly, perhaps, because the issue was not so commonly belabored in the press. In the middle of the war, February 1951, NORC asked if "government officials in charge of our foreign policy are telling the people all they should." About 39 percent thought that they were and 49 percent thought not (NORCc). The question is not quite comparable since it refers to a less readily identifiable quantity than the Truman Administration and does not specifically mention the war, but the data do suggest, nevertheless, rather less of a credibility problem in the earlier war. A similar question asked during World War II found far less of a credibility gap (Cantril and Strunk 1951:1130, 1135; Erskine 1971–72).[14]

[13] GOI 71, NYT May 23, 1971. As the *Times* article notes, the president had made efforts to improve his credibility on the war issue in the period between these polling dates.

[14] With a considerable degree of regularity over several decades poll respondents have been asked what they happen to feel is "the greatest problem facing the country today." The reaction to this question has varied considerably: a problem, popular this month, may be of little concern the next. Almond (1950) has argued that this is evidence of an instability of mood on foreign affairs, although the evidence could be used as well to demonstrate an instability of mood on domestic concerns. This notion has been rather effectively attacked by Caspary who argues from other evidence such as that in Table 4.7 that "American public opinion is characterized by a *strong* and *stable* 'permissive mood' toward international involvements" (1970:546).

The "most important problem" question, an open-ended one, seems to stagger many respondents with its charming ingenuousness: the breathtaking assumption that from all the horrors of human existence detailed daily in the press, one can extract one that stands out above all the rest. Fortunately for the respondents, editors have the same problem when they must decide

4.7 CONCLUSIONS

The state of the data has rather effectively kept the analysis in this chapter from being in any sense tight or neat. Nevertheless, it does seem to be the case that the major conclusions of the previous chapter still hold true after this rather detailed examination of miscellaneous poll questions related to the wars in Korea and Vietnam. By and large, the popular support for and response to the wars has been about the same.

Also the consideration of the question-wording problem has been extended and the "follower" group has been introduced. The next chapter investigates the inclination of members of various social groupings to be in support of, or in opposition to, the wars in Korea and Vietnam. As part of this discussion, the notion of the follower mentality will be further developed.

each day what problem merits lead coverage. Hence the public's opinion about "today's greatest problem" tends to reflect yesterday's largest headline.

Under these circumstances the "importance" of international problems can show a considerable fluctuation depending on the events of the day and on the fortunes of the domestic competition: strikes, riots, unemployment, crime, pollution, and scandal. (For plots, see Caspary 1970:541 and GOI 45 and 78.)

Therefore to use the question to say much about attitudes toward the wars in Korea and Vietnam seems a bit hopeless. A special problem, in addition to those already discussed, arises in attempting to separate out concern for the war from other international worries (and vice versa). Concern over the wars also seems to be manipulable by politicians. In the course of the 1952 presidential campaign, the Republicans were remarkably successful in increasing the importance of Korea as a problem (Harris 1954:25).

CHAPTER 5

Sources of Support for the Wars

The last two chapters have assessed the way the general public has responded to various questions about the wars in Korea and Vietnam. Generally, it has been found that the trends and patterns of these reactions are quite similar for the two wars although, judged from the remarkable difference in the amount of vocal opposition inspired by the two wars, one might expect far less similarity of popular response.

In this chapter the analysis is extended to deal with the reactions to the wars of various subgroups of the population. Because of the way in which polls are usually constructed, much of this analysis can sort the population only into a series of fairly standard social and economic categories (education, age, sex, race, party, and the like). Often, however, efforts will be made to suggest popular inclinations of a more psychological nature for which the standard categories can sometimes be taken to be cloudy but fairly sincere reflections. The analysis will make use both of the "mistake" question of Chapter 3 and also of the questions about war policy options which were central to the discussion in Chapter 4.

As suggested in Chapter 4, to do justice to this topic, it is profitable to avoid the unidimensional hawk-dove conception. Rather, it appears that this is the source of only one of a number of cues that influence public attitudes toward the wars. Specifically, at least three categories of cues seem important: those that activate "partisans," those that activate "followers," and those that activate "believers." These three forces, which sometimes complement and sometimes oppose each other, seem to be vital factors in an understanding of popular support for a war or a war issue. Efforts will be made, using the standard poll categories, to illustrate the kinds of people most likely to respond to each of the cues.

5.1 THE PARTISAN MENTALITY

It is not surprising to learn—but it *does* seem easy to forget—that much of the public's response to the wars has been influenced by the position taken by the leadership of the political parties. Very simply, many people use their party identification as a shortcut method for arriving at a position on an issue. Rather than sort through the intricacies of argument on the issue, they prefer to take as cues the word of the leadership of their party. It is their method for minimizing information costs.

Partisanship is evident on an issue like the "mistake" question that asks if "we" or "the U.S." did the right or wrong thing in getting involved in the war. Partisans seem to see the query as one asking for the approval or disapproval of an action of the administration, which for most of the course of both wars was Democratic. Accordingly, Democrats are found to support the wars on this dimension to a greater degree than Republicans. Some of the data for this are plotted in Figures 5.1 and 5.2 and the complete data are given in Table A.1 in the Appendix, on pp. 270–271.[1]

Partisan differences were relatively small at the beginning of the wars, presumably under the influence of a sort of nonpartisan consensus at a time of national emergency. Differences broadened

---

[1] The plots include only the support percentages for the various groups. As will be seen, this sometimes maximizes apparent group differences. To keep the drawings from being hopelessly confusing, the Korean plots contain only data from the AIPO-SRC surveys (Column A in Table 3.1 on p. 45, line A in Figure 3.1, and part B in Tables A.1 and 5.5). Since the question wording is constant, this means that the Vietnam and Korean plots are directly comparable. The text, however, will also deal with the NORC data from the Korean period which will be found in part A of Tables A.1 and 5.5. For reasons of cost or availability, a few surveys used in the analysis in Chapter 3 are not included in the breakdown in Tables A.1 and 5.5.

considerably once the wars were underway, becoming entirely un-ambiguous after the Chinese intervention in Korea and by the second year of the war in Vietnam.

5.1.1 Partisans, Hawks, and Doves

An alternative interpretation of these data, of course, would be that Democrats are simply more likely to be hawks than Republicans. However, the data from the Nixon Administration demonstrate quite clearly that it is the partisan, not the hawk-dove, cue which is most important in this case. For it certainly seems that, if conditions alter, polarity can be reversed as readily in politics as in physics. During the Johnson Administration Democrats were persistently more inclined to deny that "we" made a mistake in getting into the fighting there. By October 1969, however, Republicans had become more supportive of the war than Democrats on this measure. In a fairly important sense, then, by the time the new administration was a year old, Johnson's war had begun to become Nixon's war. Part of this change was due, of course, to the increasingly single-minded opposition to the war from prominent Democratic spokesmen, including some who had been active in the Johnson Administration.[2]

It is possible that this same reversal of polarity would have occurred in the Korean case if the war had dragged on longer than it did into the Eisenhower tenure. Since the war came to an end in 6 months, however, it remained a purely Democratic war in the public mind. Unaltered polarities can be seen in the data in Table A.1, and they are found also in party breakdowns for the NORC question, labeled *C* in Table 3.1, which was asked during the last year of the war and into the postwar period (NORCc).

Perhaps as a way to rationalize their policy position, supporters of the president's own party are also more likely to anticipate that his programs will be successful than are adherents of the opposition. Thus, during the Truman and Johnson administrations, Democrats

---

[2] This change in the war's identification is also seen in responses of the public as a whole when asked which party would be more likely to keep the United States out of World War III. The Republican party enjoyed a large advantage on this measure when Nixon attained office. The gap was considerably closed within a year, was eliminated entirely by mid-1971 (GOI 74), and was reversed by the end of August 1971 (GOI 75).

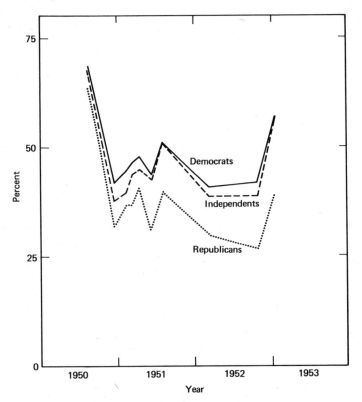

Figure 5.1 Trends in support for the Korean War, by partisanship. For complete data, see Table A.1, p. 270.

were less likely than Republicans to be pessimistic about the progress being made in the wars and in the peace talks. This is also a topic on which polarities can be reversed: of the partisan groups, Republicans were more pessimistic that the war in Vietnam would be ended in 1967, but Democrats were more pessimistic that it would end in 1969 (GOI 19, 43). In 1968 Democrats were more likely to perceive the Paris peace talks to be making headway; as early as February 1969 Republicans were more inclined to be captivated by such visions (GOI 39, 43, 46).

Further evidence to indicate that the hawk-dove continuum has little relevance to the partisan one comes in an examination of partisan response to the questions about escalatory and deescala-

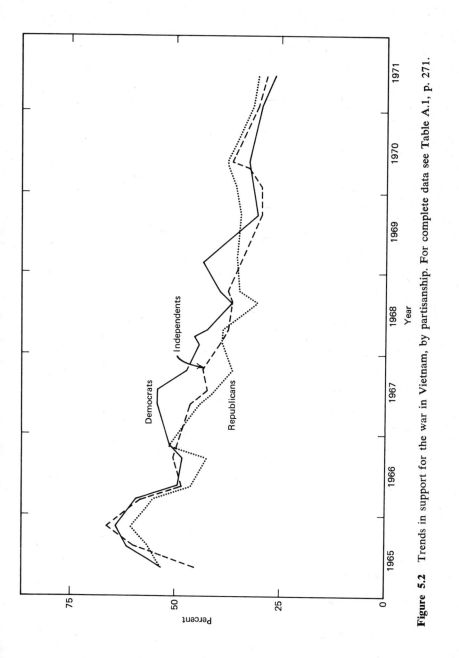

Figure 5.2 Trends in support for the war in Vietnam, by partisanship. For complete data see Table A.1, p. 271.

tory options that were arrayed in Tables 4.4 and 4.5 in the previous chapter. Throughout the course of the Truman and Johnson administrations there was remarkably little difference in response to these hypothetical war policies, a reflection of the simple fact that the leadership of the two parties—with some exceptions— did not differ markedly on these issues.[3] One rather dramatic example of this can be seen with respect to the escalation issue during the Korean War. Republicans were strongly inclined to voice their preference for General MacArthur's position in his controversy with President Truman (Belknap and Campbell 1951–52), an issue of some importance in Chapter 9. Despite this, however, in the election atmosphere of 1952, which was dominated by the rather vague war policy of General Eisenhower, Republicans were only a little more likely than Democrats to select a policy option that reflected the MacArthur position: "Take a stronger stand and bomb Manchuria and China" (Hamilton 1968:441).

There are two periods in which this absence of party polarization on war strategy does not hold true—one rather ephemeral, one quite solid. Both reflect division at the top. The first is the 1964 election period in which strong Republicans were inclined to accept Senator Goldwater's preference for stronger measures in Vietnam (Hamilton 1968:444; Patchen 1966:300).

The other is the Nixon period, when, for the first time in either war, the visible leadership groups of the two parties differed quite clearly on war policy. Accordingly after 1969, partisan differences on the rate of withdrawal often reached toward 20 percentage points.[4]

Party polarization on an issue therefore depends on the degree to which the positions of the leaders of the parties differ and the degree to which the question makes the difference obvious. Where

[3] For examples of partisan differences as well as other demographic breakdowns on these questions, consult the *Gallup Opinion Index* references for Table 4.5. For Korean War data on the partisan mentality and for further discussion, see Scott and Withey (1958:145–46) and Belknap and Campbell (1951–52). See also Key (1963: Chap. 17).

[4] Such shifts are in no sense uniquely American. For example, a major shift in partisan opinion on a foreign policy issue occurred in Canada in 1963 when party leaders, after months of artful vacillation, finally came down on opposite sides of the issue (Mueller 1967:874).

there is little visible difference, little partisan cleavage will be noted in the population. Where the president has a policy and the opposition is unclear in its position, there will be moderate polarization as presidential partisans are attracted disproportionately to support their leader on the issue. Where leadership divergence is clear, polarization in popular opinion will be quite intense.

As Belknap and Campbell (1951–52) have noted, partisan polarization (measured in their case by voting intention) is likely to be more intense among well-informed people than among poorly informed ones. This seems to be partly because the well-informed are more likely to know what their party's position on an issue happens to be. Thus the well-informed seem to be quite willing to take party cues as a shortcut to policy thinking, and they seem generally to prefer this method of thinking to the application of personal ideological perspectives. It is often easier to predict a well-informed partisan's position on a question of war policy by assuming he will adopt his party's position as his own than it is by assuming he will apply his own predilections toward, say, isolationism or internationalism or toward war or peace.

It is often possible to see the importance of information and party referents in a simpler way—by artificially informing the respondent about the position of the leadership and seeing how this alters response patterns. One then finds opinion on "policy x" to be barely polarized; opinion on "the president's policy x" to be quite polarized. As can be seen, the ability of the poll question writer to manipulate in order to generate interesting newspaper copy is considerable.

5.1.2 Independents

With a delicate sense of appropriateness, those who identify themselves as Independents respond as a group almost always somewhere between the Republicans and the Democrats. This can be seen quite clearly in the data for the "mistake" question tallied in Figures 5.1 and 5.2 and in Table A.1. A couple of bare exceptions are instructive. At the very beginning of the war in Vietnam and, for the NORC data only, at the beginning of the Korean War, Independents were found to be less supportive of the war than either partisan group, and it took them a while before they found their "natural" position (or until the partisans found theirs). This finding may suggest that rally-round-the-flag appeals are more influential with partisans, even partisans of the opposition party. But it probably reflects at least as much the rather amorphous and polyglot nature of the "Independent" category, which makes it, as a group of people with countervailing sympathies, less susceptible to special events and appeals.

The other exception to the Independents' preference for a middling position occurred as Nixon took over the Vietnam War. While partisans were puzzling themselves over whose war it was after all, the Independents briefly found themselves once again to be less supportive of the war than either party group. By 1970, however, the proportions were fairly well sorted out again.

5.2 THE FOLLOWER MENTALITY

The follower mentality is discussed at some length in Chapter 4, particularly in Section 4.1.2. As noted there, followers are people who take as cues for their own opinion the issue position of prominent opinion leaders. As such, partisans could be considered to be a special breed of followers. But what is of particular interest at this point are followers who cue on the position of the president, regardless of party preference.

When presidential war policy shifted, whether in an escalatory or deescalatory direction, swarms of followers have obligingly accepted the President's lead. As with the partisan situation, then, the follower phenomenon suggests complications concerning the view that war opinion can be discussed simply in hawk-dove terms.

At this point the discussion of followers is extended to include an investigation of the war attitudes of the kinds of people most susceptible to follower appeals.

5.2.1 Followers and the Educational Groups

Of the sample subgroups easily separated out by polling methods, it is the well-educated segment of the population that most nearly typifies the follower mentality. Thus, contrary to a common belief, it has been the well-educated members of the society who have most consistently supported the prosecution of the wars in Korea and Vietnam. This is shown in Figures 5.3 and 5.4 and in the appropriate columns of Table A.1 (pp. 272–273). There is a consistent and usually pronounced tendency on the "mistake" question for the better educated to support the wars to a greater degree and for them to oppose it to a lesser degree that the more poorly educated. This relationship generally holds true for the entire course of both wars and, unlike the case with partisans, did not alter when a new party took over the presidency—and the Vietnam War—in 1969.[5]

"Education" in this context, of course, is at least partly a sort of surrogate for social class, since the well educated are generally among the financially better off. The education variable is far easier to work with than those dealing with occupation or income, since the classification methods used by the polling agencies for dealing with the latter two variables vary considerably over time and from agency to agency. Educational groupings differ in at least two respects from the other social class components: (1) the education variable more sharply differentiates the better informed from the poorly informed (Key 1961:332–36); and (2) the better educated tend to be disproportionately young (Stouffer 1955: Chap. 4; Key 1961:337n). It should also be borne in mind that the average educational attainment in the American population rose somewhat in the period between the two wars. Of course, a considerable rise in median income also occurred.

At any rate, as the embodiment of the follower mentality, it is suggested that the better educated tend to possess the characteristics of that view as detailed in Chapter 4: a comparatively close identification with the nation, its leadership, and its destiny; an awareness of and a sympathy for the problems of dealing with other countries in a unified manner; and, consequently, a susceptibility to leadership appeals on issues of international policy. In addition, they are likely to know what the present policy *is* and thus can line themselves up in the appropriate column with a certain efficiency.

The Assertion Phenomenon. It is important to notice that the support and opposition differences in Table A.1 are not equal. As

---

[5] It was noted in Chapter 1 that, because of sampling procedures in use at the time, lower status people would be somewhat underrepresented in most of the AIPO surveys during the Korean War. Because of the way the educational groups break down on the "mistake" question, this means that the measured support for the Korean War may have been slightly *over*estimated in comparison with that of the Vietnam War. (See also Glenn 1970.) The argument of Chapter 3 that the Vietnam War was no more unpopular than the Korean War until its costs had surpassed those of the earlier war becomes therefore, if anything, *stronger.*

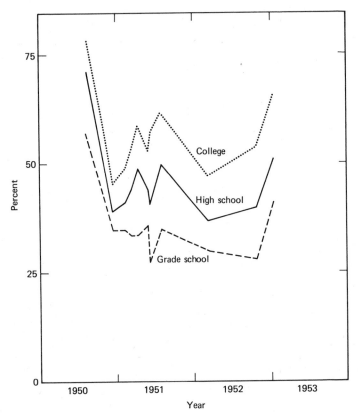

Figure 5.3 Trends in support for the Korean War, by education. For complete data, see Table A.1, p. 272.

can be seen in the data, the differences among the educational groups are consistently greater for the support scores than they are for the opposition scores. For example, in the 1965 data from Vietnam reported on p. 273, one finds that college-educated respondents are some 20 or 30 percentage points more likely to voice support for the war than those with only a grade-school education. At the same time the poorly educated are only some 5 to 15 percentage points more likely to express opposition to the war. The slack is taken up in the "no opinion" percentage, which is always higher for those with less education. Thus, the difference comes not so much because the poorly educated are willing to assert their *op-*

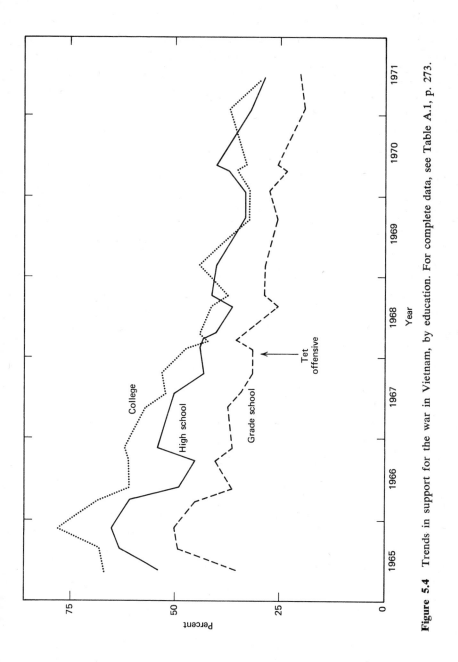

Figure 5.4 Trends in support for the war in Vietnam, by education. For complete data, see Table A.1, p. 273.

position to the war as because they are far less willing to assert their *support* for it.

Hence, here is another opportunity for the dedicated data manipulator. If one wishes to demonstrate a disagreement among education groups, one publishes only the support figures (as in Figures 5.3 and 5.4). If one wishes to minimize the gap, one publishes only the figures for those in opposition. In addition there is a special danger in dichotomizing this (and, as will be seen, other) questions for aggregation with other questions in an opinion scale. If one simply records whether a given respondent did or did not support the war, the scale will have a built-in tendency to emphasize differences among educational groups; if the dichotomy indicates whether the respondent did or did not oppose the war, the differences will be minimized.

Followers versus Aginners. It could be argued that the follower phenomenon is misconceived that, instead of the better educated's being followers, the poorly educated are dedicated "aginners," acting from a position of societal alienation perhaps. There is no doubt some merit to this proposition, but it does seem that the more dynamic aspects of the relationship are stressed by viewing things from the follower perspective. The assertion phenomenon suggests this. If the poorly educated were actively pursuing an antagonistic course, one might expect more difference of opinion on the oppose dimension than on the support dimension. As noted, this is not the case.

The activity of the well-educated followers can also be seen in the behavior of the trend lines for the "mistake" question. For both wars, far the greatest sensitivity to events and developments occurs in the support trend lines for the better educated. In the Korean case, support of the war for all educational groups dropped sharply with the Chinese entry into the war. From there on out, however, the poorly educated altered their opinion on the war almost not at all. The relatively minor alterations of opinion in reaction to events in 1951 and 1952, noted in Section 3.3, were largely furnished by the better educated groups.

In Vietnam, the gradual decline of support is mostly contributed by the disillusionment with the war that occurred among the better educated, especially the college group. Once the war was well under way (from 1966 on) the poorly educated, as in Korea, moderated their support for the war very little. At the time of the Tet offensive it was the best educated whose support (and opposition) was affected.

Albert Cantril (1970:15) has noted a similar phenomenon. Contrary to the notion that the less educated tend to react precipitously to events and presidential appeals, he observes that it was the well educated who dramatically rallied to President Johnson's support after he had begun the bombing of oil dumps in Hanoi and Haiphong in 1966.

The impression one garners from such phenomena is of a well-educated group reacting in an active and attentive manner to the war and its consequences, and to the arguments of opinion leaders; and of a poorly educated group responding to the survey stimulus viscerally and in a half-aware, semirandom and, consequently, rather unperturbable fashion. Nevertheless, it was the poorly educated groups whose reaction to the wars was ahead of the time in this case: in the end the well-educated groups came to respond to both wars in the way the poorly educated had at the beginning.[6]

Followers, Hawks, Doves. An important consideration in this discussion of the follower mentality parallels one in the analysis of partisans: the relationship to the hawk-dove continuum. The concern is of special importance because several studies have argued that the well educated and the better off are inclined to be hawks on the war (Hamilton 1968; Rosenberg et al., 1970: Chap. 3; Converse and Shuman 1970). The argument here, of course, is that they are followers, not hawks.

For evidence to support this proposition we must consider questions about war strategy and tactics, since both followers *and* hawks will deny that the United States made a mistake in getting into the war. It is essential in this analysis to consider survey questions that

[6] A very similar process occurred in the mid-1940s on the degree to which Americans were willing to trust the Russians to be cooperative in world affairs. The poorly educated were substantially less trusting than the well educated as World War II came to a conclusion. Trust among all groups declined as the cold war began, but it declined mostly among the well educated until by 1948 they were in entire agreement with the poorly educated (Caspary 1968:34–36).

cover the *entire range* of alternatives in the hawk-dove continuum from extreme escalation to extreme deescalation. The problem in many studies has been that the hawk end of the scale has been truncated, with extreme escalation not included.

Tables 5.1, 5.2, and 5.3 present opinion on a number of policy options asked about during the two wars with breakdowns not only by education but also by occupation and income. Higher-status groups tend to reject *both* plans for withdrawal *and* plans for extreme escalation. The differences are clearest cut in the educational breakdowns. Those of upper status support the war not because they are necessarily enamored of force as a way of solving problems, but because they see the war as "ours": their country is at war and in such circumstances they are inclined to support their country and its leadership.[7]

In the hawk-dove question posed by Gallup between 1967 and 1969 (should we "step up" or "reduce" "our military effort in Vietnam") reported in Table 4.6 (p. 107), the flexibility is neatly seen. In 1967 the well educated tended to identify themselves as hawks (GOI 32). However, with the shifts in presidential policy after 1968 from hawkish to a dovish perspective (in terms of the question), educational differences on the question completely broke down (GOI 54).

---

[7] A follower of purest cast would, of course, be inclined to accept policy options advocating a continuation of the present policy in the various multi-option queries listed in Tables 4.4 and 4.5 in the previous chapter. In addition, particularly when the war is not going satisfactorily, follower groups such as the well educated are attracted to mildly escalatory options such as those urging the government to take a "stronger stand"—to do more of the same, except perhaps tougher. This position probably most nearly rationalizes the war they support. Hence the necessity for extending the hawk end of the scale to include items concerning extreme measures of escalation. In some cases, however, "stronger stand" options accepted by high-status groups have included quite belligerent riders. In the SRC examples that Hamilton (1968) examines, the entire wording of the "stronger stand" option in the Korean case was "Take a stronger stand and bomb Manchuria and China," and in Vietnam, "Take a stronger stand even if it means invading North Vietnam." It would appear, however, that it is the "stronger stand" aspect of these options that garnered the disproportionate higher status support; when asked as a distinct issue, the bombing of China and the invasion of North Vietnam tend to be rejected more by higher status people than by lower status people. See Table 5.3 for data on Korea and GOI 30 for data on Vietnam.

TABLE 5.1 Opinion on the Use of Atomic Weapons in Vietnam, by Education, Occupation, Income

Some people say we should go all out to win a military victory in Vietnam, using atom bombs and weapons. Do you agree or disagree with this view? (AIPO)

	March, 1968			May, 1967		
	Agree	Disagree	No Opinion	Agree	Disagree	No Opinion
	(In Percent)					
National	27	65	8	26	64	10
Education						
College	21	75	4	20	76	4
High school	29	64	7	24	65	11
Grade school	30	57	13	33	54	13
Occupation						
Professional and business	21	75	4	23	73	4
White collar	33	60	7	21	69	10
Manual	26	66	8	26	64	10
Farmers	31	60	9	28	53	19
Income						
$10,000 and over	24	73	3	23	72	5
7,000 and over	24	70	6	22	71	7
5,000 to 6,999	33	63	4	26	63	11
3,000 to 4,999	28	59	13	28	60	12
Under 3,000	29	59	12	31	53	16

Source. GOI 24, 34.

TABLE 5.2 Support for Three Policy Options in Vietnam, by Education, Occupation, Income; October 1967

	Military Escalation Plan[a]			Deescalation Plan[b]			Withdraw-Now Plan[c]		
	Favor	Oppose	No Opinion	Favor	Oppose	No Opinion	Favor	Oppose	No Opinion
				(In Percent)					
National	42	48	10	24	65	11	35	56	9
Education									
College	38	56	6	22	71	7	23	70	7
High school	42	50	8	23	68	9	37	55	8
Grade school	46	36	18	28	52	20	46	40	14
Occupation									
Professional and business	37	57	6	24	68	8	28	65	7
White collar	42	52	6	21	70	9	37	59	4
Manual	42	48	10	26	63	11	39	53	8
Farmers	54	32	14	16	72	12	38	54	8
Income									
$10,000 and over	38	55	7	23	70	7	29	66	5
7,000 and over	40	53	7	23	71	6	29	64	7
5,000 to 6,999	46	45	9	27	59	14	38	54	8
3,000 to 4,999	43	42	15	26	62	12	42	47	11
Under 3,000	37	46	17	22	57	21	46	39	15

TABLE 5.2 (Continued)

Source. GOI 29.

[a] Let the heads of the army run the war as they see fit, giving them all the men they say they need. Increase the pressures on enemy troops and step up the bombing of North Vietnam. Add new targets that have not been bombed thus far, such as the harbor of Haiphong. Go all out and use atomic weapons and bombs if the army believes we should. Do you favor or oppose this plan? (AIPO)

[b] Stop bombing for a fairly long period of time even if North Vietnam does not make any promise as to what they will do in return. See if this action on our part will bring the North Vietnamese to the peace table. Try to win support from Communists in South Vietnam for a peace solution by offering long range economic aid and benefits. Do you favor or oppose this plan? (AIPO)

[c] The war in Vietnam is not worth the cost in lives and money. We should withdraw our troops now. Even if we win, the South Vietnamese will start fighting among themselves as soon as the war is over. And if we don't get out now we may get involved in World War III. Do you favor or oppose this plan? (AIPO)

TABLE 5.3 Support for Various Policy Options in the Korean War, by Education, Occupation, and Income

Here is a list of things that might be done in handling the Korean situation. Which of these things do you feel the United States should do and which ones shouldn't we do? June 1951 (SRC)

	Get Out of Korea and Stay Out			Drive the Enemy Out of South Korea			Drive the Enemy Out of All Korea			Bomb Bases in China			Invade China		
	Yes	No	DK	Yes	No	DK	Yes	No	DK	Yes	No	DK	Yes	No	DK
							(In Percent)								
National	19	63	18	72	6	22	52	21	27	42	26	32	20	51	29
Education															
College	14	74	12	83	6	11	52	25	22	42	36	22	14	71	15
High school	16	68	16	77	5	18	53	22	24	44	26	29	21	51	28
Grade school	24	53	22	62	7	31	51	18	31	40	22	38	23	41	36
Occupation															
Professional	12	71	17	78	5	17	54	31	15	37	41	22	19	69	12
Managers	20	70	11	84	4	12	56	23	21	49	28	23	23	60	16
Clerical, sales	13	75	12	81	6	13	60	20	20	49	29	22	29	51	20
Skilled, semiskilled	17	66	17	71	7	22	53	21	26	43	27	30	19	50	32
Unskilled	19	52	28	62	6	32	42	21	37	38	22	41	17	44	39
Farm operator	28	54	18	62	4	33	51	15	34	38	17	45	18	46	35

TABLE 5.3 (Continued)

	Get Out of Korea and Stay Out			Drive the Enemy Out of South Korea			Drive the Enemy Out of All Korea			Bomb Bases in China			Invade China		
	Yes	No	DK	Yes	No	DK	Yes	No	DK	Yes	No	DK	Yes	No	DK
							(In Percent)								
Income															
$5,000 and over	12	74	14	82	6	12	57	24	19	56	28	16	23	62	15
2,000 to 4,999	17	67	16	73	6	20	54	21	25	43	27	30	20	51	28
1,000 to 1,999	22	54	23	67	6	27	48	20	32	34	26	41	17	46	38
500 to 999	32	48	20	71	5	23	46	23	30	30	30	39	14	48	38
Under 500	36	32	32	44	2	54	36	14	50	28	14	58	28	28	44

Source. SRCc.

Further evidence for this notion is furnished in Table 5.4. The data here are quite striking when juxtaposed with the last breakdown in Table 5.2. While higher status people rejected withdrawal as a policy option at that time (both before and after Tet), the status difference seems to break down and, perhaps, to reverse when the question is simply reframed to say, in essence, "Suppose withdrawal *were* government policy, would you go along with it?"

Lower status people, from this evidence, seem to adopt a sort of all-or-nothing preference rather than a consistent dove or hawk pose. In part, this point of view may reflect some of the aspects of

TABLE 5.4 Support for a Governmental Decision To Withdraw from Vietnam, by Education, Occupation, and Income

If our government were to decide at this time that the best thing for us and the Vietnamese would be for United States forces to stop the bombing and the fighting and gradually withdraw from Vietnam, would you approve or disapprove of this decision? February 1968 (AIPO).

	Approve	Disapprove	No Opinion
	(In Percent)		
National	56	34	10
Education			
College	62	33	5
High school	55	36	9
Grade school	52	31	17
Occupation			
Professional and			
business	58	34	8
White collar	58	34	8
Manual	55	34	11
Farmers	67	24	9
Income			
$10,000 and over	61	33	6
7,000 and over	57	35	8
5,000 to 6,999	53	35	12
3,000 to 4,999	53	35	12
Under 3,000	61	27	12

Source. GOI 34.

the "working-class authoritarian" personality as described by S. M. Lipset (1960:114–15): the desire for "immediate gratification" in life and for "immediate action" in politics.

The assertion phenomenon makes such propositions a little too neat, however. For, as can be seen in the tables, it is not so much that lower status people favor withdrawal or extreme escalation; rather, they are usually far less likely to *oppose* them. Again, the active element in the response cadences seems to belong to the higher status people.

Hard Hats. The antipathy of blue collar workers to student anti-war demonstrators during the Vietnam conflict has been often re-marked on. It is easy to conclude from such evidence that, since the demonstrators are doves, their antagonists must be hawks. On the other hand, it has sometimes been found that withdrawal sentiment on Vietnam referendums is particularly high in lower class neigh-borhoods (Hamilton 1968:442n; Hahn 1970a and 1970b).

The evidence presented here should help to clarify these matters. As seen in the data in Tables 5.2 and 5.3, blue collar workers can be called hawks because they do favor major measures of escalation —or, rather, are relatively less likely to oppose them. However they *also* are inclined to favor plans for immediate withdrawal—or, rather, are relatively less likely to oppose them. Clearly, viewing such relationships from a follower perspective is sounder than trying to apply the hawk-dove continuum as an explanatory and classifica-tory tool.

Education and Internationalism. It has often been observed that the well educated are strongly inclined to be internationalist. They are willing to support free trade, initiatives for international agree-ments, alliance commitments, and foreign aid, and are particularly inclined to be favorable toward the United Nations (Hero 1966: 455–59; Scott and Withey 1958:116–29; Key 1961:336–38).

Of course, most of this is fully explainable within the follower concept, since these policies have been fairly consistently advocated by successive Presidents and opinion elites since the late 1940s. And the concept explains quite well the puzzle Patchen (1966: 302–08) uncovers in a 1964 survey. He finds the well educated willing, on the one hand, to support hypothetical presidential initiatives to increase contacts with Communist China. But, on the other hand, they are inclined to oppose agreements with China to neutralize Vietnam (where no presidential initiative is suggested) and to favor the use of American forces in Vietnam if necessary to carry out present policy there.

But on some issues the internationalism seems to go well beyond presidential policy. In particular, the well educated have been considerably more supportive of the idea of admitting Communist China to the United Nations than the more poorly educated although, of course, until 1971 official policy in the United States was opposed to such a measure (Hero 1966:460; GOI 65). The poll data from the wars fairly clearly indicate that such adventurous conciliatory leanings among followers are successfully mitigated when the President stresses the need for military firmness to carry out an official foreign policy objective. And, of course, a considerable element in the internationalist perspective as it has usually been defined has been a willingness to see American forces based overseas to enforce the policy of containment (Key 1961:562).

5.2.2   Followers and the Age Groups

Most of what has been said for the educational groups can also be said for the age groups—with young people, very much contrary to most of the generation gap discussion, adopting a follower perspective.[8]

Trends for the age groups for the "mistake" question for the two wars are given in Table A.1 (pp. 274–275) and in Figures 5.5 and 5.6. The young, like the well educated, have tended to support the wars and have been similarly relatively sensitive to events and developments in the wars. The assertion phenomenon remains in effect with older people usually only somewhat more likely to oppose the wars, but far less likely to support them. And data like that in Tables 5.1, 5.2, and 5.3 could be marshaled to show that the young are reacting as followers, not hawks.

Of course, some of this is to be expected because, as pointed out

---

[8] This point has also been noted for Vietnam by Erskine (1970:134–35), Converse and Schuman (1970), Rosenberg et al. (1970: Chap. 3), and A. Cantril (1970). For an able dissection of the "generation gap" discussion, see Adelson (1970).

above, young people also tend to be better educated than older ones. But even when education is controlled, an age effect remains (Rosenberg et al. 1970:66).

In comparison with the education figures, however, the differences among age groups are usually smaller and less focused. This is especially the case when one moves to a consideration of questions concerning alternative strategies.

And, unlike the situation with the "mistake" question where age differences remained reasonably constant for the course of the wars, there was some tendency for these differences to diminish on strategy questions during the course of the Vietnam War. In the early years of the war, fairly pronounced differences could be found (Patchen 1966:299; GOI 12). But they were smaller toward the end of the 1960s. In the case of the bombing issue in late 1967 and early 1968, there was some tendency for young people to be relatively favorable to a bombing halt as reflected in their responses to questions like those listed in Table 4.3, while the better educated as a group continued to oppose it.[9] Even earlier, in the first months of 1967, the young began to be noticeably critical of President Johnson's handling of the war, reversing an earlier favorable inclination. The Cambodian invasion of 1970 found young people disproportionately opposed (GOI 60; Harris 1971:121–2).

But no case can be made for the popular proposition that "youth" was in revolt over the war. This notion was based on the prominence of young people in the antiwar movement, but young people are the most obvious element of almost any political movement presumably because of their physical energy and their lack of occupational and familial obligations—in 1964, it may be recalled, journalistic pundits professed to see an attraction of young people to the Goldwater movement. The poll data argue that, although *some* young people may have been deeply opposed to the war, "youth" as a whole was generally more supportive of the war than older people. This topic is considered at greater length in Chapter 6.

In fact, much of the small change that was observed in some of the attitudes of young people toward the war can be explained by the follower concept. Antiwar protests were so widely touted and

---

[9] This can be seen in the breakdowns in the *Gallup Opinion Index* reports cited in Table 4.3.

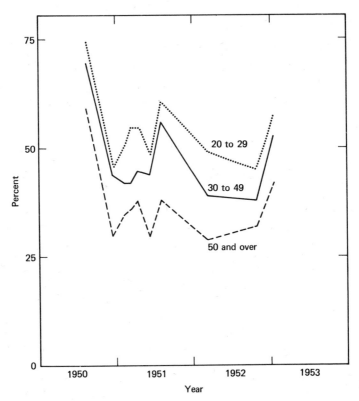

Figure 5.5 Trends in support for the Korean War, by age. For complete data, see Table A.1, p. 274.

accepted as special movements of and for the young, that some young people may have come to believe it themselves and may have began to conform to the popular view of what they should think. This notion is supported by some data gathered in the wake of the Cambodian invasion of 1970. In May, when the massive youth-oriented protest was under way, people under 30 were found to be substantially more likely than their elders to express serious doubts over the invasion and to declare it unjustified. By July, however, the "generation gap" was considerably narrowed (Harris 1971:121–22). Predictably, the one area in which such a gap did develop solidly was in attitudes toward the youthful protesters.

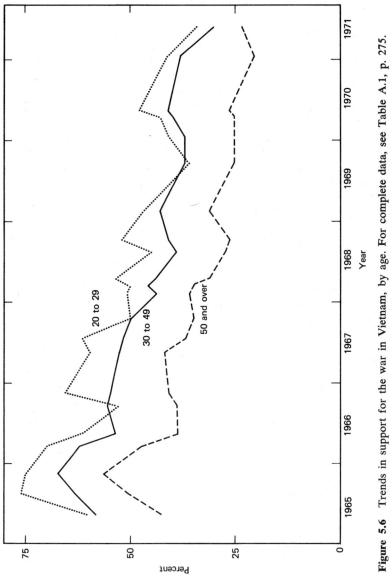

Figure 5.6 Trends in support for the war in Vietnam, by age. For complete data, see Table A.1, p. 275.

Young people were noticeably more likely to approve of this method of protest than were older people (GOI 61).

5.3 THE BELIEVER MENTALITY

On issues of war support and policy, those called partisans are inclined to cue on the expressed views of their party's leadership while followers tend to cue on the expressed policy of the country's leadership, regardless of party. Both groups, however, find their cues in something extraneous to the content of the issue itself. Democrats will tend to support a war they identify as a Democratic one, but to oppose it if they see it as a Republican one. Followers will tend to support a policy when it is advocated by the president, but to oppose it when he shifts his position.

There are people, however, who cue on the issue itself regardless of what the leadership of their party or country happens to think. These people we can call believers and the phenomenon, the believer mentality. Believers can be said to arrive at their position on an issue by applying a set of preestablished beliefs to it. At least three sources for these beliefs seem relevant to war attitudes. First, it is possible to discern the effect of ideology on the war attitudes of some people. Second, there is, at last, the hawk-dove continuum—the varying belief in the use of force as a method for solving international problems. A third possible belief source is self-interest.

5.3.1 Ideology

Some people do have a fairly well worked out perspective on political choices and can be expected to opt for, say, the liberal or conservative position on any given issue. If the president or a party leader is pursuing a course of action in harmony with their ideological perspective, they will support him; if not, they will oppose him on the issue.

Although a great deal of philosophical speculation about ideological perspectives has been generated, it is important to observe that most empirical analysis of public response finds that, even under quite generous definitions, ideologues constitute only a very small minority of the population (Campbell et al. 1960:188–265; Converse 1964b).

As pointed out in Section 2.3.8, the intellectual Left seems to have viewed the wars in Korea and Vietnam differently: support for the earlier war, increasingly vehement opposition to the later one. Yet this sharp alteration for position by an important ideological group has been reflected in none of the data thus far examined: neither in the aggregate figures sorted through in Chapters 3 and 4 nor in the subgroup totals thus far examined in the present chapter. This should help to suggest how little mass opinion is ideologically inclined.

Jews. Obviously if one had a battery of questions capable of isolating the ideologues from the rest of the population, one could look at the intellectual Left and trace its change of heart. But no sound measure of ideological position has been devised and consistently administered in the polls. The best one can do is to look at the responses of Jews as a sort of imperfect surrogate for the liberal position on most issues. And here one can see a notable shift. As documented in Table 5.5 Jews strongly supported the Korean War but have tended to oppose the war in Vietnam. In fact, Jews seem to be the only subgroup of all those usually sorted out by poll questions whose position on the two wars clearly differs. Since Jews are such a small minority of the population—a few percent—their shift in support, which of course was hardly unanimous anyway, would not appreciably affect the aggregate support for the wars.

For Vietnam, the observation of Rosenberg et al. (1970:74) is sound: "it is clear that Jews have been by some fair quantitative margin more distinctly dovish than any other simply defined group in the electorate." This fact is found "consistent with other data showing that American Jews tend to take a liberal position on the broad range of political issues." Although the Korea data will not allow any casual necessary association of Jews (or liberals) with dovishness, clearly Jews have opposed the Vietnam War as a policy and have been consistently favorable to pleas for withdrawal. Table 5.6 supplements the data in Table 5.5.[10]

The Jewish shift, then, illustrates the shift of the intellectual Left. But it was the intellectual Left that acted in an ideological manner.

[10] For somewhat comparable data from Korea showing a lack of support among Jews for withdrawal from that war, see Hamilton (1968:441).

TABLE 5.5 Support for the Wars, by Religion, Race, Sex

For each group, the numbers represent, in order, the percentages in support of the war, in opposition, and with no opinion

	Religion			Race and Sex			
	Protestant	Catholic	Jewish	White Men	White Women	Black Men	Black Women

A. NORC polls from Korean War (Column B in Table 3.1)

	Protestant	Catholic	Jewish	White Men	White Women	Black Men	Black Women
July 1950	58 31 10	63 29 08	63 25 13	76 20 04	76 19 04	78 18 04	58 39 03
September 1950	61 29 11	69 24 07	85 11 04	86 10 04	80 15 05	64 23 13	60 26 12
December 1950				61 34 05	52 37 12	45 45 10	39 36 23
February 1951				64 28 08	51 36 13	54 32 14	43 40 17
March 1951				66 27 07	55 34 11	60 26 13	48 37 15
April 1951				67 25 08	62 26 11	51 37 12	43 40 17
May 1951				68 25 07	53 34 13	55 33 12	53 33 15
Late August 1951				66 28 06	56 31 14	57 31 12	47 40 13
Early December 1951				57 35 08	54 36 11	42 42 16	28 62 09
Early January 1952				62 32 06	51 37 12	50 44 06	56 29 14
March 1952				55 38 07	46 41 13	51 37 12	34 47 19
June 1952	52 41 07	63 31 05	64 27 09	59 34 07	50 42 07	62 33 06	59 31 11

B. AIPO polls from Korean War (Column A in Table 3.1)

	Protestant	Catholic	Jewish	White Men	White Women	Black Men	Black Women
August 1950				72 17 09	61 21 16	69 19 13	46 25 27
December 1950				43 50 07	36 49 13	32 53 12	24 46 29
February 1951				46 45 08	37 52 10	35 45 21	30 44 26
March 1951				51 40 09	37 48 15	46 42 12	29 40 27
April 1951				57 33 11	37 41 21	34 32 34	24 35 41
Early January 1951	40 42 18	50 38 13	68 18 15	48 37 15	39 44 17	32 42 26	29 37 34
Mid June 1951				46 40 13	34 45 19	37 37 25	19 52 28
Early August 1951				55 37 08	42 45 13	43 46 11	23 56 21
March 1952	36 51 13	39 48 12	53 35 12	43 47 09	32 52 15	52 32 16	13 58 28
Late October 1952	35 54 19	40 40 19	44 29 26	44 40 15	31 46 22	36 33 29	24 45 31
January 1953				54 35 10	46 37 17	58 32 10	38 42 20

TABLE 5.5 (Continued)

C. AIPO polls from war in Vietnam (Table 3.3)

	Religion									Race and Sex												
	Protestant			Catholic			Jewish			White Men			White Women			Black Men			Black Women		
May 1965	49	27	24	59	23	18	59	21	20	58	27	15	48	27	25	55	23	22	31	18	51
August 1965	57	26	17	71	19	11	69	16	15	63	26	11	61	22	18	67	26	07	37	26	37
November 1965	62	23	15	70	16	14															
March 1966	57	26	17	64	22	14	56	34	09	65	26	09	54	26	20	53	24	23	43	13	45
May 1966	46	37	17	57	32	11	33	50	17	54	36	10	47	37	16	24	52	24	21	30	49
September 1966	46	37	17	55	27	19	44	38	17	56	33	11	43	37	20	41	24	35	35	35	29
November 1966	49	31	20	58	27	15	38	43	20	58	29	13	48	31	21	47	29	24	25	50	24
May 1967	47	39	14	59	32	09	54	28	18	60	31	09	46	36	17	28	59	14	13	74	12
July 1967	46	42	12	55	35	09	35	50	15	52	40	08	45	42	13	35	52	13	43	39	18
October 1967	42	47	10	52	41	07	29	60	12	49	45	07	39	48	12	53	37	10	29	60	11
December 1967	43	47	10	54	37	07	36	53	09	48	43	07	44	45	10	33	54	12	24	59	14
Early February 1968	41	50	09	48	45	07	29	67	04	43	51	07	42	48	09	36	56	08	23	60	17
March 1968	41	49	10	47	44	09	20	74	07	41	51	08	40	49	12	38	43	19	11	52	36
April 1968	40	48	12	43	48	09															
August 1968	35	53	12	38	50	12															
Early October 1968	37	54	09	42	49	09	16	80	04	42	51	07	34	55	11	25	56	19	29	60	10
February 1969	39	51	09	45	48	07	30	62	08	42	51	07	39	51	10	34	55	10	27	50	23
September 1969	32	57	10	34	50	16	23	62	15	35	55	10	29	56	15	27	60	13	27	68	05
January 1970	30	54	16	36	55	09	15	76	09	35	54	11	28	56	16	29	60	18	24	60	16
April 1970	35	49	16	40	49	12	03	84	13	41	49	10	30	51	18	27	60	13	19	61	20
March 1970	37	54	09	35	57	08															
January 1971	31	58	11	36	57	07															
May 1971	29	60	11	28	62	10															

Source. See Tables 3.1 and 3.3.

TABLE 5.6 Support for Various Vietnam Policy Options, by Religion

Have you been paying any attention to what is going on in Vietnam? Those answering yes were then asked: Which of the following do you think we should do now in Vietnam? (Interest question not asked as a filter after 1966.) (SRC)

	Pull Out of Vietnam Entirely	Keep Our Soldiers in Vietnam but Try to End the Fighting	Take a Stronger Stand Even if It Means Invading North Vietnam	Don't Know	No Interest
			(In Percent)		
1964					
Protestants	9	24	30	16	21
Catholics	8	26	34	14	18
Jews	16	34	18	21	11
1966					
Protestants	8	35	36	14	8
Catholics	10	39	39	6	6
Jews	19	44	33	5	0
1968					
Protestants	18	36	35	11	
Catholics	20	39	32	9	
Jews	36	36	19	9	
1970					
Protestants	30	34	25	12	
Catholics	35	30	25	10	
Jews	50	21	14	14	

Source. SRC.

Whether Jews as a whole cued on the issue, and thus acted as believers, or took the cue of the Left's opinion leadership, and thus acted as a special breed of followers, cannot be determined from the data. But it does seem that Jews were the only group of those usually sorted out in the polls that joined the intellectual Left in its shift on the wars.

Jewish attitudes toward the war in Korea are difficult to analyze in depth because a religion question was only occasionally incorporated into surveys of the time, as the very large data gaps in Table 5.5 suggest. And, although general patterns are clear, Jews represent such a small number of respondents on the average survey that one must expect a greater degree of unreliability in the numbers generated and therefore must be wary of pushing the data too far. (This holds, of course, also for the Vietnam data.) In general, Jews seemed to have reacted to the Korean War more as Democratic partisans than anything else. They were close supporters of the president's policy, spurning both withdrawal and expansion, and strongly preferred his position in the controversy with General MacArthur.

Protestants and Catholics. The data for Protestants and Catholics are presented for comparison with the Jewish figures. By themselves, they are not particularly relevant to the ideology or believer issues. Instead, the two groups seem to reflect mild partisan differences, a disclosure hardly surprising. On the "mistake" question, Catholics express somewhat greater support for the Democratic wars. As is familiar from the partisan discussion, little difference is found between the two groups on abstract policy options like those in Table 5.6 until the party polarizations began under the Nixon Administration (for example, GOI 57, 69). Predictably, of the two groups, Catholics were somewhat more likely to expect progress toward peace in 1967, Protestants more likely to expect progress in 1969 (GOI 19, 43).

5.3.2 Hawks and Doves

A hawk is someone who approves the use of force as a method for solving international problems; a dove disapproves, preferring instead peaceful and conciliatory measures. At the extreme, hawks will advocate not only increased troop commitments or more extensive bombing missions but also outright invasions and the use of nuclear weapons. At *their* extreme, doves will approve not only cease-fires and negotiated settlements but also immediate withdrawal. In either case the cue is on the issue. No matter what the party leadership suggests, no matter what present policy is, hawks are persistently more willing to sanction the application of force or the increased application of force to solve problems.

Of the groups easily separated out by the usual polling methods, two seem particularly relevant to the hawk-dove discussion: sex and race. Specifically, men tend to be hawks and women doves; whites tend to be hawks and blacks doves. Trends on the "mistake" question for the racial and sex groups are given in Table 5.5.

Sex. Male-female differences on the "mistake" question are documented, controlling for race, in Table 5.5. The assertion phenomenon is in effect, at least for whites, as the sexual difference is mostly manifested in women's relative unwillingness to voice support for the wars, not in their expressed opposition to them.

On other questions about the wars a consistent hawk-dove pattern is found, modified slightly by the assertion phenomenon. Women generally are less favorable to escalation than men, but only slightly more opposed to it; and women are less opposed to withdrawal than men, but only slightly more in favor of it.[11]

The situation in which men are inclined to favor the use of physical force and women to shy away from it presumably is based on society's preferred sex roles in which men are expected to be firm and aggressive, women quiet and demure. The sexual difference also shows up rather repeatedly in bargaining experiments in which it is found that women prove to be notably bad bargainers because they are likely to seek ways to avoid the bargaining conflict itself, thereby reducing joint and individual profits (Mueller 1969: 90–91).

Fortuitous evidence from a 1953 survey suggests that an effect of women's liberation could be to diminish this sexual difference on war policy by making women more hawkish. However, the inference is a bit oblique. That survey contained a question about a proposed use of atomic artillery shells in the Korean War. The respondents were also asked whether the then-current Kinsey report should be discussed so widely and openly. The rather surprising result when these two questions were cross-tabulated was that those favorable to the Kinsey discussion were *also* more inclined to favor the use of atomic weapons in Korea. Suspecting a contaminating effect from sex in this relationship, since men tended to approve both the Kinsey discussion and the weapons, the relation was looked at separately for the two sexes. When this was done, it

---

[11] For similar data from the World War II period, see Cantril (1947:223).

was found that attitudes about the Kinsey discussion were entirely unrelated to war policy preferences among men, but that those women favorable to the discussion, presumably the relatively liberated ones, were distinctly more like men on the atomic weapon issue than their unliberated peers (RC).

Although this relationship should be investigated with more current data, it suggests, again, that mass attitudes are not necessarily well reflected by the pronouncements of vocal activists. The women's movement, of course, has been associated with the peace movement. However, if the effect of women's liberation is to change the attitudes of women, making them more assertive so that they can compete in a male-oriented society, a correlative result may be to make them more hawkish on war and foreign policy.[12] In this view, the quintessential dove among women is not the liberated activist, but the unassertive little old lady who can't bring herself to support wars because they aren't "nice."

Race. Another social variable that relates rather persistently to war policy is race. Relative to whites, blacks react to the wars as doves, both on the "mistake" questions documented in Table 5.5 and on questions about escalation and withdrawal.[13]

[12] See Gornick (1971), especially the exchange on p. 82.

[13] Poll data for blacks are notoriously unreliable. There are several reasons for this. First, blacks represent only 10 or 15 percent of the population, and thus the size of the black sample in a national survey is rather small. Second, like other groups largely in the lower classes, they tend to be underrepresented in the sample. And third, they live, at least for the Korean period, disproportionately in rather remote rural areas thus increasing sampling difficulties. Therefore, although the general patterns on war support are quite clear in the data, too little reliance can be placed on the data to trace trends or to spot the influence of events on black attitudes toward the wars.

The support percentages are given for men and women separately to eliminate a sex bias that would occur if racial figures were presented in the aggregate. Specifically, black men are severely underrepresented in many of the surveys, particularly from the Korean period, and therefore a "Negro" sample would be disproportionately female. Partly because of the small sample size for black men, the support figures for them fluctuate from survey to survey considerably. Nevertheless it is clear that, in general, among blacks as well as among whites, men have been more supportive of the war than women—an observation, incidentally, that does not fit particularly well with notions about the supposedly influential matriarchal family structure among blacks.

The opposition by blacks to the war in Vietnam has often been noted, and suggestions are frequently made that this phenomenon is related to the racial upheaval taking place in the country at the same time as the war (Rosenberg et al. 1970:74–75; Converse and Schuman 1970:22; Verba et al. 1967:325, 331). The problem with the explanation, however, is that poll data like that in Table 5.5 show blacks to have had the same relative position on the Korean War. In fact, data from World War II show much the same thing (NORC 1942). Furthermore this relationship remains reasonably firm when social class or information level are controlled for.[14]

The causes for black opposition to the Vietnam War, therefore, are not found simply in the facts of the racial turmoil of the 1960s. They must go much deeper into the black experience.

5.3.3 Self-interest

In many areas self-interest, treating the concept in a rather material sense, can influence a respondent's opinion and, thus influenced, he will respond as a believer: that is, his cue will be on the issue, not on the recommendations of party or opinion leaders. Thus, few would be startled to learn that farmers tend to favor farm price supports and that workers are inclined to oppose wage controls.

In international affairs, it is sometimes difficult to sort out particular survey groups who stand to derive benefit or harm from a given action. On the tariff issue, perhaps, one could separate out interested groups, but it is less easy to do so, for example, on an issue like admitting Communist China to the United Nations.

For the wars, however, there are people who have a definite self-interest in peace: young men and their relatives. It has been

---

[14] As noted above, members of the lower classes have responded to the wars in a manner indistinguishable from doves except that they have been unwilling to reject measures for extreme escalation. Blacks, as consistent doves, *do* reject these measures. Some data from the Korean period to supplement the Vietnam data included in the references in the text may be helpful. Asked in 1953 whether atomic artillery shells ought to be used in the war should peace talks break down, the favorable/unfavorable percentages for white men were 65/20; for white women, 49/26; for black men, 46/26; for black women 37/30 (RC).

suggested that the support sometimes found in blue collar neighborhoods for Vietnam withdrawal referendums is because sons from these areas stand a greater chance of induction and of drawing combat duty (Hahn 1970a:205). A rather remarkable finding, based however on rather sketchy evidence, is that self-interested groups do not appear to be particularly likely to be dovish on the wars.

A hint of this is suggested in findings already discussed. In Section 5.2.2 it was found that young people have been supporters of the wars in the follower sense. And in Section 5.3.2 it was shown that women, who are not eligible for the draft, are more dovish than men, who are.

The questions in Tables 5.7, 5.8, and 5.9 approach the issue more directly. In various ways and at various points in the Korean and Vietnam wars, opinions on the war and on various warlike postures are assessed for groups that differ in their presumed self-interest in peace. Although there are some puzzles, on the whole the data do not suggest that self-interest is a very good predictor of hawkish or dovish attitudes. Similarly, a study in 1968 of Columbia University students found that support for American withdrawal from Vietnam was completely unrelated to the draft status of the respondent (Barton 1968:348–50).

A couple of investigations before the American involvement in World War II found the same situation. In 1939, Rugg and Cantril (1940) observed that members of families with potential soldiers were no less interested in getting entangled in the European conflagration than anyone else. They postulated that this might change once the United States became involved in the war, thus making the conflict less remote. The data in Tables 5.7 and 5.8 (albeit from different wars) do not support their expectation. A Gallup study conducted more than a year after the one by Rugg and Cantril (still before Pearl Harbor, however), generated the same puzzling data (AIPOr May 28, 1941).

It seems clear that, however inclined the self-interested may be toward peace, this inclination is effectively counteracted by other forces. For the draftable themselves, this may be partly the tendency of the young to be followers and men to be hawks; and conceivably some of this rubs off on the people who are close to them. Furthermore respondents with draftable members in their

TABLE 5.7 **Relation of Vietnam Attitudes to Presence of a Family Member in the Armed Services (SRC Election Study 1968)**

Have any members of your immediate family served in the armed forces in the past five or six years? Has he served any time in Vietnam?

	No Member in Service	Member in Service, not Serve in Vietnam	Member in Service, Serve in Vietnam
Do you think we did the right thing in getting into the war in Vietnam or should we have stayed out?			
Right thing	30%	31%	34%
Should have stayed out	52	50	49
No opinion, other	18	19	17
Which of the following do you think we should do next in Vietnam?			
Pull out of Vietnam entirely	21%	16%	21%
Keep our soldiers in Vietnam but try to end the fighting	37	36	30
Take a stronger stand even if it means invading North Vietnam	32	37	36
No opinion, other	10	11	13

Source. SRC.

immediate family are likely to be younger on the average than those in families without them and thus are more likely to be followers. Neither explanation is much help, however, for self-interest does not emerge as an important factor even when age or sex are controlled for (as in Table 5.8, Barton 1968, and Rugg and Cantril 1940).

TABLE 5.8 **Support for Withdrawal from Korea by Presence of Draftable Family Member, August 1950 (AIPO)**

Is there any man in your immediate family who would be affected by such a law [Universal Military Training] during the next few years?	Some people say that the United States should pull our troops out of Korea and stop fighting there. Other people say we should go on fighting in Korea. With which point of view do you agree?		
	Withdraw	Continue Fighting	No Opinion
	(In Percent)		
Women with no draftable family member	13	75	13
Men with no draftable family member	9	83	8
Women with draftable son	10	78	12
Men with draftable son	10	83	6
Women with draftable brother	11	84	5
Men with draftable brother	21	77	2
Women with draftable husband	19	77	4
Men who are themselves draftable	17	77	7
Total population	11	80	9

Source. RC.

There may be a force of rationalization at work to counteract any pacifistic leanings: an unwillingness to admit that the war one's family member is, was, or may be caught up in is unwise or unjust. And there may simply be an unwillingness to view the wars in personal terms; the war is seen as an abstract, remote affair that may affect other people, but not oneself.[15]

---

[15] Those who have some reason to identify with the enemy may also be said to have a particular self-interest in the war. Specifically, one might expect the polls to show that German-Americans and Italian-Americans differ from other citizens in their support for, and approach to, World War II. One brief study conducted by the National Opinion Research Center a couple of

TABLE 5.9   Support for Defense of Norway and Iran by Presence of Draftable Family Member, July 1951 (NORC)

Suppose the Russian army *invaded* Norway and tried to take over that country. Should the United States do anything about it?	Is anybody in your immediate family likely to be called into the armed forces during the next year or so?		
	Yes, Self	Yes, Other Person	No, Nobody
Yes, take action	63%	53%	54%
No, do nothing	20	24	26
No opinion	17	23	20
If Communist armies were to attack Iran (Persia), do you think the United States should stay out of it or should we defend them? (If "defend":) Should we send American troops to help them or just send military supplies?			
Stay out if Iran attacked	31%	35%	34%
Defend, send troops	36	25	22
Defend, send military supplies only	16	15	22
Defend, don't know about troops	5	5	3
No opinion whether should defend Iran	12	20	19

Source. NORCc.

months after Pearl Harbor has looked into this matter (1942b). In it the responses of those with one or both parents born in Germany or Italy are compared to those from respondents with native-born parents. The results are more puzzling than definitive, and the relationship could certainly bear further study. Respondents with parents from Axis countries were less willing than those with native-born parents to trust the British, but about equally trusting of the Russians. They were more likely to believe the Allies had sunk merchant ships without warning, but no different in their beliefs that the Allies had used poison gas or spread disease germs; they were just as willing to believe that the Axis powers had sunk merchant ships without warning while only respondents with *both* parents born in Germany were noticeably inclined to deny that the Axis powers had spread disease germs. German-Americans were no more likely than those with native-born parents to urge that most of the American military effort should be concentrated on Japan rather than Germany, but Italian-Americans *were*. Also those with parents born in Axis countries were more likely than those

5.4 OTHER MENTALITIES

The partisan, follower, and believer mentalities seem to emerge rather clearly from the kinds of cross tabulations possible with public opinion surveys.[16] Most of the standard demographic variables are incorporated in these concepts: party identification, race, sex, age, religion and, correlated with education, occupation and income.

Left out of the analysis have been two geographic variables: the region in which the respondent resides and the concentration of people at his place of residence—whether rural or urban. Because of shifts of definitions (Is Tennessee in the South? Is a city "big" at 100,000 or 1,000,000?) and the muddiness of conceptualization (Does it make sense to bunch residents of a small Vermont town either with Bostonians because they share the same region or with citizens of a small Mississippi town because they have the same number of neighbors?), little was done with these variables, though perhaps a more careful and refined analysis would be beneficial (see Hero 1965). At any rate the wars in Korea and Vietnam do not seem to differ much in the degree to which they garnered support from different geographic locales although, imperfectly reflecting the liberal shift, there may have been more hostility in the Northeast to Vietnam than to Korea.

Here and there, traces of an "all-or-nothing" mentality were found: a kind of believer who finds either immediate withdrawal or unlimited escalation preferable to middle range courses. Among the demographic groups, the mentality seems to be most nearly typified by farmers. In general, farmers have been in fairly consistent opposition to the wars as judged by responses to the "mistake" question; also they have often been unusually willing, compared to other occupational groups, to endorse proposals for drastic escalation and immediate withdrawal. The data in Tables 5.1, 5.2, 5.3, and 5.4 furnish suggestive, if less than conclusive, evidence of this.

---

with native-born parents to see Japan as the number one enemy, to favor leniency toward the enemy after victory, and to anticipate that the war would end in a draw (although few in any group said they expected an Axis victory).

[16] See also the approach of Modigliani (1972) and of Suchman (1953).

5.5 CONCLUSION

This chapter has investigated the ways various subgroups of the population have responded to the wars in Korea and Vietnam. It has been found helpful to distinguish at least three "mentalities" that have affected war attitudes: the partisan mentality in which respondents find cues for their own opinion in the recommendations of party leaders; the follower mentality in which the cues come from national opinion leaders, especially the president; and the believer mentality in which the cues come from the issue itself.

By using most of the demographic breakdowns possible with standard poll data (party identification, education, age, income, occupation, religion, sex, and race), it has been possible to illustrate the kinds of people most likely to respond to these different cues. Of course, a single individual is a complex entity susceptible to a number of influences, and each person will weigh the influences differently.

However, while the use of these three mentalities as an analytic device may simplify reality, the approach seems far more useful than the usual reliance on the monochromatic hawk-dove continuum. It has been shown at several points that this reliance can lead to substantial confusions and to highly dubious inferences.

As for an ongoing theme of this book, the comparison of support for the wars in Korea and Vietnam, it has been found that the wars each inspired support and opposition from the same sectors of the population. One striking exception to this was the Jewish subgroup which supported the Korean War but opposed the war in Vietnam. This phenomenon is taken to be a reflection of the attitudes of the intellectual Left, a group of central concern in the next chapter.

CHAPTER 6

The Similarity of Support for the Wars: Some Explanations and Commentary

It is time to tie up some loose ends. The last three chapters have been devoted partly or mainly to a comparison of popular support for the wars in Korea and Vietnam. In general, it appears that this support was highly similar. As shown in Chapter 3, both wars began with about the same amount of support as judged by responses to the "mistake" question. This support was found to decline as a logarithmic function of American casualties, a function that was remarkably the same for both wars. While support for the war in Vietnam did finally drop below those levels found during Korea, it did so only after the war had gone on considerably longer and only after American casualties had far surpassed those of the earlier war.

In Chapter 4 other measures of war support were assessed, particularly questions probing attitudes toward alternative war strategies. Although these measures were less satisfactory than the "mistake" question for a number of reasons, it does seem that the wars still register at about the same degree of unpopularity when these other poll questions are examined.

Furthermore, in Chapter 5 it was found that the kinds of people likely to turn up in the support or opposition camps were much the same in the two wars. And they seemed to appear there for much the same reasons. This, despite the seemingly unique political movements among the young and among blacks that occurred during the war in Vietnam.

This similarity of support might seem surprising, for grand proclamations about the extreme unpopularity of the war in Vietnam are common. James Reston once called it "the most unpopular American war of this century"; a study group for the National Commission on the Causes and Prevention of Violence has declared that it "commands less popular support than any previous American international war"; and journalist David Wise has disclosed that in the Vietnam War, the nation entered "the most unpopular war in its history."[1] The poll evidence suggests that Vietnam has, at least, one rival for these unhappy distinctions.[2]

Vietnam is seen by some to be a more unpopular war than Korea, even from its beginning, probably because, as discussed in Section 2.3.8, *vocal* opposition as judged by demonstrations, petitions, and organized political campaigns was far greater during the later war. Of course all the anti-Vietnam demonstrators, petition-signers, and campaign workers together represent only a few percent of the American adult population, and thus cannot be expected, by themselves, to exert a measurable effect in a cross-sectional poll. But one might expect their existence to be symptomatic

---

[1] *New York Times*, June 21, 1968; *ibid.*, June 6, 1969; Wise (1968:27). All these statements were made before Vietnam support fell below that of Korea.

[2] On the other hand, one possible indicator, the morale of American troops, would suggest that the earlier war was the more unpopular. Social commentators during the Korean War were fond of attributing the low morale they discerned to miscellaneous notions about the crusading spirit of the American people, who were unable to support a war unless there were some Great Ideal at stake. Vietnam was surely no more a crusade than Korea yet, at least until the withdrawal phase, morale apparently was comparatively high. One seeks, therefore, more prosaic explanations for the supposed low morale in Korea: the men thrown into the Korean War, especially in its early stages, were very disproportionately World War II veterans extracted from peacetime preoccupations just when they were getting used to them. Bitterness under these circumstances is hardly surprising. The army desertion rate, incidentally, appears to have been considerably higher in Korea than in Vietnam. And it was much higher yet during World War II when massive mobilization brought in less "select" recruits. See *New York Times,* February 14, 1968.

of a much larger discontent. The data suggest, however, that although the opposition to the war in Vietnam may have been more vocal than that in Korea, it was not more extensive until the war had far exceeded the Korean War in casualties.

6.1 SOME EXPLANATIONS

One must account, therefore, not for increased *popular* opposition in the Vietnam case, but for increased *vocal* opposition. Several suggestions can be made.

6.1.1 The Intellectual Left

As noted in Chapter 2, most of the vocal opposition to the war in Vietnam seems to have come from the intellectual, nonunion Left. For the reasons discussed there, it seems likely that this small group did view the wars differently: Korea seemed an unpleasant, but necessary, episode in the cold war against Stalinist Russia; however, an anti-Communist war in Vietnam, under the substantially altered cold war atmosphere of the mid-1960s, was not found to be worthy of support.

As discussed in Chapter 5, it is difficult in the poll data to measure this shift among intellectual liberals because no questions designed to sort them out from the rest of the population were consistently posed. Looking at the responses of Jews as a surrogate for the liberal position on the issue, however, a notable shift was evident: Jews strongly supported the Korean War but tended to oppose the war in Vietnam. In fact, Jews seem to be about the only subgroup of all those usually sorted by demographic questions in surveys whose position on the two wars differs.

The years between the Korean and Vietnam wars had seen the gradual emergence of the intellectual Left as a force with political, though not necessarily electoral impact. This seems to have grown out of the opposition to McCarthy and then developed in the late 1950s with movements urging arms-control measures such as atomic test bans, unilateral disarmament initiatives, and alliance readjustments. In the early 1960s it had as a major inspiration the opposition to President Kennedy's fallout shelter program (see Levine 1963).

Around 1963, the intellectual Left moved from a preoccupation with international cold war issues to an alignment with the fast-emerging civil rights forces. In part, this was a result of the attractive dynamism of the movement and of its aggressive and inspired leadership. And, in part, it was due, after the 1962 Cuban missile crisis, to the notable thaw in the cold war. This seemed to make international threats and issues less pressing. The near evaporation of the arms control movement at this point is quite ironic, since the improved diplomatic atmosphere made it likely that pressure for arms-control measures would finally prove effective.[3]

In its association with the civil rights movement, the intellectual Left picked up and helped develop effective new techniques for political expression: passive disobedience, peaceful mass protest, the use of the media, and obstructionism.

As important legislative and judicial victories were won in the civil rights struggle, as the issue became more technical and cloudy, as blacks showed themselves capable of handling their own movement and, in some quarters, became rather resentful of (even friendly) white interference, and as the movement developed into the destructive, but possibly cathartic and vital, riot stage—as these developments occurred, the civil rights issue became less attractive to the intellectual Left.

Vietnam became at first a competitive cause, then a dominating one, until by 1968 the intellectual Left was almost entirely preoccupied with it. The new techniques of political expression were refashioned and redeveloped to fit the new cause and were put into action. The seeming efficacy of the movement generated a certain attractive inertia, swelling the ranks.

Thus *the "new Left" of the late 1960s seems, in this analysis, to be the old Left with new methods of expression, a new vocalism*. It is not "young people" brought up in the shadow of the bomb or of John Dewey. As stated in Chapter 5, young people are the most obvious element of any political movement presumably because of their physical energy and their lack of occupational and familial obligations. In fact, it was found that young people were generally more inclined to support the wars than their elders.

As the Vietnam issue itself faded in 1970 with declining Ameri-

---

[3] Indicative of the change was the collapse of the *Journal of Arms Control* after two issues in 1963. It proved to be the wrong journal at the wrong time on the wrong subject.

can combat activity and with the continuing withdrawals of United States forces from Vietnam, the intellectual Left—except for a spurt of activity in connection with the Cambodian invasion in the spring of 1970—for the most part moved on to new areas, most notably the environmental one.

This is not simply to say that the intellectual Left is fickle about its causes. Rather, because it is limited in size and energy, it does not seem able effectively to fight full force on two fronts at the same time and must choose its priorities: the race issue, it was common to hear in the late 1960s, can never be solved until the war in Vietnam is brought to an end.

Thus the difference in vocal opposition between the wars can be traced in part to a shift in attitude by one political group and to the effective use by that group of newly learned techniques of expression. However, none of this is to deny the political impact of the agitation on important elite groups, including those that finance political campaigns (Robinson 1970:9). The message here is simply to warn against the assumption that intellectual agitation is the same thing as a mass movement.[4]

6.1.2 McCarthyism, the Korean War, and Academic Economics

If there were people on the Left in opposition to the Korean War, their expression of dissent may have been smothered by the pall of McCarthyism.[5] In the early 1950s, a war opponent risked the danger of being labeled a Communist. In the 1960s the climate had changed enough so that such labeling was less likely to occur and, more importantly, less likely to be effective if applied.

For academicians, an important element of the intellectual Left, economic considerations may have reinforced these pressures, thus discouraging any inclined to oppose the Korean War from loudly voicing their point of view. The academic marketplace of the early 1950s was an extreme buyers' market as the generation born in predepression days, embellished by somewhat older people whose

---

[4] That demonstrators have not been representative either of the general public or of nondemonstrating activists in their attitudes toward the war in Vietnam is suggested by the evidence presented by Verba and Brody (1970).

[5] It has been suggested that the fear politicians had of McCarthy was somewhat unrealistic. See Polsby (1960).

graduate education had been postponed by World War II, entered the academic profession to find only the depression generation to teach. Thus job insecurity may have made political protest economically unwise and may have made the academic profession peculiarly susceptible to McCarthyite intimidation.

By the mid-1960s, however, the situation was reversed. The post-World War II babies were going to college while depression babies were entering the academic profession which then became a sellers' market. Thus academicians could protest, threaten to resign, and speak freely and impertinently, always aware that jobs were open somewhere. In part, therefore, academic courage may have an economic base.

While the fear of McCarthyite attack might have kept Korean War opponents from publicly expressing a point of view that could be interpreted as pro-Communist, it does not appear that the McCarthy camp was a notable source of support for the war. Table 6.1 displays some data on this. Those who adopted a McCarthy point of view were no more likely than others to find the war worthwhile either while it was being fought or after it was over, although (at least in 1953) they did have an escalatory vision of what strategy should be pursued there.

The 1954 survey in Table 6.1 (NORC 365) also included a large number of questions concerning areas of foreign policy other than Korea. By and large, they show little difference between approvers and disapprovers of McCarthy—even on such issues as trusting Yugoslavia, defending Formosa if under Communist attack, or recognizing Communist China. Nor do the groups differ markedly on their willingness to volunteer whether "most people can be trusted." Similar results are generated by a survey conducted in the last months of the Korean War (NORC 340). While those intent on rooting out domestic Communists were, comparatively, somewhat opposed to dealing with and compromising with the Russians, they did not differ from others on trading with Communist China or on the wisdom of intervening militarily in other countries to stop international Communism.

6.1.3 The Attentive Public

It may be the case, as James Rosenau has suggested, that the size of the attentive public has been increasing in response to ad-

TABLE 6.1 McCarthyites and the Korean War

	Do you think membership in the Communist party should be forbidden by law?		
December 1950	Should	Should Not	DK
In view of the developments since we entered the fighting in Korea, do you think the United States made a mistake in deciding to defend South Korea, or not?			
Yes, a mistake	50%	49%	45%
No, not a mistake	39	40	24
No opinion	11	11	31
Now that Communist China has entered the fighting in Korea with forces far outnumbering the United Nations troops there, which ONE of these two courses would you, yourself, prefer that we follow:			
Pull our troops out of Korea as fast as possible	63%	60%	60%
Keep our troops there to fight these larger forces	22	23	15
Qualified	8	10	5
No opinion	6	7	21

TABLE 6.1 (Continued)

January 1953

	Do you think such people [Communists or disloyal people in the State Department] have done any serious harm to our country's interests, or not?	
	Serious Harm	No, or Don't Know
As things stand now, do you think that the war in Korea has been worth fighting, or not?		
Has been worth fighting	40%	38%
Has not	55	50
No opinion	5	12
Which of these three things comes closest to *your* idea of what we should do in Korea?		
Pull our troops out of Korea and bring them home	19%	27%
Keep our troops in Korea and hold the present line there	25	29
Go ahead and attack the Chinese Communists	48	32
No opinion	8	12

TABLE 6.1 (Continued)

November 1954
As things stand now, do you feel that the war in Korea was worth fighting, or not?

All things considered, would you say you think favorably of Senator McCarthy, or un-favorably?

	Favorably	Unfavorably
Was worth fighting	40%	43%
Was not	54	49
No opinion	6	6

Source. RC, NORCc.

vances in education, technology, and communication. These increases would not be enough to register markedly in public opinion polls, but they might show themselves in the increased scope of organized political protest (Rosenau 1968).

6.1.4 The Vietnam Protest as Counterproductive

Finally, it should be considered that the protest against the war in Vietnam may have been counterproductive in its impact on public opinion: that is, the war might have been somewhat *more* unpopular if the protest had not existed.

To assess this proposition, it would be useful to recall a repeated finding from Chapters 4 and 5: many people, in arriving at a position on an issue, do not cue on the elements of the issue itself so much as on the expressed preferences of various opinion leaders. Instead of paying high information costs by sorting through the intricacies of argument of the issue, they prefer to take the word of people and institutions that they have reason to trust. Thus the public does not view an issue in the simple debating-manual sense with arguments pro and con neatly arranged. Rather the issue comes attended by certain public figures who array themselves on various sides and whose visible presence at an issue position may influence public opinion more than any element of the issue itself.

For a war, then, public opinion is going to be influenced by who is for it and who is against it. Now it happens that the opposition to the war in Vietnam came to be associated with rioting, disruption, and bomb throwing, and war protesters, as a group, enjoyed negative popularity ratings to an almost unparalleled degree. This has been shown in a number of studies and is, perhaps, most dramatically evident in the public's reaction to the 1968 Democratic Convention disorders, which was overwhelmingly favorable to the Chicago police (Robinson 1970; Converse et al. 1969:1087–88).

That negative reference groups can harm a cause's impact, a sort of negative follower effect, is quite clear. Cantril reports a poll from 1940, before the United States entered World War II, in which it was found that 57 percent of the American public expressed its agreement with the idea that the country should try to have friendly relations with Germany if she won the war in Europe. However, when the name of Charles Lindbergh, a prominent isolationist leader, was associated with this idea, support for it dropped to 46 percent while opposition climbed 16 percentage points (1947:41).

Thus it seems entirely possible that, because their cause became associated with an extraordinarily unpopular reference group, any gain the opposition to the war in Vietnam may have achieved by forcefully bringing its point of view to public attention was nullified.[6] But, again, it must be observed that the protest may still have been effective in a general political sense if it was successful in altering attitudes among elites and decision-makers.[7]

6.2 SOURCES OF THE ANTI-VIETNAM PROTEST

Studies indicate quite clearly that the young people who did oppose the war, as well as their well-educated older colleagues, were very disproportionately associated with the "better" colleges in the country (Converse and Schuman 1970:23–25). In cross-sectional polls, however, their attitudes are overwhelmed by the

[6] Much of the negative rating may have been inevitable. There seems to have been a rather low tolerance among the public for antiwar protest in general. In 1966 only 35 percent agreed with the right "to demonstrate against the war" (Lipset 1966:24). The SRC 1968 election study found only 20 percent approving of "taking part in protest meetings or marches that are permitted by the local authorities" as a way for "people to show their disapproval or disagreement with government policies or actions" (Converse et al. 1969:1105n).

Opinion on civil liberties, however, seems to be one of the many that are quite sensitive to question wording. Thus, the Harris Poll finds considerably more than 35 percent willing to grant the right to undertake "*peaceful* demonstrations" (WP December 18, 1967) and one wonders whether "approval" in the SRC question was taken to apply to the legitimacy of the demonstrators' actions or their point of view. As noted in Section 1.3, the percentage willing to "not allow" speeches against democracy was once found to be 16 points higher than the percentage willing to "forbid" them (Rugg 1941:92). Studies on this subject, perhaps extending those done during the McCarthy period such as Stouffer (1955), are much needed. There does not appear to be any data in existence to compare the Korean and Vietnam periods in the degree to which dissent was tolerated. The closest thing to extended trend data is given in Table 1.2 (p. 14).

[7] One cannot easily conclude, however, that politicians who lead or strongly support stop-the-war movements are forever damaged by such unpopular and "unpatriotic" associations. In Britain David Lloyd George actively opposed the Boer War and J. Ramsay Macdonald fought against World War I; each later became Prime Minister (see Richardson 1948:151, 159). In the United States Abraham Lincoln opposed the Mexican War of 1848.

legions among the young and the educated who enjoy no such association. It is of interest to consider why these associations should correspond with opposition to the war and the president's policy there.

One element in the explanation concerns the relatively liberal and left-liberal atmosphere at the better universities. Since, as noted above, political liberals were inclined to oppose the Vietnam War, it is not surprising to find opposition to the war in Vietnam centered at places where liberals are concentrated: the better universities (see Armor et al. 1967).

But in part this begs the question. What must be discussed is why the better universities are relatively liberal places. It could be that the more intelligent a person is, the more likely he is to adopt the liberal philosophy. However comforting this thought may be to liberals, it is of questionable validity, since in decades past the better universities were often bastions of conservatism. Or, it may be that pliable student minds are being bent to the Left by a band of liberal professors. But this explanation fits poorly with studies that find student values and attitudes in the aggregate not to be affected in any such gross way, if indeed they are affected at all, by the college experience (Jacob 1957; Goldsen et al. 1960; Feldman and Newcomb 1969). Nor does it fit with those that find faculty members to be particularly ineffective when changes do occur (Feldman and Newcomb 1969:330–31 et passim.). Nor does it fit with those that find college-bound high school seniors already to differ markedly in attitude from their peers (Langton and Jennings 1968:866).

A better explanation might draw on an observation made in Chapter 5 about the liberalism of Jews. Outside of a few sections in a few cities, the only easily identifiable places that Jews are found in strikingly disproportion are the colleges and universities of the land—and very particularly the better ones. Thus the liberalism of those associated with the better universities may not derive from anything endemic in the university situation. Rather, it may stem from the influence of a major subpopulation in the university community inclined toward liberalism and war opposition regardless of its association with the college.[8]

[8] A survey conducted by the President's Commission on Campus Unrest

6.3 TV

Many have seen Vietnam as a "television war" and argue that the vivid and largely uncensored day-by-day television coverage of the war and its brutalities made a profound impression on public attitudes.

The poll data used in this study do not support such a conclusion. They clearly show that whatever impact television had, it was not enough to reduce support for the war below the levels attained by the Korean War, when television was in its infancy, until casualty levels had far surpassed those of the earlier war.[9] Furthermore the television coverage of the 1968 Democratic Convention, although favorable to the demonstrators, was not capable of generating popular sympathy for them or their cause (see Section 6.1.4).

A study conducted by the National Opinion Research Center during World War II seems to be consonant with these findings. In the study realistic war pictures were shown to 112 respondents. Their reactions to a number of poll questions were then ascertained and compared to a matched sample of unexposed respondents. The exposure seems to have increased favorable attitudes toward a realistic news policy, but it affected attitudes toward the war itself not at all (NORC 1944).

---

found that campus disturbances occurred most often at large, eastern, liberal arts colleges with high admissions standards (*New York Times,* November 5, 1970).

[9] For an excellent discussion, see Arlen (1969). The Harris Poll once reported, "For most Americans television helps simplify the enormous complexities of the war and the net effect is that when they switch off their sets, 83 percent feel more hawkish than they did before they turned them on" (*Newsweek,* July 10, 1967, p. 22). The question on which this observation is based, however, was "Has the television coverage of the war made you feel more like you ought to back up the boys fighting in Vietnam or not?" (Letter from Louis Harris Political Data Center, University of North Carolina, September 10, 1969.)

CHAPTER 7

Retrospective Support for the Wars

Public opinion data can generate limited information about the popularity of wars after they are over. The major conclusion seems to be that such retrospective popularity ratings are quite sensitive to events occurring at the time of the poll. Ensuing events do not change the facts about the war, but they can alter how the public recalls and evaluates it. A small amount of data is available about the retrospective popularity of the two World Wars and about the war in Korea. This material is briefly surveyed in this chapter.

7.1 WORLD WAR I

The sensitivity to events can be seen quite clearly in the popularity of World War I as measured by polls in the late 1930s and early 1940s (see Table 7.1).

In the retrospective sense, it appears that World War I was as unpopular as any war of the century, for in 1937 and again after World War II broke out in Europe in the fall of 1939, only 28 percent were found to support the earlier war—a support score lower than any ever attained by comparable measures for the war in Korea, while a figure that low for the Vietnam War was only attained in mid-1971 after American casualties (though not battle deaths) had far surpassed those suffered in World War I. However, after the successful German invasion of France in mid-1940, the

TABLE 7.1 Support for World Wars I and II

Do you think it was a mistake for the United States to enter the last war (World War I)?	Support War	Oppose War	No Opinion
	(In Percent)		
January 1937	28	64	8
February 1939	37	48	15
October 1939	28	59	13
November 1940	42	39	19
January 1941	44	40	16
March 1941	43	39	18
April 1941	48	39	13
October 1941	47	35	18
December 1941	61	21	18
Do you think you, yourself, will feel it was a mistake for us to have entered this war (World War II)?			
February 1944	77	14	9
Do you think it was a mistake for the United States to enter World War II?			
April 1946	77	15	8
October 1947	66	24	10

Source. Erskine (1970:136–7).

popularity of World War I rose noticeably among the American public and then soared at the time of Pearl Harbor.

In this way, then, the growing American involvement in World War II seems to have caused support for the earlier war to increase. This may appear curious because one might expect that the very necessity for World War II would have demonstrated the futility of World War I, billed as "the war to end war." But, apparently, the growing recognition that the Germans must be opposed reinforced the idea that the policy of opposing them in 1917 had been a sound one.

7.2 WORLD WAR II

The highly limited data from World War II are also given in Table 7.1. Although all the numbers support the notion that World War II was a comparatively popular war (see also Section 3.6), the drop of support between early 1946 and late 1947 suggests a certain disillusionment of the kind presumably experienced earlier for World War I.

This decline is almost certainly tied to the rise of the Cold War as East Europe came under Soviet control and the United States reacted with the containment policy formalized in the Truman Doctrine of March 1947. To some, the recent war must have been considered as a bloody, futile process in which one enemy was defeated only to have its place taken by another almost immediately. Poll data show a precipitous drop in American willingness to trust the Russians during this period.[1] The Pearl Harbor hearings of 1946 may also have generated some doubt about the wisdom of the war.

7.3 KOREAN WAR

Postwar data for the Korean case can be found in the listings in Table 3.1 (p. 47). They suggest some disillusionment with the truce in mid-1953 since the initial reaction to it, according to the NORC index in Column C, was for noticeably fewer people to find the war "worth fighting" than had held this opinion when the killing was still going on.

However, this phenomenon does not seem to be the result of a specific resentment to the truce itself. Although some politicians and journalists at the time denounced the settlement as a sell out, the public was found by NORC to prefer the armistice to continued fighting by a 75 to 15 percent margin (NORCc). The popular discontent may have derived from the widely held opinion that the armistice would not be successful and that the war would soon erupt again. As seen in Table 7.2, many seemed to be inclined toward this view at the time of the truce and the view prevailed for several months thereafter. The public had learned to be skeptical.

At any rate, after this initial reaction, support for the war rose. By the last months of 1953, as measured by NORC's questions in Columns B and C of Table 3.1, war support had risen to as high a

[1] See Tables 1.2 and 2.4 and Caspary 1968. See also Scott and Withey (1958:184); ON, April 1, 1948, pp. 3–11, April 15, 1948, pp. 8–11.

TABLE 7.2 **Belief that the Korean War Was Really Over, 1953 to 1954**

Do you think the fighting in Korea is really over, or will the war there start up again in the near future? (NORC)

	Really Over	Will Start Again	Don't Know
	(In Percent)		
August 1953	24	58	14
September 1953	21	62	16
November 1953	20	59	20
January 1954	35	46	19

Source. RC.

level as any since China entered the war. Doubt over the wisdom of the war apparently had begun to be replaced by a need to rationalize the losses sustained in it.

However, when the question represented in Column C was again posed a year later, in November 1954, it was found that support for the war had not risen at all. Only in 1956, substantially after the peak of the McCarthy period, when this question was last asked of the public did a majority of those Americans with opinions find the war "worth fighting." At that point opposition to the war on the toughest of the war support questions had dropped to a new low. Finally, years later in March 1965, when the Minnesota Poll asked if the United States had done the right thing by entering the Korean War, it was found that 67 percent thought it had while only 16 percent thought it had not.

Thus as the population slowly became convinced that the Korean War was really over, the popularity of war rose. But, although the anguish and uncertainty associated with the war did finally dissipate, this change took years. Unlike the situation with World War II, postwar events did not suggest that the war had been futile. Or, perhaps better, the futility of the Korean War was appreciated by the public while it was still going on as reflected in the low degree of support it inspired. Thus there were few left to be disillusioned, and support could rise when memories of the suffering faded a bit.

However, it is quite possible that the events in Vietnam a full 15 years later have harmed the retrospective popularity of the

Korean War. Polls of students in international politics classes at the University of Rochester in 1966 and 1969 found parallel drops in support for the two wars: 34 percentage points for the Korean War and 35 percentage points for the war in Vietnam.

In conclusion, then, it has been found for all three wars that the retrospective popularity of a war is influenced by current events. This is a bit surprising because, as found in Chapter 3, popularity trend lines during the Korean and Vietnam wars were unaffected by events to a rather remarkable degree. To an extent, this may be because opinion cues during the war are fairly well established and visible. After the war the respondent must think more for himself and, hence, last night's headlines have more of a bearing on his utterances.

7.4 ATTITUDES TOWARD FORMER ENEMIES AFTER WORLD WAR II

A related issue that might be discussed briefly is the manner in which attitudes toward the enemy changed after World War II. Old hatreds mellowed, of course, and the poll data can be used to trace this change. But they also demonstrate rather graphically how very much mellowing there was to be done.

Table 7.3 gives a rather striking example. The question probed attitudes toward dropping the atomic bombs, and it was asked *after*

TABLE 7.3   Attitudes toward Dropping the Atomic Bomb, 1945

Which of these comes closest to describing how you feel about our use of the atomic bomb? (*Fortune*) (September 1945)

5%	We should not have used any atomic bombs at all.
14	We should have dropped one first on some unpopulated region, to show the Japanese its power, and dropped the second one on a city only if they hadn't surrendered after the first one.
54	We should have used the two bombs on cities, just as we did.
23	We should have quickly used many more of them before Japan had a chance to surrender.
6	Don't know.

Source. Cantril and Strunk (1951:23).

the Japanese had surrendered, a surrender that was generally assumed to have been in response to the atomic bombing of two of their cities. An option is included for approval of the seemingly efficacious bombing policy, and indeed that option proved to be the most popular. Yet almost a quarter of the sample ignored it in preference for an option of utter vindictiveness: "We should have quickly used many more of them before Japan had a chance to surrender."

This intense hatred by a substantial portion of the population is also seen in other questions posed during the last year of the war. Asked in open-ended fashion what should be done with the Japanese and German people after the war, some 10 to 15 percent volunteered the response that the enemy populations should be exterminated (Cantril and Strunk 1951:1112–19).[2]

A double comparison is afforded in Table 7.4 where attitudes toward the two major enemy peoples were tapped at two different points in time—one in the midst of the war, one in the year after its conclusion. As can be seen, a rather substantial minority preferred to see the enemy peoples starve after the war rather than *sell,* much less give, them food. And, although attitudes were less harsh in 1946 than they had been in 1943 on the starvation column, the mellowing was fairly small. Furthermore the quantity of people willing to *give* food to starving ex-enemies did not increase at all.

At both times, the attitudes toward the Germans were somewhat less harsh than those toward the Japanese. This probably is due to several elements: a certain degree of racism, a special resentment over the "sneak attack" at Pearl Harbor, and a lack, in the Japanese case, of a clear-cut villainous leader to blame for the enemy nation's behavior.

Attitudes toward the two enemy peoples are substantially more similar in the 1946 polls than in those from 1943. It is likely that this reflects in part reactions to information about the German

---

[2] Although there are no really comparable data, it seems likely that attitudes toward the enemy in the wars in Korea and Vietnam were considerably less harsh. Gallup asked for ratings of various groups in a poll in mid-1970. Although 69 percent gave the Viet Cong a highly unfavorable rating, 76 percent gave a similar rating to the Ku Klux Klan and 75 percent to the Black Panthers. Other ratings: 42 percent for the Students for a Democratic Society, 38 for the John Birch Society, 22 for the NAACP, and 13 for the South Vietnamese. (GOI 61.)

TABLE 7.4 American Opinion on Postwar Aid to Japan and Germany

If the people of Japan (Germany) are starving after the war (at the present time), do you think the United States should:

	Sell Them Only What Food They Can Pay For	Send Them Food as a Gift If They Can't Pay for It	Not Send Them any Food at All	Unde-cided
	(In Percent)			
Japan				
January 1943	34	30	31	5
March 1946	46	30	20	4
Germany				
January 1943	41	39	16	4
March 1946	49	35	13	3

Source. ON, April 16, 1946, p. 3.

death camps which, as noted in Section 3.6, became fully disclosed and appreciated only at the war's end. In fact the percentage willing to send starving Germans food as a gift actually declined a bit between 1943 and 1946. The death camp disclosures, however, seem to have had no immediate impact on American anti-Semitism,[3] although in the longer period since the war, anti-Semitism has declined markedly (Stember et al. 1966).

[3] This is suggested by the following data. Between 1942 and 1945, NORC asked: "Do you think that Jewish people in the United States have too much influence in the business world, not enough influence, or about the amount they should have?"

	Too Much	Not Enough	Right Amount	Undecided
	(In Percent)			
July 1942	51	2	33	14
January 1943	51	2	34	13
November 1943	54	1	31	14
December 1944	58	2	29	11
December 1945	58	1	30	11

(*ON*, March 1, 1948, p. 7.)

Although the data in Table 7.4 indicate that attitudes toward ex-enemy people did not soften quickly, a mellowing did finally take place, of course. In 1942 and again in the 1960s, Gallup presented a list of 23 adjectives to his respondents and asked them to select the words that best described the German, Japanese, or Russian people. Virtually all the negative qualities attributed to the enemy peoples in the 1942 poll were selected far less frequently in the 1960s, and most of the positive qualities gained noticeably in popularity. Something of a reverse pattern occurred for the Russian image. The data are displayed in Table A.2 on pp. 276–277.

PART 2 **Presidents**

CHAPTER 8

The Admired

The importance of presidential leadership in supplying foreign policy opinion cues for many in the population was discussed in Chapters 4 and 5. Part 2 of this book looks directly at the relationship of public opinion to the presidency and to the men who have held the office, particularly in the period since World War II. To begin the focus on this relationship, the present chapter discusses polls that have attempted to assess the public's admiration for famous men. Of particular interest is the place that the presidency occupies in these admiration sweepstakes.

8.1 THE ADMIRED AMONG THE LIVING

Since World War II, Gallup has asked his respondents every year, usually in December, "What man that you have heard or read about living today in any part of the world, do you admire the most?"

The results of these surveys are given in Table 8.1. The display differs from those published by the Gallup organization in that where possible the percentages attained by each of the admired is indicated, not simply the rank order for each.[1] Anyone admired by

---

[1] There is another difference. Starting in 1969, Gallup changed the way he tallied admiration. He *combined* the results of the admiration question

TABLE 8.1 The Most Admired Men, 1946 to 1970

Date	Percent Mentioning No One	1	2	3	4	5	6	7	8	9	10	11
Spring 1946[ab]		MacA	Ike	HST	ERoos	WSC	Hoover	HWall	Dewey			
February 1947[b]	27	MacA 10	Ike 10	HST 6	WSC 5	Marsh 4	ERoos 4	Byrnes 2	Pope 2	Kenny 2		
November 1948	19	HST 21	Ike 14	MacA 8	WSC 5	Marsh 4	Hoover 3	Dewey 3	Pope 2			
November 1949	24	Ike 12	HST 12	WSC 12	MacA 5	Hoover 3	Pope 2	Baruch 2				
December 1950	19	Ike 24	MacA 16	WSC 7	HST 4	Hoover 4	Taft 3	Baruch 2	Pope 2	Bunche 2		
December 1951	30	MacA 21	Ike 18	HST 8	WSC 6	Taft 3	Hoover 2					
December 1952	21	Ike 26	MacA 10	HST 5	WSC 5	Steve 4	Pope 2					
December 1953	20	Ike 29	WSC 10	MacA 6	HST 5	Steve 5	Sheen 3	JMcC 2	Schw 2	Pope 2		
November 1954	17	Ike 27	WSC 12	JMcC 4	Steve 4	HST 4	MacA 3	Pope 3	Sheen 2	Hoover 2	Schw 2	

TABLE 8.1 (Continued)

Date	Percent Mention-ing No One	Name and Percentage for Most Admired										
		1	2	3	4	5	6	7	8	9	10	11
December 1955	27	Ike 26	WSC 11	MacA 4	HST 3	Schw 3	Pope 2	Hoover 2	Sheen 2	Graham 2	Salk 2	Steve 2
December 1956	26	Ike 27	WSC 4	Sheen	Schw	Steve	MacA	Pope	Hamskj	Graham	Salk	
Death: J. McCarthy												
December 1957	26	Ike 27	WSC 4	HST 4	Schw 4	Graham 4	Salk 3	MacA 3	Sheen 2	Steve 2	Pope 2	
Death: Pope Pius												
December 1958	17	Ike 22	WSC 8	Schw 5	Graham 4	HST 4	MacA 3	Nixon 2				
1959		Ike	WSC	Schw	HST	Pope	Graham	Dooley	Hoover	Nixon	MacA	
1960		Ike	WSC	Schw	JFK	Nixon	Graham	Steve	HST	Lodge	MacA	
December 1961	23	JFK 23	Ike 14	WSC 7	Schw 5	Graham 3	HST 2	Pope 2	Nehru 2	Steve 2	MacA 2	
1962		JFK	Ike	WSC	Schw	Hoover	MacA	HST	Pope	Steve	Graham	
Deaths: Pope John, JFK												
December 1963	23	LBJ 21	Ike 11	WSC 5	Schw 4	Graham 3	Pope 2	King 2	RFK 2			

TABLE 8.1 (Continued)

Date	Percent Mention-ing No One	1	2	3	4	5	6	7	8	9	10	11
Deaths: Hoover, MacArthur												
1964		LBJ	WSC	Ike	King	RFK	Goldw	Graham	Steve	Schw	Pope	
Deaths: Churchill, Stevenson, Schweitzer												
December 1965	22	LBJ 19	Ike 11	Graham 4	Pope 4	King 3	RFK 2	Goldw 2				
December 1966	26	LBJ 14	Ike 11	RFK 6	Graham 5	Pope 4	Thant 3	Dirksen 2	GWall 2	Romney 2	Reagan 2	
December 1967	31	Ike 12	LBJ 7	Graham 7	RFK 5	Pope 3	Dirksen 2	GWall 2				
Deaths: King, RFK												
1968		Ike	LBJ	EMK	Graham	Nixon	HHH	GWall	Pope	HST	EMcC	
Death: Ike												
December 1969	33	Nixon 16	Graham 7	EMK 3	LBJ 3	HST 3	Pope 2	HHH 2				
December 1970	35	Nixon 10	Graham 7	EMK 4	Agnew 3	Pope 3	Muskie 2	LBJ 2	HST 2			

Name and Percentage for Most Admired (columns 1–11)

TABLE 8.1 **(Continued)**

Abbreviations

Agnew:	Spiro Agnew	Kenny:	Sister Kenny
Baruch:	Bernard Baruch	King:	Martin Luther King
Bunche:	Ralph Bunche	LBJ:	Lyndon B. Johnson
Byrnes:	James Byrnes	Lodge:	Henry Cabot Lodge
Dewey:	Thomas Dewey	MacA:	Douglas MacArthur
Dirksen:	Everett Dirksen	Marsh:	George Marshall
Dooley:	Tom Dooley	Muskie:	Edmund Muskie
EMK:	Ted Kennedy	Nehru:	Jawaharal Nehru
ERoos:	Eleanor Roosevelt	Nixon:	Richard Nixon
EMcC:	Eugene McCarthy	Pope:	Pius; John; Paul
Goldw:	Barry Goldwater	Reagan:	Ronald Reagan
Graham:	Billy Graham	RFK:	Robert F. Kennedy
GWall:	George Wallace	Romney:	George Romney
Hamskj:	Dag Hammarskjold	Salk:	Jonas Salk
HHH:	Hubert H. Humphrey	Schw:	Albert Schweitzer
Hoover:	Herbert Hoover	Sheen:	Fulton Sheen
HST:	Harry S Truman	Steve:	Adlai Stevenson
HWall:	Henry Wallace	Taft:	Robert Taft
Ike:	Dwight Eisenhower	Thant:	U Thant
JFK:	John F. Kennedy	WSC:	Winston S. Churchill
JMcC:	Joseph McCarthy		

Sources. RC, GOI 56.

[a] Results are a combination of two surveys.

[b] In 1946 and 1947 the most admired *person* was asked for, hence the presence of some female names.

at least 1½ percent of the population is included. In a few of the years no percentage data are available, so for these the bare rank-order results are given.

Two observations should be made before discussing the person-

with those generated by another question: "Who is your second choice?" Thus the published Gallup listings after 1968 are not comparable with those from earlier years. The listings in Table 8.1, however, do not include the second choices and thus *are* comparable. The principal mischief generated by the Gallup switch was to propel Spiro Agnew into the admiration strato-sphere in 1969. Republicans, groping for a second choice after selecting Nixon as their primary choice (Eisenhower had died earlier in the year), settled often enough on Agnew to put him in third place (GOI 55), despite the fact that *no* respondent in the 1969 survey had selected the Vice-President as their *most* admired man.

ality ratings themselves. First, a rather large portion of the population responds to the somewhat convoluted question with stunned silence. A good 20 or 25 percent of the respondents generally seem unable to conjure up the name of even one admirable man. One should not credit much of the respondent reticence to cynicism, since this percentage is not particularly out of line for such bald-faced questions, but it does mean that a substantial number of people have declined to contribute their biases to the sweepstakes.[2] In recent years Gallup has also asked for the *second* most admired man. Around 50 percent of the respondents greet that question with blank faces.

A second observation, not immediately apparent from the table, is that there are a great number of miscellaneous nominations. Scores, even hundreds, of names from all walks received a vote or two each from the respondents. Usually about 5 percent (does that number seem high or low?) nominate their father or husband. Thus the agreement of even 1½ percent of the sample on a single name represents something of an achievement.

8.1.1 Americans First

When one scans the names of men who have generated at least that much esteem, one may be impressed first by the near-total ethnocentrism expressed. Despite the question wording which specifically invites the respondent to admit for consideration men "living in any part of the world," the lists are almost barren of non-American names. Chiefest exception is Winston Churchill—whose wisdom in always stressing before American audiences the American lineage of his mother seems confirmed by these data. Beyond this, the popes usually have made the lists, and Albert Schweitzer has made frequent appearances. But the only other foreigners, each only with one appearance, were Nehru, Hammarskjold, and U Thant.

Ethnocentrism, however, does not appeal only to Americans. Comparable survey questions asked around the world find French lists of the admired filled with Frenchmen, Swedish lists with Swedes, and British lists with British (Cantril and Strunk 1951:558, 565).

---

[2] This percentage drops, of course, when a list of notables is given the respondent for his selection. See Roper (1957:241).

8.1.2 The Presidency

Beyond their American backgrounds, the most common characteristic of the men on the lists in the table is their association with politics and very particularly with the presidency. In 1968, to take a somewhat spectacular example, eight of the ten names on the list were men who were, had been, were about to be, or had spent 1968 trying to be president of the United States. Many Americans are supposed to be politically alienated and to view politics as a dirty business; nevertheless the overwhelming fact remains that the men they can agree upon to admire are politicians.

To begin with, the incumbent president, no matter how low his popularity at the moment, always makes the list and is usually at its top. In general, his percentage rating roughly traces the patterns of presidential popularity to be discussed in Chapter 8. The declines during the second terms of Truman and Johnson, for example, are evident as is the striking ability of Eisenhower to maintain his popularity over eight presidential years.

The importance of the presidency can also be seen in the lists of admired women whose ranks are characteristically dominated by the wives, daughters, and mothers of presidents, former presidents, and would-be presidents (GOI 56).

Of particular interest is the persistent presence on the lists of the names of ex-presidents, especially when they are those of men like Harry Truman and Herbert Hoover who left the presidency in considerable popular disrepute. To an extent their post-presidential admiration results from a Republican need for a congenial president to admire during Truman's Democratic Administration and a similar Democratic need during the Eisenhower era. Nevertheless Hoover often made the list even after Eisenhower was elected, and Truman maintained much of his strength while Kennedy was president. It is interesting to note that Truman' disappearance from the admired list in 1963 coincided with the ascension to the presidency of Lyndon Johnson, a man whose public image was much closer to Truman's than was Kennedy's. Then, in the lists from the late 1960s, when Johnson's popularity had dropped considerably, Truman's name reappears.

The names of presidential also-rans and potential nominees pepper the lists. In general, their appearance is fleeting and their appeal, unlike that of ex-presidents, is quick to fade. Notice the evaporation of Dewey after 1948, Nixon after 1960, and Goldwater after 1964. Adlai Stevenson, partly because he had no Democratic Eisenhower-figure to compete with, did rather better.

8.1.3 Other Notables

Only two cabinet members ever have made the lists: George Marshall and James Byrnes from the Truman days. Like the also-rans their memory did not linger after they disappeared from public prominence.

Two generals appear on the lists: Douglas MacArthur and Dwight Eisenhower. Admiration for Eisenhower increased greatly when he began to be considered in presidential speculation and soared to the highest levels ever recorded by anyone after his inauguration in 1953. His admiration levels remained high throughout his tenure in office as noted above, and then dropped after he left office. Thus his popularity seems to be considerably more associated with his presidency than with his generalship.

The admiration inspired by General MacArthur showed signs of decline in the late 1940s, but was regenerated during the Korean War; it slowly faded away thereafter.[3] With the possible exception of Marshall, no other military heroes have ever made the lists. Americans do not seem to be obsessed with General admiration.

If there is an obsession, after the presidency, it is with religion. As indicated, the only men besides Churchill persistently able to overcome the disadvantage of foreignness have been Albert Schweitzer and the popes. They are frequently accompanied on the lists by a pair of popular American religious figures: Billy Graham and Bishop Fulton Sheen. The admiration for the pope, incidentally, seems to reflect reverance for the institution more than esteem for the particular man. The three men who have occupied the position in the period, although differing in policy, personality, style and, presumably, charisma, have engendered about the same amount of admiration from Americans.

8.1.4 The Missing

These then are the men who have been the most admired. But at least as interesting is a consideration of names that have not made the lists.

---

[3] Likes and dislikes about MacArthur are assessed at length in Roper (1957:Chap. 7).

Paranoid intellectuals may find some perverse comfort in the observation that no men known primarily as artists, writers, philosophers, critics, college professors, or genial pundits have ever made the lists and that the whole world of science is represented fleetingly by only one name: Dr. Jonas Salk, the polio preventer.[4] Howls of self-pity should be restrained, however, since it is *also* true that the lists nowhere bear the names of entertainers, athletes, astronauts, FBI directors, or television personalities while the only businessmen to appear is Bernard Baruch—and then only after he had achieved a certain fame as a diplomat.

For most people, the word, "admire," triggers thoughts of politicians, particularly those associated with the presidency, and of religious figures.

8.2 THE ADMIRED OF ALL AGES

Another sort of perspective on the admired can be gained from the data in Table 8.2. On display are the results for an array of poll questions in which the respondent in various ways was usually asked to express his admiration for figures from the past as well as those from the present. The questions vary widely in wording and purpose, but despite this some general observations are possible.

Two patterns found in the discussion in Section 8.1 above are seen to reappear in these data. First, the pronounced ethnocentrism remains, seen most clearly in a comparison of questions 8 and 9: the "greatest statesmen" in "all history" are seen by Americans to be much the same as the "greatest statesmen" in "United States history." Second, where the greatest "person" is asked for, as in questions 5 and 10, the names remain dominated by presidents. Thus for Americans the question "Who is the greatest United States President?" is nearly equivalent to, "Who is the greatest man?"

Generals MacArthur and Eisenhower continue to make the lists, but religious figures do not. Jesus Christ, an exception, was suggested by a significant number in question 5, but not in question 10, a difference probably attributable to the vagaries of question word-

---

[4] Contrary to what might be expected, intellectuals do not seem to do much better on European lists. A British list from 1946 does show some popular esteem for Bernard Shaw, and one from France contains the name of the physicist, Pierre Joliet-Curie (Cantril and Strunk 1951:558). But both men, of course, were extraordinarily prominent in the political life of their countries.

TABLE 8.2 Questions on Admiration, 1938 to 1962

	DK			Percentages					
1. 1/38 Fifty years from now whom do you think will be regarded as the greater president—Theodore Roosevelt or Franklin D. Roosevelt?	17	FDR 48	TR 35						
2. 11/42 Can you name two or three living Americans you would really call great? (White high school students.)	8	FDR 60	MacA. 58	Doolittl 6	H.Ford 6	Babe Ruth 4	Hull 4	Willkie 3	
3. 1/45 Who do you think was the greater man, George Washington or Abraham Lincoln?	8	Linc. 42	Wash. 22	Equal 28					
4. 7/45 In all the history of the United States, who do you regard as two or three of the greatest men who have ever lived in this country?[a]	3	FDR 61	Linc. 56	Wash. 46	Edis. 11	Wilson 8	Ike 7	Jeffn. 6	
5. 11/45 In your opinion who is the greatest person living or dead, in world history?	12	FDR 28	Linc. 19	Jesus Christ 15	Wash. 8	MacA. 2			
6. 1/46 Which of these four United States presidents do you think was the greatest—F. D. Roosevelt, Wilson, Lincoln, Washington?	4	FDR 39	Linc. 37	Wash. 15	Wilson 5				

TABLE 8.2 (Continued)

	DK	Percentages						
7. 9/48 Considering all the men in America who have been prominent in public affairs during the past 50 years, which one or two have you admired the most?b	16	FDR 43	Ike 16	Hoover 7	TR 7	MacA. 6	Wilson 5	Dewey 4
8. 3/49 Who would you say was the greatest statesman, or political figure in all history, past or present?	8	FDR 37	Linc. 21	Wash. 7	Church. 4	Jeffn. 2	Wilson 2	
9. 3/49 Who would you say was the greatest statesman, or political figure in United States history, past or present?	6	FDR 39	Linc. 25	Wash. 7	Jeffn. 3	Wilson 2	TR 2	Frankn. 2
10. 6/49 Could you tell me the name of a great person, living or dead, whom you admire the most? (Philadelphia residents only.)	?	FDR 42	Linc. 9	Wash. 5				
11. 7/55 From the point of view of personal ability, how would you rank the following Presidents—Coolidge, Eisenhower, Hoover, Roosevelt, and Truman? Which one would you rank first?	2	FDR 60	Ike 24	Hoover 8	Coolidge 3	Truman 3		

TABLE 8.2 (Continued)

	DK	Percentages						
12. 7/55 If Franklin D. Roosevelt were alive today and running for a second term against Dwight D. Eisenhower, which candidate would you like to see win, Roosevelt or Eisenhower?	4	FDR 52	Ike 42	Neither 1				
13. 1/56 What three United States presidents do you regard as the greatest?c	8	FDR 64	Linc. 62	Wash. 47	Ike 34	Truman 13	Wilson 13	TR 10
14. 5/56 Who, in your opinion, has been the greatest American political figure in the past 50 years?	5	FDR 54	Ike 16	Wilson 12	TR 3	Hoover 3	Truman 2	Other 6
15. 1/62 Of the last four presidents—Kennedy, Eisenhower, Truman, and Roosevelt—which one do you think of as being the best president?	8	FDR 44	Ike 30	JFK 14	Truman 4			

Sources. 1, 2, 3, 4, 6 in Cantril and Strunk (1951) at pages 758, 559, 562, 565, 590, respectively; 10 in Sanford (1951: 191); all others, RC.

a In addition, MacArthur and T. Roosevelt were selected by 5 percent, Henry Ford and Benjamin Franklin by 4 percent, and Harry Truman by 3 percent.

b In addition, Truman was selected by 4 percent and Marshall, C. E. Hughes, and Wendell Wilkie by 3 percent.

c More complete results from this question are given in Table 8.3.

ing (or of Philadelphians). There is a tendency for the respondent to think in terms of relatively recent history when confronted with these questions, and this probably accounts for the unexpectedly low frequency with which the name of Jesus Christ was proffered— it was the only name of anyone living before George Washington to attain any significant showing. At any rate, the phenomenon seems to have been sufficiently embarrassing that Gallup thereafter asked only for admirable statesmen or presidents.

How quickly and thoroughly the past can be forgotten is evident in the responses to question 4 in which the respondent is asked to name two or three great Americans. Of the 12 men mentioned by at least 3 percent, the only pre-twentieth-century figures, besides the perennial Lincoln and Washington, are Jefferson and Franklin. In the responses to question 13, about great presidents, all the presidents since Wilson (except Harding) are nominated for greatness by at least 3 percent of the sample; of the presidents before Wilson, only Lincoln, Washington, Theodore Roosevelt, and Jefferson do that well. Among the prominent Americans from pre-twentieth-century times who are missing from the lists are Andrew Jackson, U. S. Grant, Robert E. Lee, and Daniel Webster.

Intellectuals from all centuries are again found to be neglected as are popular heroes: Daniel Boone, Charles Lindbergh, Patrick Henry, Babe Ruth, and the Wright Brothers.

The lists are dominated by a single name: Franklin Delano Roosevelt. This high standing in the polls conducted shortly after his death is understandable, but more striking is the fact that the Roosevelt name retained its magic even 10 or 15 years later. Notice especially his strikingly similar standing in the quite comparable questions 4 and 13, despite the fact that they were conducted 11 years apart.[5]

---

[5] It does not seem to be the case that FDR enjoyed special esteem from blacks. Question 2, from 1942, was asked also of black high school students. Although 60 percent of the white students suggested their President as one of the two or three great living Americans, only 37 percent of the blacks did so. The slack was handily taken up by a couple of black heroes of the time: Joe Louis and George Washington Carver (Cantril and Strunk 1951: 559). Similarly, Sanford's poll of Philadelphians taken 4 years after Roosevelt's death (question 10) found that "Negroes *do not* nominate FDR to greatness nearly as often as do whites." The percentages were 27 for blacks

After FDR, the names of Lincoln and Washington (in that order: Washington is no longer quite first in the hearts of his countrymen—note also question 3) garner frequent mentions and together the three consistently dominate American perceptions of their history (compare, again, questions 4 and 13). There are signs, however, that Roosevelt's advantage over the other two may be partly due to his recent presence, as if respondents in casting about for a great name sort time in reverse chronological order, come to the name of Roosevelt, and stop the search. As Roosevelt's time becomes past, rather than recent, history, his advantage may diminish. This conclusion is suggested by a comparison of questions 6 and 9 (or 8). When the names of Lincoln and Washington (or Wilson) are specifically mentioned to the respondent, their stock rises considerably; for FDR's name this procedure brings no improvement.

The Roosevelt phenomenon is stronger when the question is in abstract terms of "greatness" than when it is put in terms of a partisan contest. Questions 11 and 12 were asked on the same survey and suggest that although FDR is found far abler than Eisenhower, this advantage diminishes noticeably when the two are hypothetically matched in an election contest. Some would rather have Roosevelt on a pedestal than in the White House. The results of the "contest" in question 12, incidentally, are astonishingly similar (except for the frequency of the no opinion response) to those generated by question 1 from 1938 in which FDR is hypothetically opposed by Theodore Roosevelt.

On the whole, then, popular admiration has shown a fair constancy. During the period analyzed, the only major change has been the rise to solid popular prominence of Dwight Eisenhower. This esteem may diminish in time, but the evidence thus far does not suggest that Americans are fickle about their chief popular heroes.

Question 15 suggests the possible emergence of another popular hero: John Kennedy. His rather strong showing after only a year of office when matched against the mighty Roosevelt and Eisenhower is rather impressive, even considering the advantage he had of recency. The final impact on popular esteem of his assassination

compared to 45 for whites with many blacks giving their votes to Carver and Booker T. Washington (1951:200–03).

remains, of course, to be seen.[6] Some preliminary efforts to assess this impact are included in Chapter 11 where the popularity of ex-presidents is discussed more thoroughly.[7]

8.3 PRESIDENT RANKING: HISTORIANS AND THE PUBLIC

Question 13 in Table 8.2, which asked each respondent to name the three presidents he regards as the greatest, allows a sort of truncated ranking of the presidents: those presidents most favored will receive votes in varying number while the unadmired will receive none. These rankings can then be compared to those supplied by panels of historians polled in 1948 and 1962 by the late Arthur M. Schlesinger (1949, 1962; see also Bailey 1966: Chaps. 2–3 and Maranell 1970). The comparison is afforded in Table 8.3.

The similarities between public and historian are greater than might be expected. The public agrees that seven of the nine presidents the historians place at the top more or less deserve that honor.

Beyond this the public shows its usual bias toward Republicans (the alternative notion, that the historians are biased toward Democrats is, of course, inconceivable[8]). Hoover, Coolidge, and especially Eisenhower (but not Harding) benefit from this latter bias. This is undoubtedly contributed largely by Republican partisans in the sample who, unable to admit admiration for a Democratic President, quickly settle on Lincoln and Eisenhower and then cast about for another congenial name to complete the required trio, some settling finally on Republican Presidents of the 1920s for whom the historians can work up no enthusiasm whatsoever.

It was noted above that the public was fairly loyal over time in its admiration. The historians, perhaps because they all read the

---

[6] A poll in 1969 of 325 students graduating from Catholic colleges and universities asked for no more than five persons "whom you admire and consider outstanding." Not surprisingly John Kennedy, selected by 41 percent, headed the list with Robert Kennedy in second place at 29 1/2 percent. Franklin Roosevelt failed to get even 3 percent of the vote. In fact, the only "historical figures" (pre–World War II) to do that well were Jesus Christ at 14 percent and Abraham Lincoln at 5 percent (Schick 1969).

[7] For other commentaries on the admired, see Modelski (1970) and Blum (1958).

[8] Except, perhaps, to Thomas A. Bailey (1966:337–39).

TABLE 8.3 President Rankings by Historians and the Public

Presidents	Rank Order Selections		
	Historians, 1962	Public, 1956	Historians, 1948
Lincoln	1	2	1
Washington	2	3	2
F. D. Roosevelt	3	1	3
Wilson	4	6	4
Jefferson	5	8	5
Jackson	6		6
T. Roosevelt	7	7	7
Polk	8		10
Truman	9	5	
J. Adams	10		9
Cleveland	11		8
Madison	12		14
J. Q. Adams	13		11
Hayes	14		13
McKinley	15	11	18
Taft	16		16
Van Buren	17		15
Monroe	18		12
Hoover	19	9	20
B. Harrison	20		21
Arthur	21		17
Eisenhower	22	4	
A. Johnson	23		19
Taylor	24		25
Tyler	25		22
Fillmore	26		24
Coolidge	27	10	23
Pierce	28		27
Buchanan	29		26
Grant	30		28
Harding	31		29

Sources. RC and Schlesinger (1949:96) and (1962).

same books, seem even more constant: the rankings generated in 1948 and 1962 are strikingly similar to each other. Unfortunately, we have no data to test this constancy over longer periods of time, but it is probably worth mentioning that, around the turn of the century, historian James Bryce placed Grant in the front rank of American Presidents (1924:83).

CHAPTER 9

Presidential Popularity

I think (my grandchildren) will be proud of two things. What I did for the Negro and seeing it through in Vietnam for all of Asia. The Negro cost me 15 points in the polls and Vietnam cost me 20.

Lyndon B. Johnson[1]

With tenacious regularity since 1945 the Gallup poll has posed to its cross-section samples of the American public the following query: "Do you approve or disapprove of the way (the incumbent) is handling his job as president?" The responses to this curious question form an index known as "presidential popularity." According to Richard Neustadt, the index is "widely taken to approximate reality" in Washington and reports about its behavior are "very widely read" there including, the quotation above would suggest, the highest circles (1960:205n).

Plotted over time as in Figure 9.1, the index forms probably the longest continuous trend line in polling history. This chapter will analyze the behavior of this line, focusing on the period from the beginning of the Truman Administration in 1945 to the end of the Johnson Administration in January 1969 during which time

---

[1] Quoted, Wise (1968:131).

the popularity question was asked some 300 times.[2] Occasional commentary on the popularity of Presidents Roosevelt and Nixon will also be included. Efforts will be made to associate four variables with a President's popularity. These include a measure of the length of time the incumbent has been in office as well as variables that attempt to estimate the influence on his rating of major international events, economic slump, and war.

To assess the independent impact of each of these variables as they interact in association with presidential popularity, multiple regression analysis is used as the basic analytic technique. Although rather sparingly applied in political science, the approach has a large literature and a long history in other fields, especially economics where it is frequently applied to the analysis of time trends and other phenomena.[3]

9.1 THE DEPENDENT VARIABLE: THE PRESIDENTIAL POPULARITY QUESTION

The presidential popularity question taps a general impression about the way the incumbent seems to be handling his job at the present moment. As Neustadt notes, the response, like the question, is "unfocused," unrelated to specific issues or electoral outcomes (1960:95). The respondent is asked to "approve" or "disapprove" and if he has "no opinion," he must volunteer that response himself. He has infrequently been asked *why* he feels that way—and many respondents when asked are able only vaguely to rationalize their position.[4] And only at times has he been asked to register how strongly he approves or disapproves.

A disapproving response might be considered a nonconstructive vote of no confidence: the respondent registers his discontent, but he does not need to state *whom* he would prefer in the presidency. Thus the index is likely to be a very imperfect indicator of electoral

[2] The presidential popularity data for most of the Johnson Administration and for all of the Nixon Administration have been taken from the *Gallup Opinion Index*. The Roosevelt data appear in Cantril and Strunk (1951:756). All other data have come from the Roper Center.

[3] For a discussion, see Ezekiel and Fox (1959); Draper and Smith (1966); Christ (1966).

[4] See, for example, the breakdowns in GOI 10, p. 4.

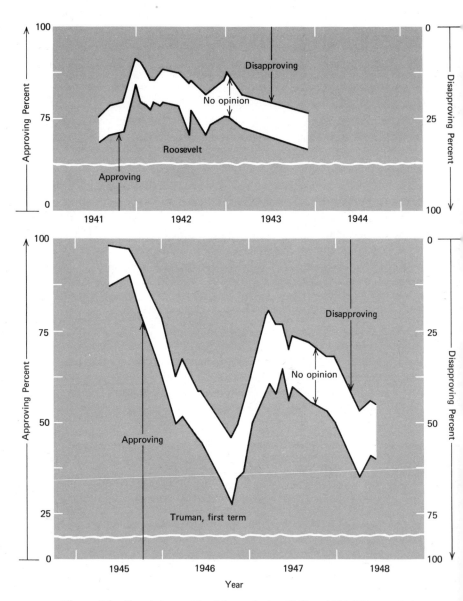

Figure 9.1 Trends in presidential popularity, 1941 to 1971. The area below the bottom line represents the approving percentage, the area above the top line represents the disapproving percentage, and the white area represents the no opinion percentage.

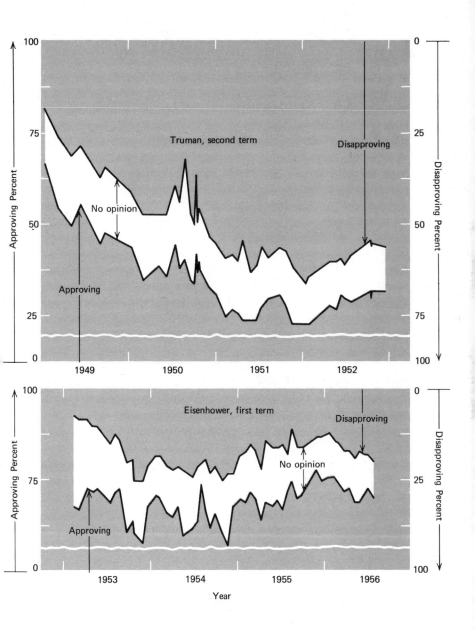

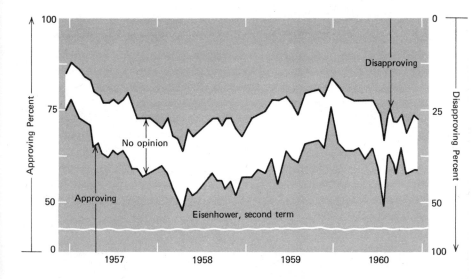

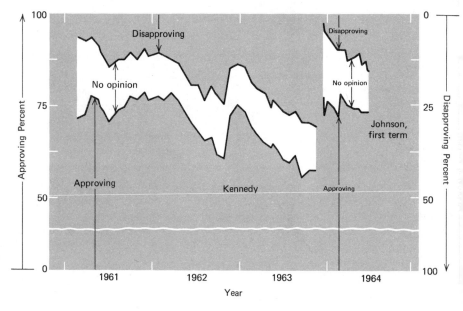

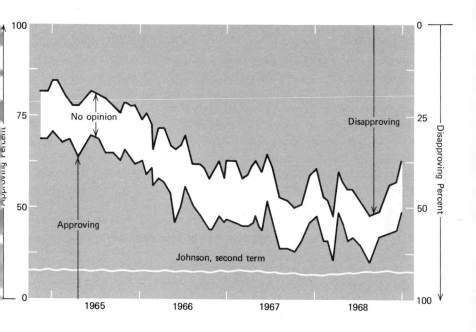

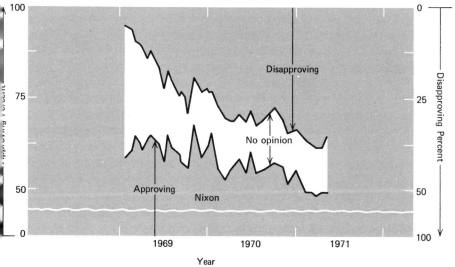

success or failure for a president seeking reelection. While approvers are doubtless more likely than disapprovers to endorse his reelection, on considering the opposition some approvers may be attracted into voting against the incumbent just as some disapprovers may be led grudgingly to vote for him.

There is also a more technical reason why the popularity index has little direct relevance to the electoral result: Gallup does not ask the question during a president's reelection campaign. Thus for the months between early summer and late fall in 1948, 1956, and 1964 no Gallup data on presidential popularity exist.[5]

Whatever peculiarities there are in this question, they are at least constant. Unlike many questions asked by the polling organizations, wording has not varied from time to time by whim or fashion. The stimulus has therefore been essentially fixed; only the response has varied.

And the variation has been considerable. Harry Truman was our most popular president in this period—for a few weeks in 1945 when more than 85 percent of the public expressed their approval—and our least popular—from early 1951 until March 1952 when less than 30 percent were usually found to be favorably inclined. Other presidents have stayed within these limits with Lyndon Johnson most nearly approaching the Truman extremes. President Eisenhower's popularity was never higher than 79 percent, but it never dropped below 49 percent either; the consistently high level of support that he was able to maintain especially throughout his first term is, in comparison with other presidents of the period, quite remarkable and is given special attention in Section 9.6 below. President Kennedy also maintained a rather high level of popularity but was in noticeable decline at the time of his death.

The proportion of respondents selecting the "no opinion"

---

[5] One other technicality is worth mentioning. There is a slight underrepresentation of data points in Truman's first years. By 1950, except for the election-year phenomenon already noted, the Gallup organization was asking the question on virtually every survey conducted—some dozen or 16 per year. Before that time the question was posed on the average only about half as frequently. Neither of these technical problems, however, is likely to bias the results in any important way, especially since so much of the analysis allows each administration a fair amount of distinctiveness.

option (represented as the space between the lines in Figure 9.1) averaging 14 percent, remained strikingly constant throughout the period.[6] This is a little surprising, since it might be expected that when opinion moves, say, from approval to disapproval of a president, the change would be revealed first in a decrease in the support figure with an increase in the no opinion percentage, followed in a later survey by an increase in the disapproval column with a decrease in the no opinion portion. There are a few occasions in which the no opinion percentage seems to rise and fall in this manner, one occurring in the early weeks of the Korean War, but by and large it seems that, if movements into the no opinion column do occur, they are compensated for by movements out of it.

This means therefore that the trend in approval is largely a mirror image of the trend in disapproval; the correlation between the two for the Truman-Johnson period is —.979. And, most conveniently, this almost means that the president's popularity at a given moment can be rendered by a single number: the percentage approving his handling of the job. The no opinion percentage is almost always close to 14 percent, and the percentage disapproving is, of course, the remainder.

There is, however, one small wrinkle. The no opinion percentage does get a bit out of hand on three highly understandable occasions—the early weeks of the Kennedy, Eisenhower, and Nixon administrations as substantial numbers of respondents felt inclined to withhold judgment of these new men (see Figure 9.1). This inordinate withholding of opinion declined in the first weeks to more "normal" levels with the result that either *both* the level of approval *and* disapproval tended to increase thus for a while showing a *positive* correlation, or else the approval rating remained constant while the disapproval rating rose.

Since one of the propositions to be tested in this study proposes that there exists a general downward trend in each president's popularity, this initial rating situation causes something of a problem. If the approved score is taken as the dependent variable,

---

[6] The standard deviation for the no opinion response for the Truman-Johnson period is 2.97. By contrast, the comparable statistic is 14.8 for the approve response and 14.5 for the disapprove response.

there will be a slight bias against this proposition; if the disapproval score is used as the dependent variable, there will be a similar bias in favor of the proposition. It seems preferable to load things against the proposition; hence, for the purposes of this study *the dependent variable is the percentage approving the way the incumbent is handling his job as President.*[7] The average approval rating for the Truman-Johnson period is 58 percent.

The size of the no opinion response at the beginning of the Nixon Administration is truly remarkable. Since the man had been prominent on the national political scene for two decades, one might expect the public to feel they knew him pretty well by the time he attained the presidency; yet far more withheld opinion on him than had for any other president, including the political neophyte, Eisenhower. Apparently, familiarity does not necessarily breed understanding.

As shown in Figure 9.1, initial popularity ratings for other terms do not show the same degree of uncertainty. Presidents Truman and Johnson entered the presidency under highly traumatic circumstances, and the public was strongly inclined to express its confidence in them: the no opinion response is relatively low and disapproval registers at a bare whisper. The other initial ratings are for second terms when, of course, the incumbent would be well known. Presidents Truman and Johnson began their second terms at almost precisely the same level of popularity, although President Johnson had done far better in the preceding reelection contest, suggesting perhaps that Senator Goldwater's candidacy contributed as much to that triumph as did President Johnson's efforts.

9.2 THE INDEPENDENT VARIABLES

If one stares at presidential popularity trend lines long enough, one begins to imagine one is seeing things. If the things imagined seem also to be mentioned in the literature about the way presi-

---

[7] Some argue that percentages should not be used in their pure state as variables but, instead, should be transformed into logits $\{Y^* = \log_e [Y/(1-Y)]\}$. The transformation was tried in the analysis, but it made little difference. Therefore, the more easily communicated percentage version has been kept. In any event, the dependent variable rarely takes extreme values. It rises to 80 percent only three or four times and never dips below 23 percent.

dential popularity should or does behave, one begins to take the visions seriously and to move to test them.

In this manner were formulated four basic "independent" variables—predictor variables of presidential popularity. They are (1) a "coalition of minorities" variable that suggests the overall trend in a president's popularity will be downward; (2) a "rally round the flag" variable which anticipates that international crises and similar phenomena will give a president a short-term boost in popularity; (3) an "economic slump" variable that associates recessions with decreased popularity; and (4) a "war" variable that predicts a decrease in popularity under the conditions of the Korean and Vietnam wars.

9.2.1 The Coalition-of-Minorities Variable

In a somewhat different context Anthony Downs (1957:55–60) has suggested the possibility that an administration, even if it always acts with majority support on each issue, can gradually alienate enough minorities to be defeated. This could occur when the minority on each issue feels so intensely about its loss that it is unable to be placated by administration support on other policies that it favors. A clever opposition, under appropriate circumstances, could therefore form a coalition of these intense minorities until it had enough votes to overthrow the incumbent.

Transposed to presidential popularity, this concept would predict that a president's popularity would show an overall downward trend as he is forced on a variety of issues to act and thus to create intense, unforgiving opponents of former supporters. It is quite easy to point to cases where this may have occurred. President Kennedy's rather dramatic efforts to force back a steel price rise in 1962, while supported by most Americans, tended to alienate many in the business community (see Erskine 1964:341 and 338). Administration enforcement of the Supreme Court's original school desegregation order tended to create intense opposition among white Southerners even though the presidential moves had passive majority support in most of the country (Fenton 1960:146).

Realistically, the concept can be extended somewhat. From time to time there arise bitter dilemmas in which the president must act and in which he will tend to alienate *both* sides no matter what he does, a phenomenon related to what Aaron Wildavsky (1968) has called a "minus sum" game. President Truman's seizure of the steel mills in 1952 made neither labor nor management (nor the Supreme Court, for that matter) happy. For the mayor of New York, situations like this seem to arise weekly.

There are other, only vaguely related, reasons to expect an overall decline in popularity. One would be disillusionment. In the process of being elected, the president invariably says or implies that he will do more than he can do, and disaffection of once bemused supporters is all but inevitable. A most notable example would be the case of those who supported President Johnson in 1964 because he seemed opposed to escalation in Vietnam. Furthermore initial popularity ratings are puffed up by a variety of weak followers. These might include leering opposition partisans looking for the first excuse to join the aggrieved, excitable types who soon become bored by the humdrum of postelection existence, and bandwagon riders whose fair weather support dissolves with the first sprinkle.[8] As Burns Roper (1969) notes, "In a sense, presidential elections are quadriennial myth builders which every four years make voters believe some man is better than he is. The president takes office with most of the nation on his side, but this artificial 'unity' soon begins to evaporate."

For these reasons the coalition-of-minorities variable, as it is dubbed here, predicts decline. "Love," said Machiavelli, "is held by a chain of obligation which, men being selfish, is broken whenever it serves their purpose."[9]

The variable itself is measured simply by the length of time, in years, since the incumbent was inaugurated (for first terms) or re-elected (for second terms). It varies then from zero to about four and should be negatively correlated with popularity: the longer the man has been in office, the lower his popularity. It is. The simple correlation for the Truman-Johnson period is −.48. The decline is assumed to start over again for second terms because the president is expected to have spent the campaign rebuilding his popular coalition by soothing the disaffected, redeluding the

[8] For the bandwagon effect among nonvoters, see Campbell et al. (1960: 110–15).

[9] *The Prince,* Chap. XVII.

disillusioned, and putting on a show for the bored. If he is unable to do this, he will not be reelected, something which has not happened in the postwar era, although twice presidents have declined to make the effort.

Actually, what one would expect then is a decline until the reelection campaign period when popularity should rise again.[10] As noted in Section 9.1, however, Gallup does not ask his question during reelection periods, so the upturn effect cannot be assessed.

The analysis will assume a *linear* decline in popularity. That is, a president's popularity is assumed to decline at an even rate for all four years of his term: if a decline of 6 percentage points per year is indicated, he will be down 6 points at the end of his first year, 12 at the end of the second, 18 at the end of the third, and 24 after four years.

There is nothing, however, in the justification for the coalition-of-minorities variable which demands that the decline must occur with such tedious regularity. At least two variants of this basic theme are entirely sensible. One, which might be called the "honeymoon" variant, would argue that the decline would be *exponential* —slow in the first year as the public gives the president a chance to show his true colors and then faster in each successive year as greater and greater portions of the public decide that they prefer different shades. If the decline is a squared function, for example, a president who lost 2 percentage points in the first year (and most of that would occur toward the end of the year), would lose 6 points more in the second year, 10 in the third, and 14 in the fourth.

The second variant would employ a *logarithmic* transformation and would postulate a slowing rate of decline as was found to be the case for war support in Chapter 3. Thus in one version using natural logarithms, a president who lost 6 percentage points between his first and third months in office would take until his seventh month to lose another 6, until the end of his second year to lose another 6, and at least until the end of his term to lose another 6.

Intuitively the justification for the coalitions-of-minorities vari-

---

[10] Such an effect is found in British data by Goodhart and Bhansali (1970).

able would tend to find the logarithmic variant more palatable than the honeymoon variant. Initial popularity ratings, it was noted, are undoubtedly inflated with many very weak supporters who are easily and very quickly turned off. After their conversion to the disaffected camp the president is left with relatively hard core supporters whom he will find more difficult to alienate. Thus decline might be expected to occur disproportionally in the early part of his term.

Happily for intuition, if not necessarily for truth and wisdom, the honeymoon variant does rather poorly when tested: the regression fit is worse, and the behavior of the predictor variables becomes more incoherent. While the logarithmic variant sometimes shows some improvement over the linear version, the improvement is usually quite minor, hence the rather general reliance here on the linear version which has the advantage of simplicity and ease of communication.

9.2.2 The Rally-Round-the-Flag Variable

This variable seeks to bring into the analysis a phenomenon often noted by students of the presidency and of public opinion: certain intense international events generate a rally-round-the-flag effect which tends to give a boost to the president's popularity rating. It is a development of the follower effect discussed in Chapters 4 and 5. As Kenneth Waltz (1967:272) has observed, "In the face of such an event, the people rally behind their chief executive." Tom Wicker (1967): "Simply being president through a great crisis or a big event . . . draws Americans together in his support." Richard Neustadt (1960:100) notes "the correspondence between popularity and happenings"; Burns Roper (1969) finds "approval has usually risen during international crises"; and Nelson Polsby (1964:25) observes: "invariably, the popular response to a president during international crisis is favorable, regardless of the wisdom of the policies he pursues." A rather clearcut example can be seen in the data in Figure 9.1 where President Roosevelt's popularity is found to soar after the Japanese attack on Pearl Harbor in late 1941.

The difficulty with this concept is in operationalizing it. There is a terrible temptation to find a bump on a popularity plot and then to scurry to historical records to find an international "rally point" to associate with them. This process all but guarantees that the variable will prove significant.

The strategy adopted here to identify rally points was somewhat different, and hopefully more objective. A definition of what a rally point should look like was created largely on a priori grounds, and then a search of historical records was made to find events that fit the definition. Most of the points so identified *are* associated with bumps on the plot—that, after all, was how the concept was thought of in the first place—but quite a few are not, and the bumps associated with some are considerably more obvious than others.

In general, a rally point must be associated with an event which (1) is international and (2) involves the United States and particularly the president directly; and it must be (3) specific, dramatic, and sharply focused.

It must be international because only developments confronting the nation as a whole are likely to generate a rally-round-the-flag effect. Major domestic events—riots, scandals, strikes—are at least as likely to exacerbate internal divisions as they are to soothe them.

To qualify as a rally point, an international event is required to involve the United States and the president directly because major conflicts between other powers are likely to engender split loyalties and are less likely to seem relevant to the average American.

Finally, the event must be specific, dramatic, and sharply focused to assure public attention and interest. As part of this, important events that transpire gradually, no matter how important, are excluded from consideration because their impact on public attitudes is likely to be diffused. Thus sudden changes in the bombing levels in Vietnam are expected to create a reaction, but the gradual increase of American troops is not.

Errors in this process could occur by including events whose importance is only obvious in retrospect or by ignoring events like the Geneva summit of 1955 that may seem minor in historical perspective but were held significant at the time. For this reason more reliance has been put on indexes of newspaper content than on broad, historical accounts of the period.[11] In general, if there

---

[11] Especially valuable was Nordheim and Wilcox (1967). Other sources

has been a bias in selecting rally points, it has been in the direction of excluding borderline cases. This was done in profound respect for the extent of the lack of public interest and knowledge on most items of international affairs as discussed in Chapter 1. For example, the 1954 crisis over Quemoy and Matsu, seen by some to have had relevance to presidential popularity, is excluded partly because fully 45 percent of the population stated after the event that it had neither heard nor read anything about the islands.[12]

At that, some 34 rally points for the Truman-Johnson period were designated. They are listed in Table 9.1. In general, they can be said to fall into six categories. First, there are the four instances of sudden American military intervention: Korea, Lebanon, the Bay of Pigs, and the Dominican Republic. A second closely related category encompasses major military developments in ongoing wars: in Korea, the Inchon landing and the Chinese intervention; in Vietnam, the Tonkin Bay episode, the beginning of the bombing of North Vietnam, the major extension of this bombing, and the Tet offensive. Third are the major diplomatic developments of the period: crises over Cuban missiles, the U-2 and atomic testing, the enunciation of the "Truman doctrine" with its offer of aid to Greece and Turkey, the beginning of and major changes in the peace talks in Korea and Vietnam, and the several crises in Berlin. Fourth are the two dramatic technological developments: Sputnik and the announcement of the first Soviet atomic test. The fifth category includes the meetings between the president and the head of the Soviet Union at Potsdam in 1945, Geneva in 1955, Camp David in 1959, Paris in 1960, Vienna in 1961, and Glassboro in 1967. Although these events are rarely spectacular they, like crisis, do generate a let's-get-behind-the-president effect. Because they are far less dramatic—even if sometimes more important—presidential conferences with other powers (for example, the British at Nassau) are excluded as are meetings with the Soviet Union at the foreign minister level.

Sixth and finally, as an analytic convenience the start of each

often consulted included the *New York Times Index* and the Chronology section of the *World Almanac*.

[12] NORC polls 370 (March 1955) and 371 (May 1955). NORCc.

TABLE 9.1   Rally Points for the Truman-Johnson Period

April	1945	Death of FDR, Truman takes office
August	1945	Potsdam Conference, Japan surrenders
March	1947	Truman Doctrine announced
Spring-Summer	1948	Beginning of Berlin blockade (reelection campaign, no polls)
November	1948	Truman reelection
September	1949	Truman announces Soviet A-bomb test
June	1950	Korean invasion
September	1950	Inchon landing
November	1950	China enters Korean War
July	1951	Korean peace negotiations begin
January	1953	Eisenhower inauguration
July	1953	Final resumption of Korean talks, truce signed
July	1955	Geneva conference of the Big Four
November	1956	Eisenhower reelected
October	1957	Sputnik I launched
July	1958	United States troops sent to Lebanon
September	1959	Talks with Khrushchev at Camp David
May	1960	U-2 incident, Paris summit
January	1961	Kennedy inauguration
April	1961	Bay of Pigs invasion
June	1961	Vienna meeting with Khrushchev
August	1961	Berlin wall erected, USSR resumes testing
October	1961	Berlin crisis, tank confrontation
October	1962	Cuban missile crisis
November	1963	Kennedy assassination, Johnson takes office
August	1964	Bay of Tonkin episode (reelection campaign, no polls)
November	1964	Johnson reelected
February	1965	Retaliatory bombing of North Vietnam begun
April	1965	United States troops sent to Dominican Republic
June	1966	Extension of bombing to north of Hanoi (oil dumps)
June	1967	Glassboro summit
January	1968	Tet offensive
April	1968	North Vietnam agrees to beginning of Vietnam talks after partial bombing halt
October	1968	Full bomb halt, talks to get substantive

presidential term is rather arbitrarily designated as a rally point. Presidents Truman and Johnson came in under circumstances that can justifiably be classified under the rally-round-the-flag rubric, although the crisis was a domestic one. The other points all involve elections or reelections that, perhaps, might also be viewed as a somewhat unifying and cathartic experience.

These, then, are the events chosen to be associated with the rally-round-the-flag variable. No listing will satisfy everyone's perspective about what has or has not been important to Americans in this 24-year period. However, in the analysis the variable has proved to be a rather hardy one. Experimentation with it suggests that the addition or subtraction of a few rally points is likely to make little difference.

The rally-round-the-flag variable is measured by the length of time, in years, since the last rally point. It varies then from zero to a theoretical maximum of about four or an empirical one of 1.9. Like the coalition-of-minorities variable, it should be negatively correlated with popularity: the longer it has been since the last rally-round-the-flag event, the lower the popularity of the incumbent. It is. The simple correlation for the Truman-Johnson period was —.16. Some experiments with curvilinear transformations of the variable were attempted but, since improvement was marginal at best, the variable has been left in linear form.

Each rally point is given the same weighting in the analysis. One effort to soften this rather crude policy was made. The rally points were separated into two groups: "good" rally points (for example, the Cuban missile crisis) in which the lasting effect on opinion was likely to be favorable to the president, and "bad" ones (for example the U-2 crisis, the Bay of Pigs) in which the initial favorable surge could be expected to be rather transitory. Two separate rally-round-the-flag variables were then created with the anticipation that they would generate somewhat different regression coefficients. The differences however were small and inconsistent. The public seems to react to "good" and "bad" international events in about the same way. Thus, to this limited extent, the equal weighting of rally points seems justified.

Writing shortly after the Glassboro summit, Tom Wicker (1967) observed, "the reality behind Johnson's improved position in the polls is that his latest short-term gain is no more likely to reverse the long-term trend than any of the others did." This expresses quite well for a specific case the relationship between the coalition-of-minorities variable and the rally-round-the-flag variable assumed to be general in this study. In tandem the concepts underlying these variables predict that the president's popularity will continually decline over time and that international crises and similar events will explain short-term bumps and wiggles in this otherwise inexorable descent.[13]

9.2.3 The Economic-Slump Variable

There is a goodly amount of evidence, and an ever goodlier amount of speculation, suggesting a relationship between economic conditions and electoral behavior.[14] The extension of such thinking to presidential popularity is both natural and precedented. Neustadt, for example, concludes that the recession in 1958 caused a drop in President Eisenhower's popularity.[15]

The economic indicator used here will be the unemployment rate. This statistic recommends itself because it is available for the entire period and is reported on a monthly basis.[16] It is used as a general indicator of economic health or malaise and is not taken simply as a comment about the unemployed. Presumably the unemployed—especially the newly unemployed—are likely to be inclined toward disapproval of the president who presides over their unhappy state but, with a maximum unemployment rate of 7 or 8 percent during the period, there simply are too few unemployed greatly to affect the president's rating; furthermore, as noted in Chapter 1, public opinion polls tend to underrepresent somewhat the poor and the unemployed, since people in those categories are

[13] Burns Roper (1969) observes that a high point of President Kennedy's popularity occurred after the Bay of Pigs invasion and concludes this fact says something special about that crisis event. But this phenomenon is due to *two* effects: the rally-round-the-flag effect *and* the fact that the events occurred very early in Kennedy's Administration when the value for the coalition-of-minorities variable was yet very low.

[14] See Campbell et al. (1960: Chap. 14); Key (1952: Chap. 20 and references); Kramer (1971); Segal (1968); Rees et al. (1962).

[15] (1960:97ff.) See also the discussion in Section 9.7 below.

[16] Data were gathered from Moore (1961:122) and, for more recent data, issues of the *Monthly Labor Review*.

harder to find and are more likely to be uncooperative respondents. The unemployment rate for the period is plotted in Figure 2.2 (p. 38).

In dealing with the relation between unemployment and popularity, one is immediately presented with a grossly unpleasant fact: there is a positive correlation—+.39 to be exact—between the two. That is, the higher the unemployment rate, the higher the popularity.

Fortunately the variable can be made to suggest sensible results, but only after it has been modified a bit. Three alterations are required.

First, notice that unemployment reached some of its highest points during the recessions under the Eisenhower Administration. The problem here, to be examined more fully in Section 9.6 below, is that Eisenhower was a *generally* popular president. Thus even though his popularity seemed to dip during the recessions—the correlation between unemployment and popularity during the Eisenhower years was a reassuring −.68—high unemployment comes to be associated with a relatively popular president. This problem can be handled rather easily within regression analysis by assigning to each of the presidential administrations a "dummy" or "binary" variable, the care and feeding of which will be discussed more fully in Section 9.3 below (Suits 1957; Draper and Smith 1966:134–41).

Second, observe that if the simple unemployment rate is used, a gross injustice is done to President Kennedy. Specifically, unemployment was very high at his inauguration; but to expect the public to blame *him* for the high rate at that point is absurd, since he won the election in 1960 in part because of discontent over the economic policies of the Republicans. Therefore, a more sensible approach is to assume that the individual respondent, in allowing economic perceptions to influence his approval or disapproval of the president, essentially does so by comparing how things are *now* with how they were when the incumbent began his present term of office. If conditions are worse, he is inclined to disapprove the president's handling of his job, if things are better, he is inclined to approve.

The economic variable, therefore, becomes the unemployment rate at the time the incumbent's term began subtracted from the rate at the time of the poll.[17] It is positive when things are worse and negative when things are better and should be negatively correlated with popularity.

But it isn't. Both the correlation coefficient and the regression coefficient, even when the effects of the other variables are taken into account, remain positive. This seems to be largely because *both* unemployment and the popularity of the incumbent president were in general decline between 1961 and 1968. The correlation for the period is .77.

Therefore, the third alteration administered to the economic variable was to set it equal to zero whenever the unemployment rate was lower at the time of the survey than it had been at the start of the incumbent's present term. The first two alterations merely took account of certain peculiarities in conception in the data, but this one is substantive and is executed as the only way the data can be made to come out "right." In essence, it suggests that *an economy in slump harms a president's popularity, but an economy that is improving does not seem to help his rating.* Bust is bad for him but boom is not particularly good. There is punishment but never reward.

Perhaps this can be seen in a comparison of the 1960 and the 1968 campaigns. In 1960, as Harvey Segal (1968) notes, "What was important was the vague but pervasive feeling of dissatisfaction with the performance of the economy, the pain that made the public receptive to JFK's appeals." In 1968, representing administrations that had presided over an unprecedented period of boom, Vice-President Humphrey seemed never able to turn this fact to his advantage.

It is important to notice that in practice this variable, which will be called the "economic slump" variable because of its in-

---

[17] One additional wrinkle, which is intuitively comfortable but makes little difference in the actual results, was to do something about the unemployment rates at the start of the first terms of Presidents Truman and Eisenhower when unemployment was "artificially" depressed because of ongoing wars. Presumably the public would be understanding about the immediate postwar rise in unemployment. Therefore, for these two terms the initial unemployment level was taken to be the level that held 6 months after the war ended, while the economic variable for the few months of the war and the 6-month period was set equal to zero.

ability to credit boom, takes on a nonzero value only during the Eisenhower Administration and during the unemployment rise of 1949 to 1950. In symbolic form the variable's peculiarities can be expressed in the following (the units are the percentage of unemployed).

$$E = U_t - U_{t_0} \quad \text{if} \quad U_t - U_{t_0} > 0$$
$$= 0 \quad \text{if} \quad U_t - U_{t_0} \leqslant 0$$

where U_t = unemployment rate at the time of the survey
and U_{t_0} = unemployment rate at the beginning of the incumbent's present term.

9.2.4   The War Variable

It is widely held that the unpopular, puzzling, indecisive wars in Korea and Vietnam severely hurt the popularity of Presidents Truman and Johnson (Waltz 1967:273 ff, 288; Neustadt 1960:97–99; Wicker 1967; B. Roper 1969). As stated in the quotation that heads this chapter, President Johnson himself apportioned 20 percentage points of his drop in popularity to the Vietnam War.

This notion seems highly plausible. The popularity of Presidents Truman and Johnson was in steady decline as the wars progressed, with record lows occurring during each president's last year in office at points when the wars seemed most hopeless and meaningless. The wars unquestionably contributed in a major way to their decisions not to seek third terms and then, when they had stepped aside, the wars proved to be major liabilities for their party's candidates in the next elections (Campbell et al. 1960: 50–51). Overall, the correlation between presidential popularity and the presence of war is —.67.

There are problems with this analysis, however. The coalition-of-minorities concept argues that decline is a natural phenomenon and, indeed, a glance at the plot of presidential popularity clearly shows Truman and Johnson in decline *before* the wars started. Furthermore, both men experienced noticeable decline (in Johnson's case, only in the disapproval rating) during their *first* terms when they had no war to contend with. The real question is then: Did the war somehow add to the decline of popularity beyond that which might be expected to occur on other grounds?

An answer can be approached through multiple regression

analysis, although there are some special problems. After allowing for a general pattern of decline under the coalition-of-minorities variable, the additional impact of a variable chosen to represent war can be assessed. It is also possible in this manner to compare the two wars to see if their association with presidential popularity differed.

The presence of war is incorporated in the analysis simply by a dummy variable that takes on a value of one when a war is on and remains zero otherwise. As in Part 1, the beginning of the Vietnam War was taken to be June 1965 with the beginnings of the major United States troop involvement (see Section 2.3.4). At that point it became an American war for the public; before that, ignorance of the war was considerable: as noted in Chapter 2, as late as mid-1964 twenty-five percent of the public admitted that it had never heard of the fighting in Vietnam.

Other war measures of a more sophisticated nature were experimented with. They increase in magnitude as the war progresses and thus should be negatively associated with popularity. They were applied in Chapter 3 to the war-support measure. One of these is the length of time since the war began. Another, closely related, but one that develops at a different pace, is the total American casualties (or the logarithm of this figure) suffered in the war at the time of the survey.

These latter measures, however, are almost identical to the coalition-of-minorities variable for the two relevant presidential terms and, hence, are all but useless in the analysis, since their independent impacts cannot be sorted out. The simple dummy variable suffers this defect in lesser measure (although the correlations still come in at around the .90 level), and thus, despite its crudities, has been used. The multicollinearity problem is discussed more fully in Section 9.4.

Although the Korean War continued into President Eisenhower's Administration, he is not "blamed" for the war in the analysis since, of course, he was elected partly because of discontent over the war. Accordingly, the war variable is set at zero for this period.

9.2.5 Other Variables

The analysis of presidential popularity will apply in various permutations only the four variables discussed above—a rather austere representation of a presumably complex process. As will be seen, it is quite possible to get a sound fit with these four variables, but at various stages in the investigation—which involved the examination of hundreds of regression equations—a search was made for other variables that could profitably be added to the predictor set.

International developments are reasonably well incorporated into the analysis with a specific variable included for war and another for major crisislike activities. Domestically, however, there is only the half-time variable for economic slump and the important but very inspecific coalition-of-minorities variable.

Accordingly, it would be valuable to generate some sort of domestic equivalent to the rally-round-the-flag variable to assess more precisely how major domestic events affect presidential popularity. Operationally, however, this is a difficult task. First, while it is a justifiable assertion that international crises will redound in the short term to a president's benefit, it is by no means clear how a domestic crisis, whether riot, strike, or scandal, should affect his popularity. Furthermore major domestic concerns vary quite widely not only in intensity and duration but also in nature over time. Labor relations, which rarely made big news in the mid-1960s, were of profound concern in the middle and late 1940s as a multitude of major strikes threatened to cripple the nation and the adventures of John L. Lewis and the Taft-Hartley bill dominated the headlines. In the 1950s, however, labor broke into the news only with an occasional steel or auto strike or with the labor racketeering scandals in the last years of the decade. On the other hand, race relations, extremely important in the 1960s made, except for the Little Rock crisis of 1957 and an occasional election-time outburst, little claim to public attention before that time. From the late 1940s into the mid-1950s sundry spy and Communist hunts were of concern, but the issue fairly well fizzled after that. Other issues had even briefer or more erratic days in the sun: the food shortage of 1947, the MacArthur hearing of 1951, and various space flights. Similarly, personal crises for the presidents such as heart attacks and major surgery for Presidents Eisenhower and Johnson and the attempted assassination of President Truman could not readily be fashioned into a predictor variable. In any event, these events seem to have far more impact on the stock market than on popularity ratings.

Scandal is a recurring feature of public awareness and thus is more promising as a potential variable in the analysis. Besides the scandals associated with alleged spies and Communists in the government during the McCarthy era and those associated with labor in the late 1950s, Americans, with greatly varying degrees of pain, have suffered through the five-percenter scandal of 1949 to 1950; charges of corruption in the RFC in 1951, in the Justice Department in 1952, and in the FHA in 1954; and scandals over Sherman Adams in 1958, over television quiz shows in 1959, over industry "payola" in the late 1950s, over Billie Sol Estes in 1962, and over Bobby Baker in 1963. While scandal is never worked into the regression analysis, some preliminary suggestions as to its relevance to a "moral crisis" phenomenon which may, in turn, affect presidential popularity are developed in Section 9.6 below.

Some thought was given to including a "lame duck" variable when it was observed that the popularity of Presidents Truman and Johnson rose noticeably after they decided not to seek third terms (see Figure 9.1). The trouble is, however, that President Eisenhower was a lame duck for his entire second term, and it was found easier to ignore the whole idea than to decide what to do about this uncomfortable fact.

One domestic variable which did show some very minor promise was a dummy variable that takes the value of one during a major strike. The variable was zero almost everywhere except in parts of President Truman's first term. After that time major strikes were rather unusual and, when they did occur, usually lasted for such a short time that there was barely time to have a public opinion survey conducted to test their effects. Despite these peculiarities, the variable did show statistical significance, although only after the Korean War dummy had been incorporated in the equation to allow for a major peculiarity of President Truman's *second* term. Substantively the variable suggests a popularity drop of less than 3 percentage points when a major strike is on and, as such a minor contributor, it is not included in the discussion below. Its small success, however, may suggest that further experimentation with the effects of specific domestic events could prove profitable.

9.3 RESULTS WITHOUT THE WAR VARIABLE

In *summary* the expected behavior of presidential popularity is as follows. It is anticipated (1) that each president will experience in each term a general decline of popularity; (2) that this decline will be interrupted from time to time with temporary upsurges associated with international crises and similar events; (3) that the decline will be accelerated in direct relation to increases in unemployment rates over those prevailing when the president began his term, but that *improvement* in unemployment rates will not affect his popularity one way or the other; and (4) that the president will experience an additional loss of popularity if a war is on.

In this section the relation of the first three variables to presidential popularity in the Truman-Johnson period will be assessed. In the next section the war variable will be added to the analysis.

The association between the first three variables and presidential popularity is given in its baldest form in eq. 1 in Table 9.2. The equation explains a respectable, if not sensational, 23 percent of the variance (the R^2 figure). The coalition-of-minorities variable shows, in conformity with the speculation above, a significant negative relationship. The equation suggests that, in general, a president's popularity rating starts at about 70 percent and declines at a rate of some 6 percentage points per year.

However, while the coefficients for the rally-round-the-flag and economic-slump variables are in the expected direction, they are not significant either in a statistical or a substantive sense. The trouble with the economic-slump variable was anticipated in the discussion about it in Section 9.2: the economic decline occurred during the relatively popular reign of President Eisenhower; although the slump seems to have hurt his popularity, even with the decline he remained popular compared to other presidents; hence, what is needed is a variable to take into account this peculiar "Eisenhower effect." To a much smaller extent the same things can be said to affect the rally-round-the-flag variable: the variable reaches somewhat higher values than usual during President Eisenhower's highly popular first term when, as can be seen from Table 9.1, little happened internationally.

To account for this phenomenon, eq. 2 mixes into the analysis a dummy variable for each of the presidents. This formulation insists that all presidents must decline (or increase) in popularity at the same rate but, unlike eq. 1, it allows each president to begin at his own particular level. Thus peculiar effects of personality,

TABLE 9.2 **Regression Results Including Administration Effects, Truman to Johnson**

	Equations			
	(1)	(2)	(3)	(4)
Intercept	69.91	55.10	68.15	72.01
Independent variables				
Coalition of minorities (in years)	−6.32	−5.43		
	(0.69)	(0.48)		
Rally round the flag (in years)	−0.35	−2.06	−1.85	−2.62
	(1.92)	(1.35)	(1.06)	(1.07)
Economic slump (in percent unemployed)	−0.17	−3.16	−5.30	−5.95
	(0.95)	(0.75)	(0.60)	(0.59)
Dummy variables for administrations				
Eisenhower		24.03	0.50	
		(1.43)	(2.28)	
Kennedy		23.69	11.34	
		(1.83)	(2.95)	
Johnson		11.43	5.41	
		(1.52)	(2.36)	
Coalition-of-minorities variable for administrations (in years)				
Truman			−11.45	−12.72
			(0.84)	(0.49)
Eisenhower			0.83	−0.03
			(0.57)	(0.46)
Kennedy			−5.96	−1.84
			(1.36)	(0.81)
Johnson			−9.52	−8.81
			(0.62)	(0.49)
Standard error of estimate	13.05	8.93	6.83	7.05
R^2	.23	.64	.79	.78

Each equation in Tables 9.2 and 9.3 is displayed vertically. The dependent variable, the percentage approving the way the president is handling his job, has a mean of 57.9 and a standard deviation of 14.8. The number of cases is 299. The figures in parentheses are the standard errors for the respective partial regression coefficients. To be regarded statistically significant, a regression coefficient should be, conventionally, at least twice its standard error. All equations in this chapter are significant (F test) at well beyond the .01 level. All equations exhibit a statistically significant amount of positive serial correlation (see Section 9.5).

style, and party and of differences in the conditions under which the president came into office can be taken into account.[18]

The addition improves things considerably. The fit is much better (the R^2 is .64) and the rally-round-the-flag and economic-slump variables attain respectable magnitudes in the right direction. The equation suggests that the presidents have declined at an over-

[18] The dummy variables formalize the sort of discussion found in Neustadt (1960:98). They account for what a singer might call *tessitura*.

all rate of more than 5 percentage points per year, but that each has done so at his own particular level. President Truman's decline is measured from a starting point of about 55 percent (the intercept figure—what remains when the dummy variables for the Eisenhower, Kennedy, and Johnson administrations are all zero). President Eisenhower declines from a much higher level, about 79 percent (the intercept plus the Eisenhower value: 55.10 + 24.03), President Kennedy also from 79 percent, and President Johnson from 66 percent.

The importance of these dummy variables clearly demonstrates that *any analysis of presidential popularity cannot rely entirely on the variables discussed in Section 9.2, but must also incorporate parameters designed to allow for the special character of each administration.* To an extent this is unfortunate. The beauty of eq. 1 is that it affords a prediction of a president's popular rating simply by measuring how long he has been in office, how long it has been since the last rally point, and how many people are unemployed. Such predictions, however, would be intolerably inaccurate because the fit of the equation is rather poor. Instead one must include the administration variables, the magnitudes of which cannot be known until the president's term is over. So much for beauty.

Because of this phenomenon, it is not possible to incorporate President Nixon's popularity into the analysis until he completes a term. Nevertheless, it seems clear from the incomplete data in Figure 9.1 that the coalition of minorities decline is very much present. Because of the extraordinarily large no-opinion percentage he inspired in his early months in office, the decline is shown more clearly in the disapproval percentages than in those in the support column. A decline can also be seen in the Roosevelt figures.

In eq. 3, administration effects are incorporated in a different manner, greatly improving fit (the R^2 is .79). In this formulation each president is allowed to begin at his own level of popularity as in eq. 2, but in addition each may decline (or increase) at his own rate: for each administration there is a different coefficient for the coalition-of-minorities variable. Three of the four values so generated are strongly significant while the magnitudes of the administration dummies drop greatly. When the administration dummies are dropped entirely from consideration, as in eq. 4, the regression coefficients remain quite firm, and the fit of the equation is scarcely weakened. Clearly, *the important differences between administrations do not lie so much in different overall levels of popularity but, instead, in the widely differing rates at which the coalition-of-minorities variable takes effect.*

The popular decline of Presidents Truman and Johnson has been almost precipitous. President Truman's rating fell off at some 11 to 13 percentage points per year while President Johnson's declined at a rate of 8 or 9 points a year. President Kennedy was noticeably more successful at holding on to his supporters. Then there is the Eisenhower phenomenon: in spite of all the rationalizations for the coalitions-of-minorities concept tediously arrayed in Section 9.2, President Eisenhower's rating uncooperatively refuses to decline at all.

It was stated in Section 9.1 that some minor bias in these results is introduced by an embellished rate of "no opinion" in the first weeks of the Kennedy and first Eisenhower terms. As this rate declined, there was a tendency for the presidents' approval *and* disapproval rates to rise. To see if this peculiarity had any major impact, eqs. 3 and 4 were recalculated by using the percentage disapproving as the dependent variable. This manipulation caused no fundamental difference, although President Eisenhower's rating behaved a little less outrageously. In the version comparable to eq. 3, his "unpopularity" rating barely rises, and in the eq. 4 version it climbs at a rate of nine-tenths of a point per year, the latter coefficient barely being statistically significant. President Kennedy's "unpopularity" rating rises 7 percentage points a year in the eq. 3 version and 3 points a year in the eq. 4 version, both coefficients significant. This rate, however, is still much less steep than the Truman and Johnson rates.

In eq. 3, presidents who served two terms were required to begin each term at the same level and their rate of decline or increase also had to be the same in each term. Liberation from these restrictions is gained in the rather cluttered eq. 5 of Table 9.3 which affords a term-by-term comparison. That is, eq. 5 is the same as eq. 3 except that each *term* is treated separately rather than each *administration*. As can be seen, President Eisenhower managed a statistically significant *increase* of popularity of some 2½ percentage points per year in his first term. His second term ratings showed a more human, but very minor and statistically nonsignificant de-

TABLE 9.3 **Regression Results Including Term Effects and the War Variables, Truman to Johnson**

	Equations	
	(5)	(6)
Intercept	72.00	72.38
Independent variables		
Rally round the flag (in years)	−4.87(1.03)	−6.17(1.03)
Economic slump (in percent unemployed)	−2.67(0.64)	−3.72(0.64)
Dummy variables for terms		
Truman, second	−15.25(3.65)	−12.42(3.53)
Eisenhower, first	−3.77(3.11)	−2.41(2.98)
Eisenhower, second	−5.30(3.03)	−4.35(2.90)
Kennedy	7.53(3.25)	7.18(3.10)
Johnson, first	4.40(4.07)	4.02(3.89)
Johnson, second	−1.28(3.02)	−1.06(3.21)
Coalition-of-minorities variable for terms (in years)		
Truman, first	−9.21(1.39)	−8.92(1.33)
Truman, second	−7.98(0.99)	−2.82(1.35)
Eisenhower, first	2.45(0.85)	2.58(0.81)
Eisenhower, second	−0.07(0.64)	0.22(0.62)
Kennedy	−5.12(1.20)	−4.75(1.15)
Johnson, first	1.24(8.81)	2.53(8.43)
Johnson, second	−8.10(0.65)	−8.13(0.79)
Dummy variables for wars		
Korea		−18.20(3.39)
Vietnam		0.01(2.77)
Standard error of estimate	6.00	5.73
R^2	.84	.86

cline.[19] When the percent *disapproving* is made the dependent variable, the results remain the same.

Nor do important differences emerge in this phenomenon when the economic slump variable, which functions mainly during the Eisenhower years, is dropped from the equation.

No matter how the data are looked at then the conclusion remains the same, *President Eisenhower's ability to maintain his popularity, especially during his first term, is striking and unparalleled.* An examination of some of the possible reasons for this phenomenon is conducted in Section 9.6 below.

The rally-round-the-flag and the economic-slump variables emerge alive and well in eqs. 3, 4, and 5 (and 6). Both are statistically significant, but their substantive importance varies as one moves from an administration-by-administration formulation of the coalition-of-minorities variable (eqs. 3 and 4) to the term-by-term formulation in Table 9.3. Specifically, the rally-round-the-flag variable gets stronger while the economic-slump variable weakens.

The rally-round-the-flag variable is very much a parasite—it is designed to explain bumps and wiggles on a pattern measured mainly by the coalition-of-minorities variable. Consequently, the rally-round-the-flag variable does very poorly on its own and only begins to shine when the overall trends become well determined by the rest of the equation. In the end, *the rally-round-the-flag variable suggests a popularity decline of about 5 or 6 percentage points for every year since the last rally point*—about the same magnitude as the coalition-of-minorities variable in its general state as in eqs. 1 and 2.

The declining fortunes of the economic-slump variable suggest that the variable in eqs. 3 and 4 was partly covering for the differences between the two Eisenhower terms: the first term was associated with increasing popularity and a smaller recession, the second with somewhat declining popularity and a larger recession. With the Eisenhower terms more thoroughly differentiated in eq. 5, the variable is reduced to a more purely economic function. The

---

[19] If the term dummies are dropped from the equation to attain a version comparable to eq. 4, the Eisenhower phenomenon holds true except that his first-term increase drops to 1.98 (still significant) and his second-term decrease is a slightly steeper −0.38 (still not significant).

magnitude of the coefficient of the *economic-slump variable* in this equation *suggests a decline of popularity of about 3 percentage points for every percentage point rise in the unemployment rate over the level holding when the president began his present term.* Since the unemployment rate has varied in the postwar period only from about 3 to 7 percent, the substantive impact of the economic-slump variable on presidential popularity is somewhat limited.

The evidence for a "second term effect" is minimal.[20] President Eisenhower began his second term at a very slightly lower level than his first and was not able to maintain his popularity as well in the second term. But President Truman, while he began his second term at a much lower level than his first, declined at a *slower* rate in the second term.

9.4 RESULTS WITH A WAR VARIABLE ADDED

Because of the multicollinearity problem as discussed in Section 9.2.4, the variable designed to tap the impact on presidential popularity of the wars in Korea and Vietnam was applied with no great confidence that it would prove to have an independent, added effect when the coalition of minorities had already been incorporated into the equation. As is obvious from a perusal of Figure 9.1, Presidents Truman and Johnson were in popular decline during their warless first terms.[21] Furthermore each was in clear decline in the first part of his second term before the wars started, and it is not at all clear that this trend altered when the wars began.

The equations suggest otherwise, however. When a war dummy (a variable that took on a value of one if either war happened to be on at the time of the survey and that was zero otherwise) was

---

[20] The concept is mentioned, without enthusiasm, by Neustadt (1960: 205–06n). See also B. Roper (1969).

[21] Regression statistics relating to President Johnson's first term are very unreliable, as the size of the standard errors suggests, because the popularity question was posed so few times during this brief period. As is clear from Figure 9.1, his "disapprove" rating ascended steeply while his approval rating held level. Regression equations comparable to eqs. 5 and 6 using disapproval as a dependent variable suggest an almost statistically significant growth in disapproval at the rate of 13 or 14 percentage points per year for this term.

appended to the equations already discussed, it emerged significant and suggested that the presence of war depressed the popularity of Presidents Truman and Johnson by several percentage points. The next step, obviously, was to set up a separate dummy variable for each war. This brought forth the incredible result documented in eq. 6: *the Korean War had a large, significant, independent negative impact on President Truman's popularity of some 18 percentage points, but the Vietnam War had no independent impact on President Johnson's popularity at all.*

When confronted with a result like this, one's first impulse is to do something to make it go away. This impulse was fully indulged. Variables were transformed and transmuted, sections of the analysis were reformed or removed, potentially biasing data were sectioned out.[22] But nothing worked. The relationship persisted. In fact, under some manipulations the relationship became *stronger*.

One's second impulse is to explain the phenomenon away as a statistical freak. Because of the high correlations that the war variables had with the term dummies and with the coalition-of-minorities variables for the Truman and Johnson second terms, it is clear that the multiple regression procedure is being strained. What one would expect under these circumstances is to see the pairs of correlated variables wiping each other out (as, indeed, happened when the nondummy war variables mentioned in Section 9.2.4, such as the casualty figures, were applied). There is some evidence of this in eq. 6 as the coalition-of-minorities variable for Truman's second term is reduced to a level that seems unrealistically low; it remains, however, statistically significant.

Nevertheless, the *same* considerable difficulties are posed for *both* dummy variables and, under those circumstances, the equation suggests the best guess as to what is going on: Korea had an *added* impact on Truman's decline, Vietnam did not have one on Johnson's decline. It probably would be unwise to make book on the precise 18 percentage point difference because some of its

[22] For example, the 1949 data were removed from consideration thereby making it appear that the Korean War started only 6 months into Truman's second term as the Vietnam War had been taken to start 6 months into Johnson's.

strength is doubtless stolen from the Truman coalition-of-minorities variable; and one may be able to trace special Vietnam effects in a more microscopic analysis of Johnson's popularity;[23] but, at least at this level, it seems that something of the sort indicated is going on in the data. Furthermore, as noted above, the war variable that did not distinguish between the wars also was found to have a significant effect, and its correlation with other independent variables was fairly low—in the .50 to .60 range.

One's third impulse, then, is to attempt to explain the result. One speculates.

The wars in Korea and Vietnam differed from each other in many respects of course, but it seems unlikely that these differences can be used in any simple manner to explain the curious regression finding. This is the case because, as seen in Part 1, public response to the wars themselves was quite similar.

Therefore, it, is probably a sounder approach in seeking to explain the regression finding to look specifically at popular attitudes toward *the president's relation to the war,* rather than to perceptions of the war itself. A comment by Richard Neustadt (1960: 97) seems strikingly relevant in this respect. "Truman," he observes, "seems to have run afoul of the twin notions that a wartime Chief Executive ought to be 'above politics' and that he ought to help the generals 'win.' "

President Johnson seems to have run considerably less afoul. In seeking to keep the war "above politics," he assiduously cultivated bipartisan support for the war and repeatedly sought to demonstrate that the war effort was simply an extension of the policies and actions of previous presidents. He was especially successful at generating public expressions of approval from the most popular Republican of them all: General Eisenhower. Vocal opposition to the war in Vietnam came either from groups largely unassociated with either party or from members of the president's own party. Then, when the latter opposition began to move from expressions of misgivings at congressional hearings to explicit challenges in the primaries, President Johnson removed himself from the battle precisely, he said, to keep the war "above politics."

---

[23] A preliminary report on some efforts to do this: Stone and Brody (1970).

And, while there were occasional complaints from the Right during Vietnam that President Johnson had adopted a "no win" policy there, they were continually being undercut by public statements from General William Westmoreland—a man highly respected by the Right—insisting that he was receiving all the support he needed from the president and was getting it as fast as he needed it.

If these observations are sound, the single event that best differentiates the impact of the Korean and Vietnam wars on presidential popularity was President Truman's dismissal of General Douglas MacArthur. That move was a major factor in the politicization of the war as Republicans took the General's side and echoed his complaints that it was the president's meddling in policy that was keeping the war from being won (Spanier 1959; Neustadt 1960; Higgins 1960).

That the public was strongly inclined to support General MacArthur in the dispute seems apparent from the data in Table 9.4.[24]

TABLE 9.4 Public Attitudes on the Truman-MacArthur Controversy, 1951

Date Survey Sent To Field	Do you approve or disapprove of President Truman's action in removing General MacArthur? (AIPO)			Do you think President Truman was right or wrong in dismissing General MacArthur? (NORC)		
	Approve	Dis-approve	DK	Right	Wrong	DK
	(In Percent)			(In Percent)		
April 14	25	66	9			
April 18				28	58	14
May 17	29	56	15			
May 24				34	49	17
June 14	29	55	17			
June 29				39	48	13
August 27				32	54	14
October 2				28	59	13
November 22				27	61	12
December 28				29	60	11

Source. RC.

[24] See also the data in Belknap and Campbell (1951–52). Notice especially

The first two polls, conducted as the General was making his triumphal, "old soldiers never die" return to the United States, suggest more than twice as many people supported the General as supported the president on this measure. As Neustadt suggests (1960:97), emotion on the issue faded during the Senate hearings on the issue which lasted until June, and this seems to have benefited President Truman's position. The Truman point of view received its greatest support in late June and early July as peace talks were begun. As the talks began to prove unproductive, however, public opinion began to revert to its previous support of General MacArthur until, by the first days of 1952 (when the polling agencies grew bored with the issue), the MacArthur position was as strongly approved and President Truman's position was as strongly rejected as ever.[25]

The differing impact of the wars on presidential popularity, therefore, seems to result from the fact that Korea became "Truman's war" while Vietnam never really became "Johnson's war" in the same sense.

One other item of speculation should be mentioned. Domestically, the war in Vietnam was accompanied by a profoundly important crisis as America confronted its long-ignored racial dilemma head on. There seems to have been nothing comparable during the Korean War. The clamor associated with McCarthyism comes to mind, but many analysts feel that, however important to politicians, intellectuals, and journalists, McCarthyism was of less than major concern to public opinion.[26] Furthermore its dramatic climax, the Army-McCarthy hearings, took place months

the strong party polarization on the issue. A sample of citizens listed in *Who's Who* were asked Gallup's question in May 1951 and were found to be far more in favor of the president's position than the general public: 51 percent approved Truman's action and 46 disapproved. The British public was found at the same time to support the president by a 55–19 margin with 26 percent undecided. AIPOr, May 16, 1951 and May 20, 1951.

[25] It is interesting, incidentally, to compare how the public responded to the slightly different questions posed by the two polling agencies in surveys conducted essentially at the same time. Americans appear noticeably more willing to say they "disapprove" actions by their president than to say he did "wrong."

[26] Stouffer (1955: especially Chap. 3); Campbell et al. (1960:50–51); Polsby (1960); E. Roper (1957:250–51).

after the Korean War had ended and more than a year after President Truman left office.

It may be, then, that the discontent associated with the racial crisis was enough by itself to cause much of President Johnson's popular decline and that the unhappiness over the Vietnam War could make little additional inroad. In the Truman case, there was no profound independent domestic source of discontent: his second term coalition-of-minorities decline is usually found, as in eq. 5, to have been less than his first term decline and when, as in eq. 6, a variable has already accounted for the war effect, his decline is quite moderate. Hence, in a sense there was "room" for the war to have an independent impact.

It would be wise in concluding this section to emphasize what has and what has not been said. It has *not* been argued that the war in Vietnam had nothing to do with President Johnson's decline in popularity, and thus the analysis cannot really be used to refute the president's own estimation of the impact of Vietnam as indicated in the quotation that heads this chapter. However, it is argued that whatever impact the war had was tapped by the other variables in the equation, especially in the coalition-of-minorities variable, which is specifically designed to account for general overall decline. When the same sort of analysis is applied in the Korean period, it is found that a variable associated with the Korean War emerges as strong and significant even after other variables have been taken into account. Therefore, the regression analysis shows that, while the Korean War does seem to have had an *independent, additional* impact on President Truman's decline in popularity, the Vietnam War shows no such relation to President Johnson's decline.[27]

9.5 THE RESIDUALS

Equations 5 and 6 can be applied to each data point in the presidential popularity series and, with the appropriate quantities

[27] There is evidence to suggest that World War II, a more popular (and much larger) war than either Korea or Vietnam, may have worked to the distinct *benefit* of President Roosevelt. In its postelection poll in 1944, NORC asked Roosevelt supporters if they would have voted for Dewey "if the war had been over." Enough answered in the affirmative to suggest that Dewey might well have won in a warless atmosphere (SRCc). E. Roper (1957: 53–54) reports similar data from a 1943 survey.

inserted for the independent variables in each case, they will generate a series of "predicted" data points that can then be compared to the actual series. An analysis of the difference between the actual and predicted data points, the residuals, finds that the equations predict worst in President Truman's first term. If that term is dropped from consideration, the equation explains 90 percent of the variance in the remaining set of data. The President's extremely high initial ratings are not well predicted, suggesting that the equation does not adequately account for the trauma of President Roosevelt's death, combined as it was with the ending of World War II and with important peace conferences. It was almost as if Americans were afraid to disapprove of President Truman. The rather extraordinary degree of admiration that Roosevelt inspired was discussed in Chapter 8.

From these spectacular highs, President Truman plunged to great lows during the labor turmoil of 1946 as is shown in Figure 9.1. These ratings are also badly specified by the equation. The Truman popularity rose in early 1947, as the labor situation eased, and then declined for the rest of the term. Thus, although President Truman's first term, like the other non-Eisenhower terms, shows an overall decline of popularity, that decline was considerably more erratic than the others. The dummy variable for strikes, discussed briefly in Section 9.2.5, improved matters only slightly.

Beyond this, the residuals are reasonably well behaved. There are small but noticeable effects from the lame-duck phenomenon at the end of the Truman and Johnson administrations and from the "no opinion" peculiarity of the initial weeks of the Eisenhower and Kennedy administrations. And here and there are data points whose magnitudes have somehow managed to escape specification by the variables in the regression equation. One can, of course, generate a unique explanation for each of these, but this procedure clutters the analysis more than it is worth. Besides, the laws of sampling insist that Gallup must have made *some* mistakes.

As noted in Table 9.2, serial correlation has by no means been eliminated in the regression equations.[28] Allowing the coalition-of-

---

[28] The Durbin-Watson statistic, which ideally should register at about 2.00, reached at best only about .70 for eq. 6.

minorities variable to be specified for each administration improved things considerably, but much is left to be desired.

9.6 THE EISENHOWER PHENOMENON

Much was made in Section 9.2.1 of the coalition-of-minorities variable with its stern prediction that a president's popularity would decline inexorably over his four-year term. This emphasis was not entirely unjustified, since the variable generally proved to be a hardy and tenacious predictor for the postwar Democratic administrations. In addition, judged from Figure 9.1, a decline of popularity was also experienced by Nixon and probably by Roosevelt.

The variable fails for the Eisenhower Administration, however, especially for the General's first term. The analysis suggests then that if a president wants to leave office a popular man, he should either (1) be Dwight David Eisenhower, or (2) resign the day after inauguration.

The Eisenhower phenomenon, noted but left dangling without explanation or rationalization in Section 9.3, deserves special examination. Why didn't President Eisenhower decline in popularity like everybody else? Since Nixon's popularity declined noticeably, the phenomenon is not simply a Republican one. A number of suggestions can be made.

1. First, credit must be given to President Eisenhower's *personal appeal*: he was extremely likeable—a quality very beneficial in a popularity contest and one lacked in abundance by, say, Lyndon Johnson. Part of this, but only part, may be because of the admiration he engendered in the public because of his war record —as seen in Chapter 8, even before he entered politics he was consistently at or near the top of Gallup's "most admired men" lists. But this could only give him a certain initial favorable inertia. Americans are fully capable of becoming disillusioned with, or at least bored with, former heroes. President Eisenhower kept them from doing so, and it took more than memories of his old record to accomplish this. As Fillmore Sanford (1951:198) has commented, "The American people, in reacting to a national leader, put great emphasis on his personal warmth"—a quality projected to an unusual degree by President Eisenhower. As part of this, he was able to project an image of integrity and sincerity that many

found to be enormously attractive (see Converse and Dupeux 1966).

2. Early in his first term, President Eisenhower was able to present to the public one sensational achievement: he *ended the Korean War*—or, at any rate, presided over its end. This accomplishment was seen by the public as he left office to be a great one[29] and was used with profit by the Republicans in a presidential campaign a full 15 years after it happened. From the standpoint of public opinion it may well have been the most favorable achievement turned in by any postwar president. As such, it may have tended to overwhelm the negative impact of anything else the president did, at least for the first years of his administration. Some credit for this is given in the regression analysis, since the signing of the truce is counted as a rally point, but this may be a totally inadequate recognition.

There is another aspect of President Eisenhower's first term that may not be sufficiently accounted for in the rally-round-the-flag variable: the euphoria of the "spirit of Geneva" period toward the end of this term when the president's popularity should have been at its lowest ebb.

3. President Eisenhower's *amateur status* may also have worked to his benefit, at least for a while. He entered office an unknown political quantity. Under these circumstances, the public may be more willing to grant the benefit of a doubt, to extend the "honeymoon" period, than it would for a president who is a political professional. It is also easier under these circumstances for the president to appear "above the battle," an image fostered in a number of ways, and thus to be blamed only belatedly and indirectly for political mishaps, thereby softening their impact.

4. President Eisenhower may have been curiously benefited by the fact that, especially on the domestic front, *he didn't do anything.* As Irving Kristol (1968:16) argues, ". . . when a conservative administration does take office, it pursues no coherent program but

---

[29] In December 1960, the public was asked what it believed was Eisenhower's greatest accomplishment. The ending of the Korean War was mentioned by 11 percent and a related comment, "he kept us out of war," was suggested by an additional 32 percent. No other specific accomplishment was mentioned by more than 5 percent; only 3 percent mentioned anything having to do with the domestic scene (RC). See also Neustadt (1960:98).

merely takes satisfaction in not doing the things that the liberals may be clamoring for. This, in effect, is what happened during the two terms of President Eisenhower. . . ." Indeed, analysts of the Eisenhower Administration often argue that its contribution lies in what it *didn't* do. The times called for consolidation, they argue, and President Eisenhower's achievement was that he neither innovated nor repealed, but was content to preside over a period of placidity in which he tacitly gave Republican respectability to major Democratic innovations of earlier years: the programs of the New Deal domestically, and the policies of the Truman Doctrine internationally (see Rossiter 1960:161–78).

In the justification for the coalition-of-minorities variable, as discussed in Section 9.2.2, such behavior could have a peculiar result. It was assumed, in part, that the president would enact programs which, while approved by the majority, would alienate intense minorities that would gradually cumulate to his disadvantage. But, suppose the president doesn't do anything. Those who want no change are happy while, if things are sufficiently ambiguous, those who support change have not really been denied by an explicit decision and can still patiently wait and hope. At some point, of course, those who want change begin to see that they are never going to get their desire and may become alienated, but this will be a delayed process. Also, if the demands for change are intense enough, delay can be harmful to a president's popularity—as Herbert Hoover found. Perhaps this happened to President Eisenhower when he confronted the recession of his second term: "Eisenhower, once so satisfying as a 'man above the struggle,' apparently collided during 1958 with yearnings for a president who made his presence felt" (Neustadt 1960:97). But in moderate, placid times, a conservative policy may dissipate some of the power of the coalition-of-minorities phenomenon. If polls were available, one might find that President Warren Harding maintained his popularity as strikingly as President Eisenhower.

5. Although it might be difficult to sort out cause and effect, it is worth noting that President Eisenhower's first term (and most of his second) coincided with a *period of national goodness*. In a brilliant article Meg Greenfield (1961) has observed that "moral crises" as appraised and bemoaned by intellectuals seem to follow a cyclic pattern: we go through a period in which the popular

journals are filled with articles telling us how bad we are after which there is a period of respite.

Miss Greenfield's main indicator of these ethical cycles is exquisite: the number of items under the heading, "US: Moral Conditions," in the *Readers' Guide to Periodical Literature.* The pattern, elaborated and duly pedantified, is given in Table 9.5. As she points

TABLE 9.5   The Greenfield Index

Number of Items under the Heading,
"US: Moral Conditions" in the
*Readers' Guide to Periodical
Literature,* 1945 to 1968, by year

Year	Items	Year	Items
1945	1	1958	0
1946	0	1959	9
1947	8	1960	32
1948	1	1961	23
1949	1	1962	10
1950	3	1963	11
1951	35	1964	5
1952	17	1965	6
1953	1	1966	7
1954	4	1967	18
1955	2	1968	10
1956	0	1969	14
1957	7	1970	25

out, our first moral crisis in the postwar period arose in the early 1950s and was associated with " 'five percenters,' deep freezes, mink coats, the Kefauver hearings, and a series of basketball fixes," while "the symbols of our present (1961) decline are Charles Van Doren, payola, cheating in school, and the decision of Francis Gary Powers not to kill himself." We never recovered as thoroughly from that crisis as we did from the earlier one for, as the crisis showed signs of waning, new elements—Billie Sol Estes, Bobby Baker, President Kennedy's assassination, campus revolts, the hippies, and the city riots—proved once again that we have a "sick society." Our moral crises are regenerated every 8 years and seem largely to coincide with the end of presidential administrations.[30]

[30] It may, or then again may not, be worth noting that presidential elec-

Of course, objective indicators of public morality have not been careening in this manner. Even the most alarmist of crime wave enthusiasts would never argue that crime rates fluctuate in such a wild pattern (see Wilson 1966). Church attendance, measured by Gallup since the mid-1950s, shows only the smallest of changes (GOI 31; Lipset 1959). And careful sociological studies of American sexual practices found little sign of revolution during the period.[31]

Much of the fluctuation in the Greenfield index is, no doubt, due to journalistic fad. A sensational fraud, scandal, or disruption causes theologians, journalists, and other intellectuals to sociologize: society is sick. Others pick up the idea, and it blossoms into a full moral crisis. In a year or two the theme no longer sells magazines and the space is filled with other profundities, for example, the generation gap. Fraud, scandal, and disruption continue, but the moral crisis eases.

But—and this is a logical and empirical leap of some magnitude —to the extent that these patterns reflect and influence public attitudes, they may be relevant to presidential popularity. The early Eisenhower years are notable for their absence of moral anguish, and they differ from other between-crisis periods in an important respect: not only were we not demonstrably bad, we were positively good for we were undergoing a religious revival. Miss Greenfield looked at the items under the heading, "US: Religious Institutions." She finds only six items in the 1951 to 1953 period, but 25 in the 1953 to 1955 period, while "in the 1955–57 volume, at the height of our virtue . . . the religious listings reached thirty-four with twenty-eight 'see also.' "

If we were so good ourselves, how could we possibly find fault in our leader?

9.7 FURTHER RESEARCH

A regression equation has been generated, based on only four rather simple variables, that fits quite well the erratic behavior over

---

tions in which the incumbent party was removed (1952, 1960, and 1968) occurred during moral crises, but the elections in which the president was retained (1948, 1956, and 1964) all took place during times of relative goodness. This relationship, however, is undoubtedly much too beautiful to be true.

[31] See *The Public Interest*, Spring 1968, pp. 93–95.

24 years of the presidential popularity index. There is, however, much room for improvement and refinement.

Little has been done to separate out from the coalition-of-minorities variable the specific and divergent influences of domestic events on presidential popularity. One variable is designed to account in a general way for changes in the economy, some limited analysis is made of the relevance of major strikes, and comments are interjected about the role of scandal and "moral crisis." But domestic life is considerably more complicated than this, and more precise indicators can be sought.

It would also be of value to get better estimates of the impact of different *kinds* of international events on presidential popularity—although, as already suggested, such analysis may find that all dramatic international events affect popularity in much the same way no matter how they may differ in historical significance. It may prove valuable to attempt to see how spectacular and cumulative international events and shifts in governmental policy—to use the distinction made by Deutsch and Merritt (1965)—differ in impact.

The analysis strongly suggests that presidential style, as well as the ideological and political nature of the administration and the times, can make a sizeable difference in popularity ratings. A more precise assessment of these relationships along the lines developed by James Barber (1968) would be most desirable.

By the end of the analysis, the economic variable, though significant, proved to be of less than major importance. Experiments with other economic variables, such as price indexes and personal income figures, might prove valuable (see Goodhart and Bhansali 1970 and Kramer 1971). Furthermore, the only lag applied was one in which the respondent, it was supposed, compared the current state of the economy with the one that prevailed when the incumbent President was elected. Other lags such as a moving-six-month comparison, might prove more sensitive.

A major defect in the equations, as noted, was the high degree of serial correlation that remained. Various lagging procedures could be used in an effort to reduce this.

It would be interesting to extend the analysis to other bodies of data. Although the popularity question was posed with far less regularity during the Roosevelt Administration (and was largely dropped during World War II) and although there are problems with varying question wording, students of President Roosevelt's popularity ratings emerge with findings that fit well with those of this study. Wesley C. Clark (1943:41, 28, 35) has found some relation between a measure of Roosevelt's popularity and the state of the economy in the 1937 to 1940 period. He also notes a general "downward slant" in the rating over time and finds a rise of popularity during international crises. And V. O. Key (1952:596) has observed that during 1940 "the popularity of Roosevelt rose and fell with European crises" (see also B. Roper 1969 and E. Roper 1957: Chaps. 2 and 3).

The popularity ratings of governors and senators in states with active statewide polls can also be analyzed as can data on national leaders from countries such as Britain, Canada, and France. In their investigation of British data, Goodhart and Bhansali (1970) have applied economic variables and ones similar to the coalition-of-minorities variable to good effect (see also Durant 1965). Extensive data from France on the popularity of General De Gaulle have been published (GOI 33), and a study by Howard Rosenthal (1967) has investigated regional aspects of the General's popularity.

The analysis in this chapter deals entirely with general popular approval of the president. Unexamined are the ways population groups differ in their approach to the president. The next chapter considers the reaction of the partisan groups—Democrats, Republicans, and Independents—to the presidential popularity question.

9.8 SUMMARY

Presidential popularity is investigated in this chapter, and multiple regression analysis is applied to the behavior of the responses to the Gallup poll's presidential popularity question in the 24-year period from the beginning of the Truman Administration to the end of the Johnson Administration. Predictor variables include a measure of the length of time the incumbent has been in office as well as variables that attempt to assess the influence on his rating of major international events, economic slump, and war. Despite the austerity of this representation of a presumably complex process, the fit of the resulting equation is very good: it explains 86 percent of the variance in presidential popularity.

This degree of fit can only be attained, however, by allowing the special character of each presidential administration to be expressed in the equation. Thus it does not seem possible to predict a given president's popularity well simply by taking into account such general phenomena as the state of the economy or of international affairs.

The first variable, dubbed the coalition-of-minorities variable, found, as expected, the popularity of most presidents to be in decline during each term. The important differences between administrations do not lie so much in different overall levels of popularity but, instead, in the widely differing rates at which this coalition-of-minorities variable takes effect. Specifically, the popular decline of Presidents Truman and Johnson was quite steep, but President Kennedy seems to have maintained his popularity somewhat better. President Eisenhower's popularity declined only slightly during his second term and not at all during his first term.

In considering this Eisenhower phenomenon, a combination of several causes may be relevant: the president's personal appeal, his ending of the Korean War, his amateur status, his domestic conservatism at a time when a policy of this kind was acceptable, and his fortune in coming to office at a time of national goodness.

The second variable, the rally-round-the-flag variable, predicts short-term boosts in a president's popularity whenever an international crisis or a similar event occurs. The variable proves to be a sturdy one and suggests a popular decline of about 5 or 6 percentage points for every year since the last "rally point."

Economic effects are estimated in the third variable. The variable can only be made to function if it is assumed that an economy in slump harms a president's popularity, but that an economy in boom does not help his rating. A decline of popularity of about 3 percentage points is suggested for every percentage point rise in the unemployment rate over the level holding when the president began his present term.

The fourth variable attempts to take into account the influence of war on presidential popularity. It is found that the Korean War had a large, significant independent negative impact on President Truman's popularity of 18 percentage points, but that the Vietnam War had no independent impact on President Johnson's popularity. It is suggested that this difference may result from the relationship between the presidents and the wars: President Truman was less able than President Johnson to keep the war "above" partisan politics, and he seemed to the public to be interfering and restraining its generals. The absence in the Truman case of a domestic crisis comparable to the racial turmoil of the Johnson era may also be relevant.

CHAPTER 10

Presidential Popularity for the Party Groups

The analysis in Chapter 9 traces patterns of presidential popularity for the American population as a whole. The approach developed there is applied in this chapter to the party groups. That is, presidential popularity is assessed separately for Democrats, Republicans, and Independents.

In one respect, however, the analysis in this chapter is not directly comparable to that in the previous chapter. The party identification question was not regularly posed by the Gallup organization until mid-1946. This means that, although the analysis of Truman's first-term popularity in the previous chapter covered the entire term, the discussion in this chapter must be restricted to the last 2½ years of that term. As shown in Figure 9.1, the first part of Truman's tenure included the time of his spectacularly high popularity after Roosevelt's death and then a monumental plunge. Therefore, by starting the consideration of Truman's first term in mid-1946, at a low point in his popularity, one gets the erroneous impression that his rating *rose* over the course of the term. For completeness, the data for this term are included in the equations but, because of the peculiar data bias, the term is largely ignored in the discussion.

10.1 TRENDS IN PARTY IDENTIFICATION SINCE 1946

The Gallup party identification figures as generated on polls since mid-1946 are displayed in Figure 1.1 (pp. 4–7). As can be seen, the overall pattern is one of rather remarkable stability (see also Campbell et al. 1960: Chap. 6). While party proportions in the vote for Congress and the presidency have shifted considerably over this period of time, only small changes in party identification are evident. In fact, as discussed in Section 1.4.3, the one rather abrupt, permanent change in the identification proportions (at the end of 1952) seems to have been caused by changes in Gallup's sampling procedure. However, within this general stability, certain patterns of ebb and flow are worth discussion.

In Table 10.1 trends in party identification percentages are given for each term, based on the data from Figure 1.1. Compared to the term slopes for the coalition-of-minorities variable as displayed in Table 9.3 (p. 224), these numbers are small indeed.

One regularity is evident. Except for the remarkable first term

TABLE 10.1   Change in Party Identification, 1946 to 1970

Term	Percentage Point Change per Year in Party Identifiers		
	Republicans	Independents	Democrats
Truman, first (starting mid-1946)	0.5	0.7	−1.0
Truman, second	0.3	1.3	−0.5
Eisenhower, first	0.5	0.3	−0.7
Eisenhower, second	−1.1	−0.3	0.8
Kennedy	−0.2	2.2	−1.7
Johnson, first	0.5	−2.0	1.5
Johnson, second	0.9	1.6	−2.7
Nixon (to spring 1970)	−0.2	−0.1	0.3

Each number in the table represents the percentage point change in party identifiers for each year of the relevant term. For example, during Truman's second term, the number of people identifying themselves as Republicans increased at a rate of 0.3 percentage points per year, or 1.2 for the course of the entire 4-year term. Meanwhile, Democratic identifiers declined at a rate of 0.5 percentage points per year (2.0 percentage points for the term) and Independents grew at 1.3 percentage points per year (5.2 percentage points for the term).

of Eisenhower and the very short one of Johnson, all presidents have experienced a decline in the number of congenial party identifiers during their time in office: Democrats for Truman, Kennedy, and Johnson; Republicans for Eisenhower and Nixon. To an extent, this probably is a reflection of the coalition-of-minorities phenomenon described in Section 9.2.1. A successful presidential candidate finds his bandwagon boarded not only by fair-weather admirers but also, to a lesser degree, by whimsical party identifiers.

In one case, however, there is considerably more to it than this. During Johnson's second term, Democratic identifiers declined at a record rate of 2.7 percentage points per year, an accumulated decline of 11 percentage points over the term. This may well be associated with the growing dissention over Johnson's Vietnam policy. As noted in Section 9.4, this debate took place largely within the Democratic party. As argued in Section 9.4, Johnson may have been able to keep the war from having an independent adverse impact on his popularity by keeping it out of *partisan* politics. But the data in Table 10.1 suggest that his policies did have a cost *within* his party, causing a considerably higher defection rate than one would normally expect.[1]

One other development should be noted. During the Kennedy-Johnson tenure from 1961 to 1969 there was a rather considerable increase in the portion of the population that identifies itself as Independent. A growth at a rate of more than 2 percentage points per year during the Kennedy Administration, arrested during Johnson's brief first term, was then continued at a fair clip during his second.

Early data from the Nixon Administration suggest that both these trends have been halted and, perhaps, reversed. Democrats were found to be increasing slightly and Independents to be in barely perceptible decline. Thus the trends may have been associ-

---

[1] The decline of Democrats during Truman's second term may be underestimated in Table 10.1. As discussed in Section 1.4.3, changes in sampling procedures instituted by Gallup near the term's conclusion caused a boost in the number of Democrats sampled at that time. The NORC figures for Democratic identifiers during the Korean War period, also plotted in Figure 1.1, suggest a somewhat greater decline of Truman identifiers, although probably not as great as during Johnson's share of the war in Vietnam.

ated with the administrations under which they occurred and were not expressions of a long-term pattern.

10.2 PRESIDENTIAL POPULARITY FOR THE PARTY GROUPS

In Table 10.2, a regression equation comparable to eq. 6 in Table 9.3 (p. 224) is displayed for each of the party groups. The first column is the equation for identifiers of the party that hold the presidency at the moment, the middle column is for the Independents, and the last column is for identifiers of the out-party. Since Democrats in office tend to respond to the president more like Republicans in office than like Democrats out of office (see, for example, Section 5.1.1), this method of display and analysis seems appropriate.

The fit for the equations is excellent: around 90 percent of the variance is explained in each case. While the partisan groups may differ on some things, their response to the presidency seems to be influenced by much the same factors and these, in turn, are similar to those that influence the public as a whole.

10.2.1 The Rally-Round-the-Flag, Economic-Slump, and War Variables

The results for the rally-round-the-flag and economic-slump variables could not be cleaner. All identifiers are affected by these phenomena, but out-party identifiers are considerably more susceptible—that is, more easily alienated—than in-party identifiers, while Independents fit neatly in between.

Specifically, support from the out-party drops off at the rate of 5.3 percentage points a year after a rally point while support from the in-party identifiers drops off at a rate of only 3.6 points per year. And a one percentage point rise in the unemployment rate is associated with a 4.3 percentage point drop in affection among the out-party, but with only a 1.6 point drop among a president's own partisans.

The results for the war variable are similar for the three groups to those found for the general public in Chapter 9: a large, significant, independent impact of the Korean War on President Truman's popularity, and little or no impact of the Vietnam War on President Johnson's popularity. There is a suggestion in Table 10.2 that the effect observed for the rally-round-the-flag and economic-slump variables may also apply to the war variables. As

TABLE 10.2 Presidential Popularity Regression Equations for the Party Groups, 1946 to 1969

	Party Identifiers		
	In-Party	Independents	Out-Party
Intercept	58.1	35.3	32.5
Independent variables			
Rally round the flag (in years)	−3.6*	−4.1*	−5.3*
Economic slump (in percent unemployed)	−1.6*	−3.7*	−4.3*
Dummy variables for terms			
Truman, second	15.8*	18.6*	5.8
Eisenhower, first	29.2*	33.8*	25.1*
Eisenhower, second	29.3*	33.3*	19.1*
Kennedy	32.1*	40.3*	31.2*
Johnson, first	23.0*	36.1*	40.8*
Johnson, second	25.7*	27.5*	20.0*
Coalition of minorities variable for terms (in years)			
Truman, first (starting mid-1946)	1.9	3.7	3.3
Truman, second	−2.9*	−3.9*	−3.0*
Eisenhower, first	2.8*	3.3*	0.9
Eisenhower, second	0.8	0.3	−1.4
Kennedy	−3.2*	−5.5*	−8.5*
Johnson, first	10.7	−3.9	−22.0*
Johnson, second	−7.0*	−8.0*	−6.8*
Dummy variables for wars			
Korea	−15.5*	−14.4*	−15.7*
Vietnam	−1.7	0.2	−2.3
Mean for dependent variable	75.86	55.50	40.79
Standard deviation for dependent variable	15.29	16.94	16.21
Standard error of estimate	4.77	5.73	5.77
R^2	.91	.89	.88

As with Tables 9.2 and 9.3, each equation is displayed vertically. Except for the absence of party data for the early part of Truman's first administration (before mid-1946), the equations are comparable to eq. 6 in Table 9.3 and relate the independent variables to presidential popularity as seen by each of the three party groups. The number of cases in each instance is 268. Coefficients at least twice their standard error are marked with an asterisk.

can be seen, the coefficients for both wars are somewhat more strongly negative for the out-party identifiers than for the in-party. This phenomenon emerges more clearly when the percent *disapproving* the president replaces the percent approving as the dependent variable. The Korean and Vietnam variables then suggest changes of disapproval of 9.2 and −0.2, respectively, for the in-party identifiers and 13.9 and 3.7 for the out-party identifiers.[2]

10.2.2 The Coalition-of-Minorities Variable

The party groups differ substantially in the degree to which they approve the president. This can be seen quite clearly in the mean approval rating for each group as shown toward the bottom of Table 10.2: while 76 percent of the in-party identifiers have, on the average, approved of the president, only about 41 percent of the out-party identifiers have done so—a rather impressive difference of 35 percentage points.

There is no way of determining from such summary figures how these differences were arrived at. It could be, for example, that each group began at the same level with the out-party support declining at a much faster rate; or it could be that parallel rates of decline in popularity are found with out-party approval rates being uniformly lower than in-party rates.

The second of these two suggestions proves to be more nearly typical. In Table 10.3 the dummy variables, the intercept, and the coalition-of-minorities variables from Table 10.2 are combined (and rounded off) to give a picture for each term. For example, the data for the in-party group indicate that support for Truman in his first term can be taken to have begun at 58 percent (when all term dummies in Table 10.2 are zero) and to have risen at 2 percentage points per year while, in his second term, a decline of 3 percentage points per year was registered starting at a level of 74 (58.1 + 15.8).[3]

---

[2] Independents fit between for the Korean War—the coefficient is 11.9—but not in Vietnam where the coefficient is −0.6.

[3] As would be expected from the discussion in Section 9.4, the rate of change figures for Truman's second term are higher when the war dummies are removed from the equation. For the in-party, Independents, and out-party they are −7, −8, and −7, respectively, similar to those for Johnson's

TABLE 10.3   Coalition-of-Minorities Effects for the Party Groups,
by Term, 1946 to 1969

	Party Identifiers					
	In-Party		Independents		Out-Party	
	Starting Point	Rate of Change	Starting Point	Rate of Change	Starting Point	Rate of Change
Truman, first						
(starting mid-1946)	58	+2	35	+4	33	+3
Truman, second	74	−3	54	−4	38	−3
Eisenhower, first	87	+2	69	+3	58	+1
Eisenhower, second	87	+1	69	+0	52	−1
Kennedy	90	−3	75	−6	64	−9
Johnson, first	81	+11	71	−4	73	−22
Johnson, second	84	−7	63	−8	53	−7

For the most part, the big differences between the party groups occur in starting point figures, not in the rates of decline or increase. Thus *the coalition-of-minorities phenomenon has typically affected each of the party groups in much the same way: declines or increases occur at different levels, but not at different rates.* However, *within* the party groups most of the interesting variations occur on the rates, particularly if the Truman terms are set aside. This, of course, was the pattern found for the population as a whole in Chapter 9.

Study of these starting point figures, then, shows that, except for the 1961 to 1964 period encompassing the Kennedy and first Johnson terms, the differences are very substantial, running a solid 29 percentage points or more between the in-party and the out-party identifiers. That this should be the case for Eisenhower is rather impressive. Apparently his efforts to appear "above the party battle," while effective in helping to prevent a coalition-of-minorities decline (see Section 9.6), did not keep Democrats from seeing him as a Republican.

The Kennedy figures suggest that there may be more of a relationship between the starting point and rate of change figures than is evident from the data for the other terms. In the Kennedy case, the starting point differences between the in- and out-groups

second term. No other numbers in the equations change much when the war dummies are dropped.

are slightly smaller than usual, 26 points. However, the rates of change also differ in a way to offset this initial advantage. Specifically, the rates of decline are higher for the Independents and Republicans so that, within a year or so, the party differences were as substantial as those for any other term. It is as if the rate of change figures have moved to compensate for an initial abnormality. The pattern of the rate of change figures for the Kennedy Administration, moving neatly from −3 to −6 to −9, are reminiscent of the pattern found for the rally-round-the-flag and economic-slump variables.

An extreme example of what appears to be the same pattern occurs in the data from Johnson's first, very short, term. Here the differences in starting points are very small but are very quickly compensated for by vastly different rates of change as Johnson's popularity seems to have grown among Democrats while it plunged at a rate of 22 points per year among Republicans.[4]

Actually, what seems to be occurring in this instance is a rather extreme rally-round-the-flag phenomenon. By coming to office under the circumstances of the Kennedy assassination, Johnson gained unusually high initial support, even from opposition partisans. In fact, out-party identifiers were more willing than Independents to approve the president at the start, a finding nowhere duplicated in the table. In this respect, one is reminded of a similar observation in Section 5.1.2, where Republicans were found to be more supportive of the wars in Korea and Vietnam at their outset than Independents. In short order, however, everything falls into place as out-party support quickly declines.

10.3 CONCLUSION

The regression formulation developed in Chapter 9 for the presidential popularity series has been applied separately in this chapter to the party identification groups. The application seems to give

---

[4] The difference is as spectacular when the percentage *disapproving* Johnson is made the dependent variable. Then Democratic disapproval is found to rise at a rate of 6 percentage points per year from a starting point of 3 percent. Republican disapproval began at almost the same low level, 5 percent, but then proceeded to ascend at 35 percentage points per year. Disapproval among Independents began at 7 percent and then rose at 12 percentage points per year.

a sound fit, since the subgroups and differences among the party groups display themselves in coherent patterns.

While all party groups are found to be susceptible to the rally-round-the-flag and economic-slump effects, out-party identifiers are much more easily alienated than in-party identifiers. That is, although everyone tends to rally to a president's support at the time of an international crisis, the party identification groups differ in the speed with which they became disenchanted: those who identify with the president's own party are slow to return to disapproving poses, but those who identify with the opposition party find such a return easy and natural. Similarly, out-party identifiers respond quickly and strongly to an unemployment rise by moving to disapproval of the president while in-party identifiers tend to be relatively forgiving.

As for overall trends on presidential popularity for the party groups, there appears to be a stern inevitability that, by the end of his term, a president will enjoy far less support from out-party identifiers than from in-party identifiers. This occurs in two ways. Most of the time the approval disparity is there from the very beginning of the term. When this is the case, presidential approval ratings change at the same rate for the three party groups—the initial disparity is simply maintained. However, sometimes the party groups more or less agree in their initial assessments of the president—a phenomenon seen most clearly in the rally-round-the-flag atmosphere following President Kennedy's assassination when all partisans agreed in their high assessment of President Johnson. In cases like this, the usual parallelism is violated. Rates of decline from these points of agreement are found to be higher for the out-party group so that in short order substantial party differences are again registered.

The discussion in this chapter suggests that application of the presidential popularity formulation to other sets of population subgroups would be valuable.

CHAPTER 11

The Popularity of Ex-Presidents

A concluding, if not entirely climactic, consideration in this discussion of presidential popularity logically might be an investigation of the popularity of ex-presidents. Logical or not, it is reported to be a major concern of many men when they occupy the presidency.[1]

In a somewhat grand way, this issue was touched on in Chapter 8, which assessed the ratings of former presidents on the various admiration scales of historians and of regular people. The purpose of this chapter is to look much more directly at this phenomenon by examining the post-presidential ratings of the recent presidents as they have been tapped by popularity questions posed in the months and years after these presidents stepped down from office.

11.1 SCALOMETER RATINGS

For this purpose, obviously, the presidential popularity question of concern in Chapters 9 and 10 is of little use, since it is entirely bound up with the public's assessment of the current president's handling of his job while in office. Instead, a more general popularity rating question must be used. At fairly regular intervals since 1951, the Gallup poll has applied for various public personalities

[1] For President Kennedy's interest in this issue, see Schlesinger 1965:675.

something known as the Stapel Scale, or scalometer. A typical version of the question is illustrated in Figure 11.1. As can be seen, it can be regarded as a purer measure of personal popularity than the presidential popularity question, since it asks simply about liking and disliking, not about the public figure's performance in office.

Here is an interesting experiment. You notice that the 10 boxes on this card go from the highest position of Plus 5—or someone you like very much—all the way down to the lowest position of minus 5—or someone you dislike very much. Please tell me how far up the scale or how far down the scale you would rate the following men:

☐ +5
☐ +4
☐ +3
☐ +2
☐ +1
☐ −1
☐ −2
☐ −3
☐ −4
☐ −5

Figure 11.1   The scalometer.

Since the scalometer is used only for living public figures, it gives no clue to the post-presidential popularity of presidents who have died in office. To examine the post-presidential popularity of Franklin Roosevelt or John Kennedy, therefore, a rather different approach will have to be used. This is done later in the chapter. But for presidents like Truman and Eisenhower, the scalometer ratings can be very helpful.

11.1.1   Harry Truman

Among recent presidents, Harry Truman's post-presidential popularity may well be of greatest interest. As seen in Figure 9.1 (pp. 198–199), his presidential popularity ratings while in office dropped to levels lower than any ever recorded for any president. Yet, he has emerged lately, according to historian Eric Goldman, as "something of a folk hero" (1969:24).

The Truman scalometer ratings are plotted in Figure 11.2 and

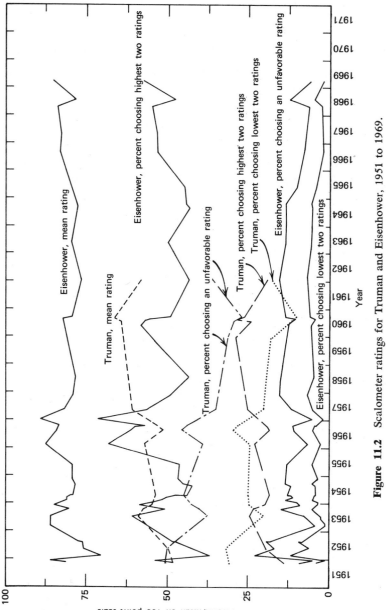

Figure 11.2 Scalometer ratings for Truman and Eisenhower, 1951 to 1969.

253

complete data are supplied in Table A.3 on p. 278. It appears that, while Truman did, indeed, become more "popular" after he left the presidency in 1953, the rise in appreciation was neither as striking nor as unambiguous as Professor Goldman might expect.

President Truman's rating on this scale reposed at its lowest level in his last years of office. As with the presidential popularity index, there was some gain after he announced in 1952 that he would not run for reelection, but his big advance on the scalometer rating was registered only in the year after he actually left office. In this period the percentage according him any unfavorable ("minus") rating dropped from 50 to 38, and the percentage giving him the lowest two ratings ("minus 5" and "minus 4") dropped from 31 to about 20 percent.

Over the next decade or so Truman's popularity tended gradually to improve, so that by 1960 only about 28 percent remembered him in an unfavorable light while only 10 or 11 percent were inclined to give him either of the two lowest ratings. This general warming hardly made Truman a "folk hero," however, for the percentage giving the *most* favorable rating ("plus five") grew only marginally during this period (see p. 278).

Furthermore, Truman's post-presidential popularity dipped precipitously whenever Truman injected himself into public controversy. Mr. Truman prominently asserted himself on two occasions: in 1956 he tried to influence the selection of the Democratic presidential nominee, and in the early 1960s he voiced his cantankerous opposition to the Southern sit-in movement. At both times his public reemergence seemed to revive old memories and old antagonisms. At any rate, his popular rating dropped abruptly to levels approached only when he had been in office and rebounded only when the controversial ex-president had again disappeared from public view.

11.1.2 Dwight Eisenhower

As would be expected from the discussion in Chapter 9, folk hero popularity is much better approximated in the scalometer ratings for President Eisenhower as displayed in Table A.3 and Figure 11.2. In addition to Eisenhower's post-presidential period until his death in 1969, the ratings encompass the time he was in office as well as a short period before he was elected in 1952. With a remarkable consistency, well under 20 percent of the American public has usually given him unfavorable ratings throughout his public life, and only the smallest minority has rated him at the bottom points on the scale.

Presumably because he generated so much esteem while in the presidency, Eisenhower's scalometer ratings, unlike Truman's, did not improve after he left office. Rather, there was a mellowing of opinion as somewhat fewer respondents gave him the highest possible ratings and virtually none gave him the lowest ones. The popularity of this ex-president, therefore, was largely unaffected by time.

Interestingly, however, there was a small dip in Eisenhower's popularity at the time of the 1968 party conventions, vaguely reminiscent of the Truman popularity phenomenon of 1956. In 1968, in a minor way, Eisenhower reasserted himself into partisan politics by public statements and a sternly anti-Communist message to the Republican convention.

As a candidate in 1952, Eisenhower seems to have generated an unusual (for him) degree of hostility as he became engaged in partisan politics. After winning, however, his ratings quickly returned to the favorable level that he was used to as a nonpolitical general.

One other point, relevant to an earlier discussion, is worth noting. Although comparisons are very crude, it does seem that the scalometer ratings attained by Eisenhower while in office trace something of the pattern of his presidential popularity as analyzed in Chapter 9. Evident especially in the two summary measures plotted in Figure 11.2, the mean rating and the percentage unfavorable, one can see Eisenhower's ability to maintain a fairly consistent popularity during his first term and, in the second term, a mild decline in the mean rating and a mild increase in the unfavorable rating associated with the 1958 recession; then a partial recovery toward the end of his administration. The notable increase in the president's scalometer rating immediately after the 1952 and 1956 elections is another indicator of this parallelism.

Data from President Johnson's tenure in office show the same pattern (GOI 53, p. 17). His decline during each term can be traced, and a temporary rise in popularity after his decision not to run again also is evident. (Unfortunately, Gallup apparently neglected to include Johnson's name in scalometer ratings after 1968, so no comparable assessment of his post-presidential popularity is possible.)[2]

It seems, therefore, that the presidential "popularity" question, although phrased to assess the respondent's approval of the way the incumbent is handling his job, is subject to some of the same influences as a question designed essentially to tap only the president's personal popularity.

11.1.3 Herbert Hoover

Very limited scalometer data on President Herbert Hoover are available, and these data appear in Table A.3 (p. 280). Although the higher "No opinion" percentages make comparison a bit difficult, it does appear that Hoover enjoyed somewhat less popularity than Truman after each had been out of office for many years. This is seen especially in the percentages assigning the lowest possible ratings to the two men: compare Hoover's scores with any for Truman after 1959. The public apparently was less forgiving—even 20 years later—about Hoover's errors (principally, for many, the depression) than about the defects associated with Truman. Of course, it is also true that Democratic anti-Hoover propaganda continued long after the man was defeated while the Republicans pretty well let up on Truman after they had captured the presidency from him. The related and curious data from 1939 given in Table 11.1 suggest that people were likely to perceive more mellowing in the attitudes of others toward Hoover than in their own.

11.2 PRESIDENTIAL VOTE RECALL

An informative, if highly indirect, method for assessing the esteem with which a president is held is to look at the percentage of people who claim to have voted for him in past elections. This approach can be especially helpful in assessing the effects on the electorate of the deaths in office of Franklin Roosevelt and John Kennedy.

Recall figures for the presidential elections from 1936 to 1968,

---

[2] Several historians were asked to rate Mr. Johnson as he was leaving office in 1969. In these early returns, he does rather well both in domestic affairs and in foreign affairs. *Newsweek*, January 20, 1969, p. 19.

TABLE 11.1 Attitudes Toward President Hoover

May 1939. Do you think Herbert Hoover is more popular or less popular today than when he ran against Roosevelt in 1932? (AIPO)

    33% More
    36   Less
    19   Same
    12   No opinion

May 1939. Do you like Hoover better today than you did in 1932? (AIPO)

    18% Yes
    47   No
    28   Same
    7   No opinion

Source. Cantril and Strunk, 1951:557.

as reported on various election-time surveys, are given in Table 11.2. For each election the winner's percentage of the two-party vote is listed together with the recall percentage as discovered on surveys that were conducted anywhere from immediately after the election to 8 years later. Because of the special care with which the samples are drawn, the surveys likely to be most accurate are those conducted by the Survey Research Center of the University of Michigan; therefore, where there is a conflict among survey results (usually a matter of only a few percentage points anyway), the SRC results are to be preferred.

As can be seen, in virtually all cases, there is a noticeable bandwagon effect as more people claim on surveys to have voted for the winner than actually did so in the election. This holds true for all winners regardless of party or size of victory.[3]

In the postwar period the bandwagon gain for the winner, except for the Kennedy case, has been 7 percentage points, plus or minus a couple—again, pretty much regardless of party or size of victory. However, although the data are not entirely consistent on this, there does seem to be a suggestion that the speed with which the bandwagon gain accrues to the winner may vary by the size of his victory. Specifically, it rather appears that big winners (Johnson

[3] See also Campbell et al., 1960: Chap. 5.

TABLE 11.2   Recall of Presidential Vote on Surveys, 1938 to 1970

Election	Winner	In the Election	Winner's Percent of Two-Party Vote					Overrecall After 4 Years (Percentage Point Difference)
			Post-election Survey	After 2 years	After 4 years	After 8 years		
1936	FDR	62.5		66 A				2.5
				65 A	65 A,R	65 N		
1940	FDR	55.0	52 A	56 A				3.0
				58 A	58 A,N			
1944	FDR	53.8[a]	53 N *FDR death*	59 A	65 S			11.2
				58 A	63 A			
1948	HST	52.3[b]	54 S	57 A	58 S			5.7
				53 A	60 A	59 S		
					56 A			
1952	Ike	55.4	58 S	63 S	63 N			8.6
			59 N	64 N	64 A,S,R,			
1956	Ike	57.8	60 S		64 S			6.2
			64 N	59 S	62 A			

TABLE 11.2 (Continued)

Election	Winner	In the Election	Winner's Percent of Two-Party Vote				Overrecall After 4 Years (Percentage Point Difference)
			Post-election Survey	After 2 years	After 4 years	After 8 years	
1960	JFK	50.1	49 S 50 A	*JFK death* 57 S	64 S		13.9
1964	LBJ	61.3	68 S	67 S	68 S		6.7
1968	Nixon	50.3c	53 S	55 S			

Source. RC, Key 1966:14.
Codes for survey organizations: A: AIPO; N: NORC; R: Roper; S: SRC.
[a] Total vote; 53.3 percent of civilian vote.
[b] 49.9 percent of three-party vote.
[c] 43.5 percent of three-party vote.

in 1968) receive their gain immediately in the postelection survey but winners with small margins of victory (Kennedy in 1960, Truman in 1948) take up to 2 years to garner the advantage. If there is a lesson, it seems to be that, while everyone may love a winner, many find big bandwagons easier to climb on than small ones.

At any rate, in the cases in which the president lived out his term, the bandwagon benefit seems to be reasonably secure by the time the winner was in office for 2 years: except for the rather puzzling data from the 1956 election, the 2-year recall figures are much the same as the 4-year (and, where available, the 8-year) figures.

Therefore, it seems safe to conclude that, had he lived out his term, John Kennedy would have had about the same overrecall figure after 4 years as he had after 2: about 7 percentage points. Thus the effect of the assassination was to double this overrecall figure to the highest ever recorded for a president: in 1964, 64 percent of the public remembered voting for Kennedy, while in 1960, only 50 percent had actually done so.[4]

The second largest overrecall figure is for Roosevelt from the 1944 election, again no doubt affected by the president's death in office. The data should not be pushed too far, but it does seem that the impact of FDR's death was somewhat less than that of Kennedy. Perhaps this was due to the extraordinary suddenness of Kennedy's death; there were, at least, rumors and speculations about Roosevelt's health before his death. It may also be that Kennedy's special appeal to the young, magnified after the 1963 tragedy, affects these figures. Voters who were under 40 in 1960 would be a larger percentage of a 1964 survey than they were at the time of the election.

A peculiarity of the Roosevelt figures from the 1944 election concerns the pace at which the bandwagon gain was attained. In 1946 the overall was only about 5 percentage points, although this figure was rather high compared to those attained by Roosevelt for earlier elections. A major additional gain was registered later,

---

[4] Some of the effect of the assassination can also be seen in the party identification figures in Figure 1.1 (p. 6). For a period after the assassination there were considerable gyrations in these figures.

between the second and fourth year, something which, as noted above, rarely happens. The full canonization of Roosevelt apparently took a little time. These data suggest that the Kennedy overrecall figures possibly may have attained even higher levels after 1964. Reliable data to test this notion, however, do not seem to exist.

These tentative meanderings with the presidential recall figures may suggest, at least, that such data are far from being simply a phenomenon of embarrassment to pollsters—who sometimes act as if they think public opinion is far firmer and more tangible than their own data demonstrate. The polls' seeming foibles, like the overrecall phenomenon, often can be helpful in understanding human attitudes.

PART 3 **Conclusion**

CHAPTER 12

Some Summary Comments

In approaching public opinion data analysis, this study has attempted to be at once irreverent and cautious. The irreverence stems from the seemingly realistic view that the poll interview is a rather primitive stimulus-response social situation in which poorly thought-out answers are casually fitted to questions that often are overly ingenuous. It stems also from a profound respect for the polls' own evidence that "public opinion" on very many issues can scarcely be said to exist.

Because of this, one must approach the analysis of such data with considerable caution. Accordingly, very careful attention is paid throughout this study to the precise nature of the stimulus—in this case the wording of the survey question. It has been observed repeatedly that changes in this stimulus can cause important changes in the response. One of the chief preoccupations of this book has been to analyze these changes carefully in order to assess the degree to which opinion on the issue can be said to be firm and, more often, to arrive at substantive conclusions about what kinds of considerations go into making up the public's response toward a given event, issue, or personality.

Although hardly the intended purpose, this book at points nearly becomes a manual on how to prove almost anything about popular attitudes with public opinion data. By an artful selection of survey questions or data arrays it has been shown how one can demonstrate great popularity for contradictory propositions, manufacture or minimize group differences, or generate congenial trend lines.

Since bias and individual peculiarities in the data cannot be avoided, therefore, the effort has been to hold them constant as much as possible and to adopt a comparative approach: comparisons over time, between subgroups, and among survey questions. When this is done it seems to be possible to see distinct regularities in the patterns of public response.

Because of imprecision both in the concept and in the instrument, it seems to be a meaningless exercise to attempt to discover at any point in time how many people supported the wars in Korea and Vietnam. However, given *constant* biases in the measures, one can determine from poll data that the wars were supported to much the same degree and largely by the same segments of the population. It has been found that support for the wars followed to a remarkable degree the same trend pattern and was a function of the logarithm of the number of American casualties.

The suggestion in the data is that in wars like these public support declines as the length and the costs of the war grow, but the decline is steeper at the early part of the war and slower toward its end. Whether this is a pattern of support typical for such limited and distant wars is a matter of speculation. But it does seem reasonable to expect the dynamic to be found in other areas.

The amount of *vocal* opposition to the war in Vietnam was, of course, vastly greater than that for the Korean War. The fact that this difference in vocal opposition seems neither to have influenced nor to have reflected a difference in popular support suggests a rather considerable discontinuity between active protesting elites and the masses that they sometimes purport to represent. It appears that political life can be carried on at several levels rather independently. Pressure groups can openly agitate for reform, leadership groups can respond or refuse to respond, and all the while mass opinion can remain relatively unperturbed. Linkages, therefore, can be extraordinarily tenuous.

It has also been found that the unidimensional "hawk-dove" continuum is a severely inadequate method for distinguishing supporters and opponents of the wars. To be sure, there are people who react to the wars in a manner suggesting that they tend rather consistently to favor or oppose the use of force in international affairs, and thus they can be characterized as hawks or doves. But there is also a small group of liberals who supported the war in Korea but not the one in Vietnam. This occurred for ideological reasons, not because of a dominating perspective on the use of force.

And, most importantly for the purposes of studying mass opinion, clearly many people do not cue on the issue at all but, instead, on the personalities associated with one side or another. Some are inclined to follow the president, others to support their party's leaders, but in either case they cannot be said to be either "hawks" or "doves," since they will support the use of force if the leader they follow supports it and will oppose such use if he opposes it. Because of this phenomenon, considerable shifts of opinion, inexplicable within the hawk-dove framework, occur when leaders make dramatic policy changes.

In considering popular attitudes toward the president, evidence has been found to further stress the high place the office has in the perceptual structure of Americans, and efforts have been made to analyze popular attitudes toward the man in office as reflected in the presidential popularity trend line.

The behavior of this line seems to be a function of several factors. First, for several reasons there is a general tendency for a president's popularity to decline the longer he is in office, a phenomenon known as the coalition-of-minorities effect. To one degree or another this seems to hold true for every president for whom there is data except President Eisenhower, who is given separate consideration. Second, there is the rally-round-the-flag effect: dramatic international crises give a short-term boost to a president's popularity. Third, the president loses additional popularity points at a time of economic slump.

With these three variables, one is able to describe quite well the rambling behavior of the presidential popularity trend line. In addition, crude variables designed to tap the effect of the wars on popularity patterns suggest that Korea had an additional independent negative impact on President Truman's popularity that Vietnam did not have on President Johnson's.

When presidential popularity is analyzed for each of the three party groups—in-party identifiers, out-party identifiers, and independents—the same variables continue to work well. The suggestion then seems to be that, at least at this level of analysis, the considerations underlying these variables have substantive meaning and firmness.

To a reasonable degree, then, regularities have been found in public response to political personalities and international events. Although the public opinion polls are far from perfect instruments, they can suggest patterns of popular response that seem to have considerable generality.

APPENDIX

TABLE A.1 Support for the Wars, by Party, Education, Age
For each group, the numbers represent, in order, the percentages
in support of the war, in opposition, and with no opinion

	Party								
	Republican			Democrat			Independent		
A. NORC polls from Korean War (Column B in Table 3.1)									
July 1950	74	23	3	78	18	4	70	24	5
September 1950	81	14	5	84	13	3	76	15	10
December 1950	42	49	9	62	30	7	56	32	13
February 1951	50	39	11	62	29	9	57	31	12
March 1951	50	40	10	66	25	9	58	31	11
April 1951	56	36	8	68	22	9	62	25	13
May 1951	54	37	9	65	26	9	58	30	12
Late August 1951	54	35	11	64	26	9	56	33	11
Early December 1951	49	43	9	59	32	9	50	40	11
Early January 1952	49	42	8	61	32	7	55	31	14
March 1952	41	49	10	56	34	10	48	41	12
June 1952	47	44	9	61	33	6	53	38	9
B. AIPO polls from the Korean War (Column A in Table 3.1)									
August 1950	64	24	11	69	18	12	68	20	10
December 1950	32	58	11	42	46	11	38	48	14
February 1951	37	55	8	45	43	11	40	51	9
March 1951	37	53	10	47	38	14	44	44	12
April 1951	41	44	15	48	32	19	45	38	18
Early January 1951									
Mid June 1951	31	55	13	44	37	18	43	39	18
Early August 1951	40	49	11	51	38	11	51	40	10
March 1952	30	61	9	41	44	15	39	47	14
Late October 1952	27	58	14	42	36	21	39	41	21
January 1953	39	46	15	57	31	12	56	31	13

TABLE A.1 (continued)

	Republican			Democrat			Independent		
					Party					

C. AIPO polls from war in Vietnam (Table 3.3)

	Republican			Democrat			Independent		
May 1965	54	27	19	54	25	21	46	29	25
August 1965	57	28	16	62	22	16	60	26	14
November 1965	61	25	14	65	18	17	67	21	12
March 1966	56	27	17	60	24	16	59	27	14
May 1966	47	42	11	50	32	18	49	37	14
September 1966	43	42	15	49	32	19	51	32	17
November 1966	52	34	14	52	28	20	50	32	18
May 1967	45	43	12	55	31	14	47	41	12
July 1967	41	51	8	55	33	12	43	46	11
October 1967	37	54	9	48	41	11	44	48	8
Early February 1968	39	53	8	45	41	14	40	47	13
March 1968	39	53	8	46	43	11	39	54	7
April 1968	39	52	9	43	43	14	38	52	10
August 1968	31	58	11	37	50	13	37	54	9
Early October 1968	35	57	8	40	52	8	38	53	9
February 1969	36	54	10	44	47	9	35	59	6
September 1969	35	57	8	31	59	10	30	60	10
January 1970	36	53	11	32	56	12	30	64	6
April 1970	38	49	13	33	49	18	33	57	10
March 1970	38	54	8	33	58	9	37	55	8
January 1971	32	61	7	30	59	11	31	60	9
May 1971	31	58	11	27	64	9	29	60	11

For each group, the numbers represent, in order, the percentages
in support of the war, in opposition, and with no opinion

	Education							
	College			High School			Grade School		

A. NORC polls from Korean War (Column B in Table 3.1)

	College			High School			Grade School		
July 1950	80	17	3	80	17	3	67	27	6
September 1950	90	7	3	84	11	4	74	18	8
December 1950	59	35	6	59	33	8	48	41	11
February 1951	69	22	10	61	32	7	49	36	14
March 1951	70	20	10	61	31	8	55	34	12
April 1951	75	20	6	69	24	8	54	32	14
May 1951	77	18	5	65	27	8	49	38	14
Late August 1951	75	17	8	63	28	9	49	39	12
Early December 1951	66	25	9	55	37	8	47	42	11
Early January 1952	69	26	6	59	34	7	49	38	12
March 1952	54	37	9	52	38	10	45	43	12
June 1952	68	26	6	57	38	5	48	42	11

B. AIPO polls from the Korean War (Column A in Table 3.1)

	College			High School			Grade School		
August 1950	79	15	6	72	20	8	57	21	22
December 1950	46	47	7	39	51	10	35	51	14
February 1951	49	45	6	41	50	9	35	52	13
March 1951	53	38	8	44	46	11	34	49	18
April 1951	59	31	9	49	38	14	34	39	27
Early January 1951	53	35	12	44	40	17	36	44	20
Mid June 1951	57	33	10	41	43	16	28	50	22
Early August 1951	62	32	6	50	40	9	35	50	15
March 1952	47	45	8	37	50	12	30	54	16
Late October 1952	54	35	11	40	43	18	28	46	26
January 1953	66	26	8	51	37	13	41	40	19

	Education								
	College			High School			Grade School		
C. AIPO polls from war in Vietnam (Table 3.3)									
May 1965	68	20	12	55	25	20	36	31	33
August 1965	69	24	8	64	22	14	50	28	22
November 1965	79	15	6	66	19	15	51	29	20
March 1966	70	22	8	62	25	13	46	29	25
May 1966	62	31	7	50	37	13	37	38	25
September 1966	62	29	9	46	36	18	41	38	21
November 1966	63	26	11	55	30	15	37	35	28
May 1967	58	34	8	52	34	14	38	45	17
July 1967	53	42	5	51	37	12	35	49	16
October 1967	54	41	5	44	48	8	32	50	18
Early February 1968	48	47	5	45	45	10	32	46	22
March 1968	43	52	5	44	48	8	36	48	16
April 1968	45	48	7	41	49	10	34	47	19
August 1968	42	53	5	37	50	13	26	60	14
Early October 1968	38	57	5	42	50	8	29	57	14
February 1969	45	50	5	41	51	8	29	56	15
September 1969	33	64	3	34	56	10	26	59	15
January 1970	33	60	7	34	56	10	28	58	14
April 1970	36	55	9	38	47	15	24	53	23
March 1970	34	59	7	41	53	6	26	60	14
January 1971	38	58	4	33	58	9	20	64	16
May 1971	31	60	9	30	61	9	21	63	16

For each group, the numbers represent, in order, the percentages
in support of the war, in opposition, and with no opinion

	Age							
	Under 30			30 to 49			Over 49		

A. NORC polls from Korean War (Column B in Table 3.1)

	Under 30			30 to 49			Over 49		
July 1950	82	16	3	76	20	4	71	24	5
September 1950	82	13	5	83	12	5	77	16	7
December 1950	64	27	9	54	37	8	44	45	11
February 1951	64	29	7	55	33	11	53	33	14
March 1951	61	32	6	63	27	10	53	35	10
April 1951	71	20	8	63	29	9	55	31	14
May 1951	67	24	9	59	31	10	52	37	11
Late August 1951	66	24	10	61	29	9	45	42	13
Early December 1951	58	34	8	55	37	9	47	41	12
Early January 1952	66	25	9	56	35	9	45	45	10
March 1952	56	35	9	49	41	10	43	44	13
June 1952	66	29	5	56	37	7	42	49	10

B. AIPO polls from the Korean War (Column A in Table 3.1)

	Under 30			30 to 49			Over 49		
August 1950	74	16	8	70	18	12	59	24	17
December 1950	46	45	9	44	47	10	30	57	13
February 1951	51	41	8	42	48	10	35	55	10
March 1951	55	34	11	42	45	13	36	51	12
April 1951	55	31	14	45	39	16	38	39	23
Early January 1951									
Mid June 1951	49	34	15	44	41	15	30	50	19
Early August 1951	61	29	9	56	32	12	38	51	11
March 1952	49	38	12	39	49	13	29	58	13
Late October 1952	45	39	16	38	42	20	32	49	20
January 1953	58	29	13	53	35	12	42	42	16

	Age							
	Under 30			30 to 49			Over 49		

C. AIPO polls from war in Vietnam (Table 3.3)

	Under 30			30 to 49			Over 49		
May 1965	61	21	18	59	23	18	43	30	27
August 1965	76	14	10	64	22	14	51	29	20
November 1965	75	17	8	68	17	15	57	25	18
March 1966	71	21	8	63	23	14	48	30	22
May 1966	62	29	9	54	32	14	39	42	19
September 1966	53	37	10	56	28	16	39	40	21
November 1966	66	21	13	55	30	15	41	36	23
May 1967	60	31	9	53	34	13	42	42	16
July 1967	62	32	6	52	37	11	37	50	13
October 1967	50	43	7	50	43	7	35	53	12
Early February 1968	51	40	9	44	46	10	36	48	16
March 1968	50	46	4	46	47	7	35	52	13
April 1968	54	38	8	44	46	10	31	54	15
August 1968	45	48	7	39	48	13	27	61	12
Early October 1968	52	44	4	41	49	10	26	64	10
February 1969	47	49	4	43	49	8	31	57	12
September 1969	36	58	6	37	54	9	25	63	12
January 1970	41	54	5	37	54	9	25	62	13
April 1970	43	50	7	40	45	15	25	57	18
March 1970	48	49	3	41	53	6	26	61	13
January 1971	41	52	7	38	55	7	20	67	13
May 1971	34	59	7	30	61	9	23	63	14

Source. See Tables 3.1 and 3.3.

TABLE A.2 Images of the Germans, Japanese, Russians, 1942 to 1966

From this list of words, which seems to you to describe the (German/Japanese/Russian) people best? (Multiple responses possible)

	Germans			Japanese			Russians		
	1942	1961	1966	1942	1961	1966	1942	1961	1966
Hard-working	62%	72%	63%	39%	47%	44%	61%	51%	45%
Intelligent	41	55	47	25	35	35	16	28	23
Progressive	32	40	33	19	24	31	24	23	19
Practical	21	27	23	9	17	17	18	14	13
Brave	30	24	19	24	21	17	48	14	10
Honest	10	24	19	2	10	9	19	7	5
Quick-tempered	25	22	18	21	11	6	10	22	13
Warlike	67	20	16	46	17	11	14	31	24
Arrogant	31	16	16	21	8	5	2	15	12
Religious	7	17	12	18	20	20	10	4	2
Ordinary	9	12	11	6	11	10	25	15	16
Cruel	57	13	10	56	14	9	9	23	13
Conceited	32	10	8	27	6	3	3	15	7
Artistic	8	12	7	19	36	31	10	6	6
Treacherous	42	9	7	73	17	12	10	28	18
Sly	21	7	7	63	24	19	7	17	15

TABLE A.2 (Continued)

	Germans			Japanese			Russians		
	1942	1961	1966	1942	1961	1966	1942	1961	1966
Aristocratic	8	7	5	21	8	6	3	3	2
Rude	19	5	5	12	4	2	6	18	11
Radical	23	7	4	12	10	4	25	23	13
Unimaginative	8	4	4	7	3	2	14	10	8
Ignorant	12	2	3	16	7	4	20	14	10
Dull	7	2	2	4	3	1	13	8	7
Lazy	1	2	2	3	3	3	5	2	1
No opinion	6	6	6	7	12	13	18	11	13

Source. GOI 13.

TABLE A.3 Scalometer Ratings for Truman, Eisenhower, Hoover

Percentage of Total

	+5	+4	+3	+2	+1	−1	−2	−3	−4	−5	DK	Top Two	Low Two	Fav-orbl	Unfav-orbl	Mean
A. Truman																
Nov 51	9	5	9	6	12	11	4	6	5	26	8	14	31	41	51	48
May 52	12	7	8	5	11	9	3	6	4	28	6	19	32	44	50	50
Jul 53	15	9	13	7	12	7	5	6	4	17	6	24	20	56	38	59
Oct 53	15	8	12	7	11	9	3	6	3	19	7	23	22	53	40	57
Dec 53	13	7	11	8	10	8	4	5	3	21	8	20	24	49	42	55
Apr 54	11	7	11	8	13	9	5	6	4	21	5	18	25	50	45	54
Feb 56	16	7	14	9	9	5	4	6	3	21	6	23	24	55	39	57
Aug 56	13	6	11	7	8	6	4	6	3	27	10	18	29	45	45	51
Oct 56	12	7	14	8	9	6	3	7	3	25	8	19	28	49	44	53
May 57	16	9	16	9	9	6	3	5	2	18	6	25	20	59	35	61
Dec 59	20	9	17	8	10	6	3	5	2	15	5	29	18	64	31	64
July 60	12	12	14	11	15	9	4	4	4	8	6	24	12	65	29	64
Aug 60	15	14	13	12	13	8	4	5	3	8	6	28	11	66	28	66
Sep 60	14	12	15	11	13	8	4	5	3	7	7	26	10	66	27	66
Jan 62	6	13	13	11	14	8	5	6	4	13	6	19	17	58	36	58
B. Eisenhower																
Nov 51	38	10	14	7	13	3	1	1	1	3	8	48	4	83	9	81
Dec 51	43	11	14	6	8	2	1	1	0	1	13	54	1	82	5	86
Feb 52	26	10	12	7	12	6	2	2	2	10	10	37	12	68	23	70
May 52	30	12	15	9	11	6	2	3	1	5	6	42	6	77	17	76
Aug 52	39	8	11	5	8	6	2	2	1	8	10	47	9	71	19	76
Aug 52	41	7	12	5	8	5	2	3	0	7	9	48	8	73	18	77
Mar 53	47	9	11	19	4	2	1	1	1	1	5	56	1	90	4	86
Jul 53	51	10	16	6	6	2	1	1	0	3	4	61	3	89	7	86
Oct 53	41	10	16	6	7	5	2	2	1	5	5	50	5	80	15	80

TABLE A.3 (Continued)

Percentage of Total

	+5	+4	+3	+2	+1	−1	−2	−3	−4	−5	DK	Top Two	Low Two	Fav-orbl	Unfav-orbl	Mean
Dec 53	48	10	16	6	5	3	1	1	0	3	5	59	4	86	9	85
Jan 54	43	12	16	5	10	3	1	2	1	3	4	55	3	86	10	83
Feb 54	41	11	18	7	5	5	2	2	1	4	4	52	5	83	14	81
Mar 54	39	12	19	7	8	2	1	3	0	4	4	50	5	85	11	81
Apr 54	35	12	21	7	8	4	2	2	1	4	4	47	5	84	12	80
Apr 54	34	9	19	8	9	4	2	3	1	3	7	44	4	80	13	79
Aug 54	30	13	23	9	10	3	2	3	1	4	5	42	4	83	12	78
Sep 54	32	13	19	8	8	3	2	3	1	4	7	45	5	80	14	78
Nov 54	35	12	18	8	10	5	2	2	1	3	5	47	3	82	13	79
May 55	34	13	18	8	7	4	2	1	1	4	8	46	5	79	13	79
Feb 56	52	16	12	4	6	2	1	1	1	2	4	68	3	90	7	88
Aug 56	49	12	11	5	6	3	1	2	2	4	6	61	5	83	11	84
Oct 56	48	12	11	6	7	3	1	2	2	3	5	60	4	84	11	83
Oct 56	46	11	13	6	8	4	2	2	1	3	6	57	4	83	11	83
Jan 57	55	16	9	5	5	2	1	1	1	1	4	71	2	90	5	89
May 57	41	15	15	6	7	4	1	1	1	4	4	56	5	84	12	82
Nov 57	39	10	18	6	6	4	2	3	1	6	6	49	7	79	15	79
Jul 58	32	12	18	7	8	5	3	2	4	1	10	43	5	76	15	78
May 60	45	13	13	6	7	3	2	2	1	5	3	58	6	85	12	82
Jul 60	44	13	15	7	6	3	2	2	1	4	3	57	5	85	12	82
Aug 60	42	13	16	8	7	3	1	2	1	3	3	55	4	86	10	82
Sep 60	37	13	19	6	8	3	2	3	1	5	4	49	6	82	13	79
Jan 62	30	14	19	9	9	4	2	2	1	6	5	43	7	80	15	77
May 63	37	13	18	9	8	4	2	2	1	4	3	50	6	84	13	80
Aug 64	31	12	19	10	9	3	2	3	1	4	6	43	5	81	13	78
Oct 64	32	12	18	9	8	2	3	3	1	5	8	44	6	79	13	78
May 65	30	14	20	12	9	3	2	2	1	3	5	45	4	85	10	79

TABLE A.3 (Continued)

	Percentage of Total															
	+5	+4	+3	+2	+1	-1	-2	-3	-4	-5	DK	Top Two	Low Two	Fav-orbl	Unfav-orbl	Mean
Aug 66	37	16	19	10	8	3	2	2	1	1	2	53	2	90	8	83
Apr 67	37	17	20	9	9	2	1	1	1	1	1	53	2	91	7	83
Apr 68	41	13	20	9	9	2	1	1	0	2	2	55	2	92	6	84
Jul 68	30	17	16	10	11	3	2	2	2	3	3	48	5	85	12	78
Mar 69	43	15	19	9	7	2	1	1	1	1	2	57	2	92	6	85
C. Hoover																
Jul 53	15	9	12	8	11	6	3	3	3	17	14	24	19	55	31	61
Aug 56	14	7	10	8	9	6	3	4	3	20	18	21	22	47	35	57
Oct 56	11	8	12	7	10	7	3	5	3	18	17	19	21	47	36	56

Source. RC.

REFERENCES

Adelson, Joseph, *1970*. "What Generation Gap?" *New York Times Magazine*, January 18.

Almond, Gabriel, *1950*. *The American People and Foreign Policy* (New York: Praeger).

Arlen, Michael J., *1969*. *Living-room War* (New York: Viking).

Armor, David J., Joseph B. Giacquinta, R. Gordon McIntosh, and Diana E. H. Russell, *1967*. "Professors' Attitudes Toward the Vietnam War" **31** *Public Opinion Quarterly* 159–75 (Summer).

Bailey, Thomas A., *1966*. *Presidential Greatness* (New York: Appleton-Century-Crofts).

Barber, James D., *1968*. "Classifying and Predicting Presidential Styles" **24** *Journal of Social Issues* 51–80 (No. 3, July).

Barton, Allen H., *1968*. "The Columbia Crisis: Campus, Vietnam, and the Ghetto" **32** *Public Opinion Quarterly* 333–51 (Fall).

Belknap, George and Angus Campbell, *1951–1952*. "Political Party Identification and Attitudes Toward Foreign Policy" **15** *Public Opinion Quarterly* 601–23 (Winter).

Bisco, Ralph L., *1966*. "Social Science Data Archives," **60** *American Political Science Review* 93–109 (March).

Blum, Richard H., *1958*. "The Choice of American Heroes and its Relationship to Personality Structure in an Elite" **48** *Journal of Social Psychology* 235–46 (November).

Bryce, James, *1924. The American Commonwealth*, Vol. 1 (New York: MacMillan).

Campbell, Angus, Philip E. Converse, Warren E. Miller, and Donald E. Stokes *1960. The American Voter* (New York: Wiley).

Campbell, Joel T. and Leila S. Cain, *1965.* "Public Opinion and the Outbreak of War" **9** *Journal of Conflict Resolution* 318–29 (September).

Cantril, Albert H., *1970.* "The American People, Viet-Nam and the Presidency." Paper delivered at the Annual Meeting of the American Political Science Association, Los Angeles (September).

Cantril, Hadley, *1967. The Human Dimension* (New Brunswick, N.J.: Rutgers University Press).

Cantril, Hadley and Associates, *1947. Gauging Public Opinion* (Princeton, N.J.: Princeton University Press).

Cantril, Hadley and Lloyd A. Free, *1968. The Political Beliefs of Americans* (New York: Clarion).

Cantril, Hadley and Mildred Strunk, *1951. Public Opinion 1935–1946* (Princeton, N.J.: Princeton University Press).

Caspary, William R., *1968.* "United States Public Opinion During the Onset of the Cold War" **9** *Peace Research Society (International) Papers* 25–46.

Caspary, William R., *1970.* "The 'Mood Theory': A Study of Public Opinion and Foreign Policy" **64** *American Political Science Review* 536–47 (June).

Christ, Carl F., *1966. Econometric Models and Methods* (New York: Wiley).

Clark, Wesley C., *1943.* "Economic Aspects of a President's Popularity," Ph.D. Dissertation, University of Pennsylvania.

Congressional Quarterly, *1967. China and U.S. Far East Policy 1945–1966* (Washington: Congressional Quarterly Service).

Converse, Philip E., *1964a.* "New Dimensions of Meaning for Cross-Section Sample Surveys in Politics" **16** *International Social Science Journal* 19–34.

Converse, Philip E., *1964b.* "The Nature of Belief Systems in Mass Publics" in David Apter (ed.), *Ideology and Discontent* (New York: Free Press), pp. 206–61.

Converse, Philip E., *1966*. "The Availability and Quality of Sample Survey Data in Archives within the United States" in Richard L. Merritt and Stein Rokkan (eds.), *Comparing Nations* (New Haven: Yale), pp. 419–40.

Converse, Philip E. and Georges Dupeux, *1966*. "De Gaulle and Eisenhower: The Public Image of the Victorious General" in Angus Campbell et al., *Elections and the Political Order* (New York: Wiley), pp. 292–345.

Converse, Philip E. and Howard Schuman, *1970*. " 'Silent Majorities' and the Vietnam War." *Scientific American* 17–25 (June).

Converse, Philip E., Warren E. Miller, Jerrold G. Rusk, and Arthur C. Wolfe, *1969*. "Continuity and Change in American Politics: Parties and Issues in the 1968 Elections" **63** *American Political Science Review* 1083–1105 (December).

Deutsch, Karl W. and Richard C. Merritt, *1965*. "Effects of Events on National and International Images," in Herbert C. Kelman (ed.), *International Behavior* (New York: Holt), pp. 132–87.

Downs, Anthony, *1957*. *An Economic Theory of Democracy* (New York: Harper and Row).

Draper, N. R. and H. Smith, *1966*. *Applied Regression Analysis* (New York: Wiley).

Durant, Henry, *1965*. "Indirect Influences on Voting Behavior" **1** *Polls* 7–11 (Spring).

Erskine, Hazel, *1964*. "The Polls: Kennedy as President" **28** *Public Opinion Quarterly* 334–38 (Summer).

Erskine, Hazel, *1970*. "The Polls: Is War a Mistake?" **34** *Public Opinion Quarterly* 134–50 (Spring).

Erskine, Hazel, *1971*. "The Polls: Red China and the U.N." **35** *Public Opinion Quarterly* 123–35 (Spring).

Erskine, Hazel, *1971–1972*. "The Polls: Information Policy" **35** *Public Opinion Quarterly* 636–51 (Winter).

Ezekiel, Mordecai and Karl A. Fox, *1959*. *Methods of Correlation and Regression Analysis* (New York: Wiley).

Feldman, Kenneth A. and Theodore M. Newcomb, *1969*. *The Impact of College on Students*, Vol. 1 (San Francisco: Jassey-Bass).

Fenton, John M., *1960*. *In Your Opinion* (Boston: Little, Brown).

Free, Lloyd A. and Hadley Cantril, *1968*. *The Political Beliefs of Americans* (New York: Simon and Schuster).

Gallup, George, *1941*. "Question Wording in Public Opinion Polls" **4** *Sociometry* 259–68 (August).

Gallup, George, *1953*. "The Future Direction of Election Polling" **17** *Public Opinion Quarterly* 202–07 (Summer).

Gallup Opinion Index (GOI) (originally titled *Gallup Political Index*) 1965– .

Gamson, William A. and Andre Modigliani, *1966*. "Knowledge and Foreign Policy Opinions: Some Models for Consideration" **30** *Public Opinion Quarterly* 187–99 (Summer).

Glenn, Norval D., *1970*. "Problems of Comparability in Trend Studies with Opinion Poll Data," **34** *Public Opinion Quarterly* 82–94 (Spring).

Goldman, Eric F., *1969*. "The Wrong Man from the Wrong Place at the Wrong Time Who May Live in History," *New York Times Magazine*, January 5, pp. 24, 82ff.

Goldsen, Rose K., Morris Rosenberg, Robin M. Williams, Jr., and Edward A. Suchman, *1960*. *What College Students Think* (Princeton, N.J.: Van Nostrand).

Goodhart, C. A. E. and R. J. Bhansali, *1970*. "Political Economy" **18** *Political Studies* 43–106 (March).

Gornick, Vivian, *1971*. "Consciousness ♀," *New York Times Magazine*, January 10.

Greenfield, Meg, *1961*. "The Great American Morality Play," *The Reporter,* June 8, pp. 13–18.

Hahn, Harlan, *1970a*. "Dove Sentiment Among Blue-Collar Workers," *Dissent*, May/June, pp. 202–05.

Hahn, Harlan, *1960b*. "Correlates of Public Sentiments About War: Local Referenda on the Vietnam Issue" **64** *American Political Science Review* 1186–98 (December).

Hamilton, Richard F., *1968*. "A Research Note on the Mass Support for 'Tough' Military Initiatives" **38** *American Sociological Review* 439–45 (June).

Harris, Louis, *1954*. *Is There a Republican Majority? Political Trends, 1952–1956* (New York: Harper).

Harris, Louis and Associates, *1971*. *The Harris Survey Yearbook of Public Opinion 1970* (New York: Louis Harris and Associates).

Hastings, Philip K., *1964*. "The Roper Public Opinion Research Center" **16** *International Social Science Journal* 90–97.

Hero, Alfred O., Jr., *1965*. *The Southerner and World Affairs* (Baton Rouge: Louisiana State University Press).

Hero, Alfred O., Jr., *1966*. "The American Public and the U.N., 1954–1966" **10** *Journal of Conflict Resolution* 436–75 (December).

Higgins, Trumbull, *1960*. *Korea and the Fall of MacArthur* (New York: Oxford).

Hochstim, Joseph R. and Karen S. Renne, *1971*. "Reliability of Response in a Sociomedical Population Study" **35** *Public Opinion Quarterly* 69–79 (Spring).

Hyman, Herbert, *1972*. *Secondary Analysis of Sample Surveys* (New York: Wiley).

Jacob, Philip E., *1957*. *Changing Values in College* (New York: Harper and Row).

Key, V. O., Jr., *1952*. *Politics, Parties, and Pressure Groups* (New York: Crowell, 3rd ed).

Key, V. O., Jr., *1963*. *Public Opinion and American Democracy* (New York: Knopf).

Key, V. O., Jr., *1966*. *The Responsible Electorate: Rationality in Presidential Voting 1936–1960* (New York: Vintage).

Kramer, Gerald H., *1971*. "Short-Term Fluctuations in U.S. Voting Behavior, 1896–1964," *American Political Science Review* 131–43 (March).

Kristol, Irving, *1968*. "The Old Politics, the New Politics, and the *New*, New Politics," *New York Times Magazine*, November 24.

Langton, Kenneth P. and M. Kent Jennings, *1968*. "Political Socialization and the High School Civics Curriculum in the United States" **62** *American Political Science Review* 852–67 (September).

Levine, Robert A., *1963*. *The Arms Debate* (Cambridge, Mass.: Harvard University Press).

Lipset, Seymour Martin, *1959.* "What Religious Revival?" *Columbia University Forum*, 17–21 (Winter).

Lipset, Seymour Martin, *1960, Political Man* (Garden City: Doubleday-Anchor).

Lipset, Seymour Martin, *1966.* "The President, the Polls, and Vietnam," *Transaction* 19–24 (September/October).

Maisel, Richard, *1969.* "The Impact of Events" **33** *Public Opinion Quarterly* 456–57 (Fall).

Maranell, Gary M., *1970.* "The Evaluation of Presidents: An Extension of the Schlesinger Polls" **57** *Journal of American History* 104–13 (June).

Miller, Warren E. and Philip E. Converse, *1964.* "The Inter-University Consortium for Political Research" **16** *International Social Science Journal* 70–76.

Milstein, Jeffrey and William Charles Mitchell, *1968.* "Dynamics of the Vietnam Conflict: A Quantitative Analysis and Predictive Computer Simulation," *Peach Research Society (International) Papers* Vol. X, pp. 163–213.

Modelski, George, *1970.* "The World's Foreign Ministers: A Political Elite" **14** *Journal of Conflict Resolution* 135–75 (June).

Modigliani, Andre, *1972.* "Hawks and Doves, Isolationism and Political District: An Analysis of Public Opinion on Military Policy," *American Political Science Review.*

Moore, Geoffrey H. (ed.), *1961. Business Cycle Indicators,* Vol. II (Princeton: Princeton University Press).

Mosteller, Frederick, Herbert Hyman, Philip J. McCarthy, Eli S. Marks, and David B. Truman, *1949. The Pre-Election Polls of 1948* (New York: Social Science Research Council).

Mueller, John E., *1965.* "Suggestions for the Use of Simple Experimental Methods in Political Research" **18** *Western Political Quarterly* 42–43 (September, Supplement).

Mueller, John E., *1967.* "Incentives for Restraint: Canada as a Non-Nuclear Power" **11** *Orbis* 864–84 (Fall).

Mueller, John E., *1968.* "Fluoridation Attitude Change" **58** *American Journal of Public Health* 1876–82 (October).

Mueller, John E. (ed.), *1969. Approaches to Measurement in International Relations: A Non-Evangelical Survey* (New York: Appleton-Century-Crofts).

Mueller, John E., *1970*. "Presidential Popularity from Truman to Johnson" **64** *American Political Science Review* 18–34 (March).

Mueller, John E., *1971*. "Trends in Popular Support for the Wars in Korea and Vietnam" **65** *American Political Science Review* 358–75 (June).

National Opinion Research Center, *1942a*. "Negro Attitudes Toward the War," *Report EW 96*, January 22.

National Opinion Research Center, *1942b*. "A Study of the Effect of German and Italian Origin on Certain War Attitudes," *Report EW 109*, May 26.

National Opinion Research Center, *1944*. "The Effect of Realistic War Pictures," *Report EW 20*, March 13.

Neustadt, Richard E., *1960*. *Presidential Power: The Politics of Leadership* (New York: Wiley).

Nordheim, Eric V. and Pamela B. Wilcox, *1967*. "Major Events of the Nuclear Age: A Chronology to Assist in the Analysis of American Public Opinion," Oak Ridge National Laboratory, Oak Ridge, Tennessee, August.

Opinion News (ON) National Opinion Research Center, *1943–1948*.

Paige, Glenn D., *1968*. *The Korean Decision, June 24–30, 1950* (New York: Free Press).

Patchen, Martin, *1966*. "The American Public's View of U.S. Policy Toward China" in A. T. Steele, *The American People and China* (New York: McGraw-Hill).

Payne, Stanley C., *1951*. *The Art of Asking Questions* (Princeton, N.J.: Princeton University Press).

Perry, Paul, *1960*. "Election Survey Procedures of the Gallup Poll" **42** *Public Opinion Quarterly* 531–42 (Fall).

Polsby, Nelson W., *1960*. "Toward an Explanation of McCarthyism" **8** *Political Studies* 250–71 (October).

Polsby, Nelson W., *1964*. *Congress and the Presidency* (Englewood Cliffs, N.J.: Prentice-Hall).

Rees, Albert, Herbert Kaufman, Samuel J. Eldersveld, and Frank Freidel, *1962*. "The Effect of Economic Conditions on Congressional Elections 1946–1958" **44** *Review of Economics and Statistics* 458–65 (November).

Richardson, Lewis F., *1948.* "War-Moods: I" 13 *Psychometrika* 147–74 (September).

Robinson, John P., *1967. Public Information About World Affairs* (Ann Arbor, Mich.: Survey Research Center).

Robinson, John P., *1970.* "Public Reaction to Political Protest: Chicago 1968" 34 *Public Opinion Quarterly* 1–9 (Spring).

Robinson, John P., Jerrold G. Rusk, and Kendra B. Head, *1968. Measures of Political Attitudes,* Survey Research Center, University of Michigan.

Rogers, Lindsay, *1949. The Pollsters* (New York: Knopf).

Roper, Burns, *1969.* "The Public Looks at Presidents" *The Public Pulse,* January.

Roper, Elmo, *1957. You and Your Leaders* (New York: Morrow).

Rosenau, James N., *1968.* "The Attentive Public and Foreign Policy: A Theory of Growth and Some New Evidence" Research Monograph No. 31, Center of International Studies, Princeton University.

Rosenberg, Milton J., Sidney Verba, and Philip E. Converse, *1970. Vietnam and the Silent Majority* (New York: Harper).

Rosenthal, Howard, *1967.* "The Popularity of Charles De Gaulle" **31** *Public Opinion Quarterly* 381–98 (Fall).

Rossiter, Clinton, *1960. The American Presidency* (New York: Harcourt, Brace).

Rugg, Donald, *1941.* "Experiments in Wording Questions: II" **5** *Public Opinion Quarterly* 91–92.

Rugg, Donald and Hadley Cantril, *1940.* "War Attitudes of Families with Potential Soldiers" **4** *Public Opinion Quarterly* 327–30 (June).

Sanford, Fillmore H., *1951.* "Public Orientation to Roosevelt" **15** *Public Opinion Quarterly* 189–216 (Summer).

Schick, Tom, *1969.* "1969 College Heroes," *St. Anthony Messenger,* pp. 19–25, June.

Schlesinger, Arthur M., *1949. Paths to the Present* (New York: Macmillan).

Schlesinger, Arthur M., *1962*. "Our Presidents: A Rating by 75 Historians," *New York Times Magazine,* July 29, p. 12 ff.

Schlesinger, Arthur M., Jr., *1965*. *A Thousand Days* (Boston: Houghton Mifflin).

Schuman, Howard, *1972*. "Attitudes vs. Actions *Versus* Attitudes vs. Actions" **36** *Public Opinion Quarterly* (Fall).

Scott, William A., and Stephen B. Withey, *1958*. *The United States and the United Nations, The Public View 1945–1955* (New York: Manhattan).

Segal, Harvey H., *1968*. "The Pain Threshold of Economics in an Election Year," *New York Times,* July 15.

Selltiz, Claire, Marie Jahoda, Morton Deutsch, and Stuart W. Cook, *1962*. *Research Methods in Social Relations* (New York: Holt).

Sheatsley, Paul B., *1966*. "White Attitudes Toward the Negro" **95** *Daedalus* 217–38 (Winter).

Sheatsley, Paul B. and Jacob J. Feldman, *1964*. "The Assassination of President Kennedy: A Preliminary Report on Public Reactions and Behavior" **28** *Public Opinion Quarterly* 189–215 (Summer).

Sheehan, Neil et al., *1971*. *The Pentagon Papers* (New York: Bantam).

Spanier, John W., *1960*. *The Truman-MacArthur Controversy and the Korean War* (Cambridge: Mass.: Belknap).

Stember, Charles H. et al., *1966*. *Jews in the Mind of America* (New York: Basic Books).

Stone, Philip and Richard Brody, *1970*. "Modeling Opinion Responsiveness to Daily News: The Public and Lyndon Johnson 1965–1968" **9** *Social Science Information* 95–122 (April).

Stouffer, Samuel, *1955*. *Communism, Conformity, and Civil Liberties* (Garden City, N.Y.: Doubleday).

Suchman, Edward, Rose K. Goldsen, and Robin M. Williams, Jr., *1953*. "Attitudes Toward the Korean War" **16** *Public Opinion Quarterly* 171–84 (Summer).

Suits, Daniel B., *1957*. "Use of Dummy Variables in Regression Equations" **52** *American Statistical Association Journal* 548–51 (December).

Sulzberger, C. L., *1966*. "Foreign Affairs: The Nutcracker Suite," *New York Times,* April 10, p. 8E.

Verba, Sydney and Richard Brody, *1970*. "Participation, Policy Preferences, and the War in Vietnam" **34** *Public Opinion Quarterly* 325–32 (Fall).

Verba Sydney, Richard A. Brody, Edwin B. Parker, Norman H. Nie, Nelson W. Polsby, Paul Ekman, and Gordon S. Black, *1967* "Public Opinion and the War in Vietnam" **56** *American Political Science Review* 317–33 (June).

Waltz, Kenneth N., *1967*. "Electoral Punishment and Foreign Policy Crises" in James N. Rosenau (ed.), *Domestic Sources of Foreign Policy* (New York: Free Press).

Wicker, Tom, *1967*. "In the Nation: Peace, It's Wonderful," *New York Times,* July 4, p. 18.

Wildavsky, Aaron, *1968*. "The Empty-head Blues: Black Rebellion and White Reaction" *Public Interest* 3–16 (Spring).

Wilson, James Q., *1966*. "Crime in the Streets," *The Public Interest* 26–35 (Fall).

Wise, David, *1968*. "The Twilight of a President," *New York Times Magazine,* November 3, p. 27 ff.

INDEX